The Vision
and the Reality

Dedication

This book is dedicated to our parents Léonie and Maitland Nicol, and Jackie and David Sayers, with love.

The Vision and the Reality

Equal Employment Opportunities in the New Zealand Workplace

Janet Sayers
and
Marianne Tremaine (Eds)

Dunmore Press

©1994   Janet Sayers and Marianne Tremaine
©1994   The Dunmore Press Limited

First published in 1994
by
The Dunmore Press Limited
P.O.Box 5115
Palmerston North
New Zealand

Australian Supplier:
Nyroca Press
P.O. Box 90, Hawksburn
Victoria 3142
Phone & Fax (03) 888-8307

ISBN 0 86469 205 6

Text. Times 10.5/12.5
Page Layout: June Mercer
Printer: The Dunmore Printing Company Ltd, Palmerston North

Acknowledgements

We would first like to thank all the contributors who wrote a chapter and those who gave their time to be interviewed. You helped turn the vision into a reality.

We also thank all those in the Department of Human Resource Management at Massey University who helped either directly, with personal support, or indirectly, by not complaining when other deadlines were stretched. We are grateful to our departmental secretaries, Christine and Marie, for their help in preparing material for this book, and to Joanne Te Awa for her help with indexing. We would also like to thank our Head of Department, Philip Dewe, who managed to squeeze money for travel and remained calm about the copious photocopying, phone and fax bills, and other sundry costs.

We are grateful to Sharmian, Murray, and the other staff at Dunmore Press for their editorial assistance and support.

Our thanks to Nicola for taking photos, to the Evening Standard for supplying photographs from their files and to Anthony Ellison for giving us permission to use his cartoon.

Janet would like to thank friends and family who listened and supported, particularly Mum, Dad, Gran – Gert Hooper, Lorraine, Shauna, John, Steve, Anne, Jacqui, and Remi.

Marianne would like to thank Allanah, Judy and Margie for their support and Karen Johnston and Lois Black for helping with information.

To all those others who were tolerant and understanding when we seemed a little wild-eyed and distracted, thanks for realising that it was only a temporary malaise.

Janet and Marianne

Contents

∾

Foreword

Tena ra koutou katoa,

Kia mihia to mano tini kua mene ki nga Hawaiki katoa, ratou te tututanga o te puehu, te whinuga o te kepu i nga wa takatu ai ratou, tatou te urpua o ratou ma, nga waihotanga mai e hapai nei i o wawata, tumanako hoki. Kia ora tatou.

Equal employment opportunity is simple to understand if you just think about those three words. The difficulty comes in looking at equal employment opportunity within a context. As soon as you take an ideal and attempt to bring it to life within a real and less than ideal world, all the complexities of linking the vision with the reality become plain.

Recognising and working with the difficulties of understanding EEO in our own context is something that we are doing at the university now that the good employer provisions of the State Sector Act have been extended to the universities.

Within the University, the Business Studies Faculty has been the first faculty to adopt an EEO policy and produce an EEO plan. We are also the faculty that introduced the first tertiary course on EEO in New Zealand.

This book, *The Vision and the Reality,* is another first and I am pleased that we are making a contribution to scholarly literature in this field. There is a need to reflect on our experience and document those reflections, particularly in an area like EEO which can change our workplaces and people's working lives for the better.

Producing a book takes a lot of commitment and energy. Janet Sayers and Marianne Tremaine have had the vision of gathering together the EEO knowledge that has been developed and publishing it as a book. Now their vision is a reality.

No reira, noho pai mai i roto i nga manaakitanga katoa.

Ralph Love
Dean, Business Studies Faculty
Massey University

Introduction

Janet Sayers and Marianne Tremaine

E qual employment opportunity (EEO) in New Zealand is at a crossroads. EEO has made a remarkable impact in its relatively short life-span. However, a number of factors such as the repeal of the Employment Equity Act 1990 and massive structural adjustment to the economy, have affected EEO's ability to create positive change in workplaces.

This book highlights the complexity of the issues EEO faces and the dangers in generalising about EEO successes across sectors and industries. Progress has been mixed and hard to quantify.

In the 1980s the way forward appeared to be simple and straightforward and involved preaching the 'one true gospel' of EEO practice. In the 1990s the way forward appears to be more complex: EEO involves multiple strategies, a recognition of and working with various organisational cultures, finding different solutions for different problems, as well as flexibility and diversity in approaches and responses.

This book highlights the close relationship between EEO and management, particularly human resource management. However, since 1991 EEO appears to have drifted behind in management priorities. Premature 'mainstreaming' of EEO resources into operational areas has hamstrung EEO progress in some settings. It is clear that the goals of EEO will not be achieved unless managers are held in some way accountable for 'good' human resource and EEO practice.

These issues have been under-debated in New Zealand. It is critical that people who work in the area of EEO take stock of where we have come from, assess EEO's impact on the workplace and strategise for the future. We hope that this book will contribute to raising debate about the directions of EEO and help improve the quality of its practice in New Zealand.

Equal Employment Opportunities – What Does it Mean?

In asking people how they define EEO we have found that there are many different ideas about what 'EEO' is. Some people work with the wording of the State Sector Act 1988. In their minds EEO is a planned, systematic results-oriented programme designed to get rid of present and past discriminatory practices. Implicit in this definition is the concept of social change. It encompasses the notion that structural inequality exists in the workforce and that discriminatory barriers at work prevent people from participating to their fullest potential in the workplace.

Working definitions of this kind have the advantage of being supported by legislation. They also have the advantage of being supported by a practical awareness of the realities of everyday business life. For progress to be made with EEO in organisations, there has to be a plan of action, and legitimation of that plan by the organisation.

In this view, EEO is organisation-based, practical and action-oriented; in essence, people are referring to *EEO programmes*.

Another way of looking at the term 'EEO' is as a vision, or as a concept. Sometimes people argue that EEO is not predetermined, that EEO *is* the vision – *equal employment opportunities*. Equal employment opportunities means what it says; a concept related to fairness and justice and a belief that all people, no matter their age, gender, culture, colour, religion, level of ability or disability, have the right to participate in working life to their fullest potential without being ground down by dogma, narrow-mindedness or outright discrimination.

EEO programmes of the planned, systematic kind as set out in the legislation are one way of achieving that vision. In the words of the planner, EEO is the objective and EEO programmes are one part of the overall plan.

Often when people talk and write about EEO they are actually talking about both things, the vision of EEO and EEO programmes at the same time. This can be somewhat confusing for someone just learning about EEO for the first time.

There is another unfortunate consequence of this tendency. This is that confusion about the nature of EEO can have negative repercussions both on the practice of implementing EEO programmes and the long-term aim of achieving the EEO vision.

Sometimes the term 'EEO' itself appears to take on responsibility for solving all the discriminatory practices in the labour market, a role that the systemic and organisational role of EEO programmes were not created to fulfil. Sometimes also, EEO is criticised for not getting higher numbers of people from 'disadvantaged' groups into management and non-traditional roles, but there is no recognition of the other factors that impact on an EEO programme's ability to create change. For instance, factors that may negatively impact on an organisation's progress might include the impact of restructuring, of gynopathy (the tendency for males to leave an occupation as it becomes 'feminised' and the drop in average income that accompanies this) or a lack of pay equity.

As Celia Briar explains in the first chapter in this book, EEO is a response to a particular historical situation. EEO is more likely to be successful if people realise its limits and focus on what it was developed to achieve.

EEO programmes cannot exist in isolation. In order to achieve the vision, they need to be part of a wider process of activities designed to achieve employment equity. These activities involve a range of strategies, 'multiple strategies' in the words of Gill Ellis, to achieve the vision of EEO. These strategies may include such issues as pay equity, democratic and accountable government and socially accountable business.

If we focus on the vision of EEO we can see just how important it is that EEO programmes are retained, strengthened and integrated into organisational life. EEO workers have added tremendously to our knowledge of EEO – its complexities, its realities, its achievements, its failures – and to our understanding of how to achieve the vision. As we continue to work in the EEO area our understanding of the term will continue to grow.

Why a Book on Equal Employment Opportunity?

Originally we saw the purpose of the book as a 'bringing together' of the expertise of people who work in the area of EEO. We needed a textbook that was based on New Zealand experience for a university course in EEO. The course was introduced in 1991 by the Department of Human Resource Management at Massey University and has proved an important contribution to education about EEO for university students taking degrees and diplomas both internally and extramurally.

As we discussed the idea of the book, we soon came to feel that its potential audience was wider than the students taking the EEO course. At the time the course was conceived the Employment Equity Act 1990 had widened the number of organisations with statutory responsibility for EEO. Consequently there were managers in the workplace who knew that EEO was something they would have to do, but they had little knowledge of EEO or of the skills required to implement a systematic programme of change. Even though the legislation was repealed the interest in the course remained which, we believe, demonstrated a continued commitment by managers to find answers to equity issues in their workplaces.

Initially there were other reasons for a book on EEO that went beyond the interest of managers and students. We were aware that some of the people who were most knowledgeable about EEO, many of whom were very generous in sharing their knowledge with us as we were setting up the course, were moving on. They were changing careers, changing organisations, going overseas, or taking time out for parenting or family responsibilities. It seemed likely that a lot of valuable EEO knowledge could be lost and we felt it was important that some of the experiences and expertise of EEO workers be recorded so that others could benefit from their insights.

The reality of life for those working in EEO is that it is a life of pressure trying to meet the demands of the organisation and the designated groups and keep faith with their personal vision of EEO. There is very little time to write or reflect on their experience. It is perhaps indicative of the need for further avenues for reflection that everyone we approached agreed to contribute to this book, and that so many practitioner voices are represented here.

We were also committed to bringing together critical perspectives on EEO from a range of stake-holders in the EEO field. EEO is consistently identified by employer organisations, unions, political parties, lobby organisations, human resource management literature and popular management magazines as a key workforce issue into the next century. However, there are very few New Zealand resources that explain EEO, analyse its key relationships such as the links between designated groups, or attempt to theorise it.

As planning for the book continued, it became clear that it could also provide a forum to discuss different views on the theory and practice of EEO and future directions.

Several themes emerged in our initial canvassing of contributors as to what they considered to be crucial issues in the development of EEO theory and practice. There were a cluster of issues such as: the 'diversity' versus 'equity' debate; the impact of managerialism on the practice of EEO; and the impact of industrial reform. A range of other issues were identified as crucial to the development of EEO, such as: the impact of more sophisticated human resource management perspectives, i.e. strategic human resource management; the relationship between EEO and strategic management operational perspectives such as workplace reform and total quality management; the inadequacy of current EEO theory to explain the practice of EEO; and the relationship between EEO groups.

Many of these issues are dealt with in this book. We believe that presenting a range of opinions in this way will provoke debate and further understanding. If this happens then the main reason for publishing this book will be achieved.

How has EEO Developed in New Zealand?

In doing we learn (Proverb).

History repeats itself (another Proverb).

As EEO develops we gain more knowledge of it; what works, what does not and how best to move forward. EEO has only a short history; we have only about ten years of accumulated knowledge in developing and implementing EEO plans. However, in that ten years we have come a long way. As Diana Crossan explains, ten years ago no one talked about EEO, but now it is part of our everyday language.

Our history of implementing EEO is relatively short, but awareness is growing. Several articles in this book help to document the way that EEO has developed in his country. Celia Briar provides a wide-ranging background to the development of EEO policies in New Zealand, showing how Australia, the United Kingdom and America's policy initiatives influenced New Zealand's own development in this area. Judy McGregor analyses part of this policy development background, the Convention on the Elimination of All Forms of Discrimination Against Women, and argues that New Zealand has been avoiding meeting these international obligations in respect of equality in employment.

A common theme in this book is the impact of the restructuring of the economy on EEO in both the public and private sectors and how it has challenged effective development of EEO programmes in New Zealand. Almost all the contributors to this compilation refer in some way to reorganisation, restructuring, down-sizing, deregulation, re-regulation and so on. The theme of EEO in an environment of change is a strong one. In her interview with Janet Sayers, Gill Ellis provides a useful background to the contexts of change, particularly in the private sector. She points to the difficulties that there have been in trying to achieve real EEO progress when organisations have had so many other compelling issues to deal with at the same time.

Marian Court gives an example of the impact of restructuring by demonstrating how EEO has taken several steps backwards in the education sector because industrial and educational restructuring has reinforced the value differential between men's work and women's work.

There is further analysis of the development of EEO in New Zealand in Pat Walsh and John Dickson's paper on the development of EEO in New Zealand. They examine the EEO Management Plans that were produced in the public service between 1988 and 1992. Their paper also provides an important historical account of the development of EEO and the ways that various pressure groups influenced the development and limitations of EEO policies.

Walsh and Dickson concentrate their analysis on the public sector, but Trudie McNaughton provides a perspective which pinpoints the particular characteristics and needs of the private sector. She talks about the strengths of business perspectives in EEO and the relevance of 'valuing diversity' strategies for companies' human resource policies. However, she also points out the tremendous amount of work still to be done in the relatively neglected private sector.

How do we Understand Different Groups' Perspectives?

EEO workers have learnt a lot by 'doing'. There has also been a considerable amount of 'political learning', the learning that occurs at the level of policy setting (see Briar chapter). An understanding of history and the forces that shape our present are essential if we are not to repeat the mistakes of the past.

Although governments, unions and policy-makers have been influential in the development of EEO policies and programmes, the most important pressures have been exerted by the four groups designated in the legislation; people with disabilities, women, Maori and ethnic groups.

The task of bringing together some perspectives from EEO groups brought into focus for us the tremendous strengths in the political, social and business perspectives of Maori, women, people with disabilities and ethnic groups and the ways that they interlink with each other. However, as a caveat, we did not ask the people we approached to write or talk on behalf of a 'target group'. We approached them because we knew of their work, admired it, and believed that they could convey the essence of target group issues through a forum such as this book.

EEO in New Zealand has focused on a range of groups. Although balancing the needs of all groups is a difficult task, our hope is that readers of this compilation will see many points of similarity as well as important matters of difference in the insights provided here. In a sense, EEO workers and the programmes they create, are the servants of the groups they represent. Their range of concerns and interests intersect at the locus of EEO.

For instance, Wendy Wick's chapter speaks of the importance of understanding the power of ideas in shaping the contexts of EEO. She provides an analysis of the social and historical construction of attitudes towards people with disabilities; how they relate to the struggle of people with disabilities for equal employment rights within the contexts of their much larger struggle for equal human rights. Robyn Hunt reminds us that the problems for people with disabilities are seldom the disabilities themselves except in a minor way. People with disabilities are affected in a much more negative way by contextual and environmental factors, by other people's discriminatory behaviours and attitudes. Of the four designated groups she feels that people with disabilities have been overlooked and that the need for action is urgent.

While the needs of Maori may not have been overlooked, many would consider that they have often been misunderstood. The perspectives of Maori have interacted, challenged and enriched the practice of EEO from the very beginning. Diana Crossan speaks of the way that the concept of EEO was first formed in New Zealand – as one that encompasses several target groups including Maori. The resource constraints of the time led to the inclusion of Maori within the State Services Commission's EEO Unit. However, Maori felt ambivalent and disturbed about being included as one group among many in the EEO context.

The reasons for this ambivalence are explored in more depth by Paul Spoonley, in his chapter 'Ambivalence and Anger'. This chapter builds a strong argument that EEO has decreased in relevance for Maori because of larger political, social and economic issues related to resource allocation. However, some Maori do see EEO as having a role to play. Joe Doherty explains the role of EEO Maori, and its limits, and argues that there are many points of interaction between Maori employment initiatives and the role of EEO. Marianne Tremaine supports this point of view in examining and explicating the relationship between EEO Maori and tino rangatiratanga.

The women's movement has been a strong force in promoting the introduction of EEO. Feminist theory provides some important insights into organisational theory, gendered relations in the workplace, and the operation of inequality as it is shaped by both capitalist and patriarchal forces. Janet Sayers describes some of the contributions of feminist theory in her chapter on EEO theory.

Other women writers in this compilation provide insight into issues for EEO groups. Nicola Armstrong, using more contemporary feminist perspectives, reminds us of the notion of 'celebrating difference' which is at the heart of radical feminist perspectives. Deborah Jones uses discourse theory, a relatively new but fertile avenue of social theory, to examine the ways that EEO practitioners talk about what they are trying to achieve. In analysing the ways that EEO practitioners communicate, she explains how adoption of the 'language of the organisation' can shape and influence one's perspective of the practitioner's role.

Balancing tactical strategies without compromising goals is an issue for Marilyn Kohlhase too. She has spent most of her working life immersed in social justice issues, as have many of the contributors to this book. Marilyn points out that in her EEO work with people from the Pacific Islands she had to struggle against the colonial legacy, the mind-set of gratitude for the 'benefits' of civilisation and for having a job, at even the most basic level. She has to consider her relationship with the Pacific Island community, with Maori and with her organisation in deciding how best to achieve results.

All of these perspectives offer insight into the nature of disadvantage and the diverse and creative repertoire of responses and analyses that come from the varied sources in the EEO field. There is incredible energy, strength and creativity in the various perspectives of groups that EEO represents. This energy has continued despite recent difficult times in the EEO movement.

How is EEO Related to Human Resource Management?

Another area where this book has found a rich vein of interest and debate is in the growing relationship of EEO to human resource management (HRM).

A common theme through the Viewpoints section of this book, which presents interviews with practitioners, is the strong relationship between the practice of EEO and HRM. Gill Ellis, Trudie McNaughton, Marilyn Kohlhase and Diana Crossan all argue that for EEO to be effective the basic human potential issues in organisations have to be resolved. That is, the organisation has to believe that people are important, that their employees are assets, and that there should be a human resource policy in the organisation (especially for the larger organisations) which is linked to the overall business objectives of the organisation. These themes are also pursued in Janice Burns' chapter on EEO and strategic human resource management. Janice explains the strengths of linking EEO to strategic human resource management, and also delineates some of the limits of such a response.

Other human resource management issues and their relationship to EEO are highlighted in this book. Some contributors provide useful strategies for the reader. Rae Torrie discusses a typical problem for EEO practitioners: the request for cost-benefit analyses. Her account of how to deal with such requests is an important contribution to the literature on human resource accounting.

Heather McDonald reports on the Work-Family Phone-In held in 1993, and argues that organisations need to respond more adequately to changing workforce demographics. The tendency for more parents and caregivers to be in employment will increase, and organisations must respond to employees' desire for 'family-friendly' workplaces.

Another issue that is of key importance to HRM is that of job evaluation. Job evaluation has become critical since the repealing of legislation dealing with pay equity. Bev Marshall explains why job evaluation is an EEO issue, demystifies the process of job evaluation, and argues for its relevance to HRM today.

Rose Ryan explores another area of relevance to EEO and human resource management, the potential contribution of workplace reform. Her article gives a general overview of the issues that can affect women when 'workplace reform' is introduced.

The theme of linking EEO to strategic human resource development is a strong one in this book. The ways to achieve this link are contestable, and the issues that need to be considered are diverse, but it is clear that EEO has spearheaded systematic HRM practice in many organisations. We hope that some of the views and research in this book will contribute to debates on strategic human resource management as well as EEO.

'Managing Diversity' versus EEO

'Managing diversity' is a theme that has come through strongly in overseas literature, particularly from American and British writers. One of our tasks in interviewing practitioners was to find out how they felt about 'managing diversity' tactics because they appear to emanate from a different philosophy from EEO. Diversity appears to be individual rather than group-based as is EEO. It has a top-down approach rather than the bottom-up one implicit in EEO

Some contributors comment on 'managing diversity' tactics and give their insights into this problematic term. The whole concept of 'diversity' has been criticised as being 'neo-racist' (see Spoonley chapter) and providing some important dilemmas for EEO (see Jones and Armstrong's chapters).

However, many do not see a contradiction between the two different approaches. Some practitioners ally themselves tactically with the message of managing diversity, although Trudie McNaughton (this volume) makes the point that:

> I tend to think of it as 'making the most of diversity' because that implies reciprocity between management and employees. That is a much more responsive and participative model (p. 308).

Managing diversity and valuing diversity programmes appear to have many of the same features as an EEO programme. The literature on managing diversity often argues for planned systematic results-oriented plans of action aimed at changing the organisational culture to make it more 'comfortable' for diverse types of people.

So in this case, the theoretical contradictions highlighted in the literature are not necessarily borne out in practice.

Where to From Here?

The roads toward realising the vision of equal employment opportunities are varied, diverse and contestable. No one has the 'right' answers. However, expertise and skills rest in the hands of a number of EEO workers and their work needs to carry on.

One of the strong messages that comes through in this book is the need to keep hold of visions, and not to get ground down by the everyday reality. Goals must be achievable and progress must be constantly reviewed. We need to nurture ourselves, and each other.

The material in this book shows that now is not a time for relaxing in a mood of self-congratulation. Some of the basic EEO work still needs to be done. Some people still stubbornly refuse to understand the basics of EEO. There are still EEO myths to be countered. People still have confused ideas that EEO is about quotas and reverse discrimination. They need to see that EEO is about carrots rather than sticks, about improving the organisation rather than conforming to an outside, imposed set of criteria.

On a more optimistic note, one of the strongest themes to come through in this book, and during our work in bringing this together, is the strong interest that there is the workplace about EEO. People are disheartened by some of larger trends that have impacted on workplaces, but they have also found new ways to create change and fairer places in which to work. There is clearly a strong interest in EEO among business people, managers, human resource specialists, academics and the general public.

This book is not definitive. We have attempted to represent many diverse voices, but a book of this size can only be a beginning. We have only scratched the surface. We hope, however, that people find it useful and that it finds life in other people's work towards equal employment opportunities.

Part One

An Overview of Equal Employment Opportunity Policy and Practice

1

Tracing the Patterns: The Development of EEO Policies in New Zealand and Overseas

Celia Briar

Introduction

T his chapter takes an overview of the historical development of equal employment opportunities (EEO): its aims, its beginnings, its underlying principles and the type of political learning that took place as it moved between the United States, Britain, Australia and New Zealand.

Equal opportunities policies were developed with the apparently ambitious brief of reducing inequality at work by breaking down occupational segregation which confined certain groups to the lowest paid and least prestigious positions in the workforce.

EEO appeared fairly radical in its early stages and has been vigorously pursued by its advocates working in the field, who have had numerous specific successes (Hunt, 1992; Korndorffer, 1992). However, despite isolated individual successes, EEO has been unable to create any overall change in long-standing patterns of structural inequality in the workforce. Part of the task of the chapter is therefore to assess some of the lessons that can be drawn from the development of EEO since World War II.

Limits and Scope of EEO

Equal employment opportunity programmes were never intended to address all forms of structural inequality in the workplace. EEO developed in a particular social and economic context. From the 1960s onwards this context included the rise of social movements such as black power, second wave feminism, gay liberation and, most recently, disability pride, coupled with the long labour shortage in most Western countries which lasted from the end of World War II until the onset of the current recession. EEO has thus been a product of its times and has been based on an analysis of current divisions within the labour market, which has not taken account of longer historical patterns of inequality in the workforce.

One of these historical patterns is the way in which some groups have historically been marginalised and used as a reserve labour force, to be drawn into the wider range of paid jobs at times of high demand for labour (such as wartime) and excluded at times of high unemployment. The largest of these groups has been married women but others have included older workers and single migrants.

Women have been used as a flexible reserve labour force over many centuries, and have been dependent on upturns in the economy to provide even limited entry to the wider range of occupations and professions ordinarily dominated by men (Hufton, 1985). Between the two world wars this century, married women were barred from paid work either formally or informally in most Western countries. Women's labour force participation rates increased markedly during World War II, and then grew during the post-war boom until the mid-1980s, although they did not reach the same levels as men's. During this period other marginalised groups, such as people with disabilities, gained greater opportunities of obtaining paid work. During the 1980s, as the recession deepened, women's labour force participation rates again began falling in OECD nations (Bakker, 1988). Women's rates of unemployment have tended to be higher than those of men and there is currently considerable hidden unemployment and underemployment in Britain and New Zealand. Since EEO has been designed to deal with discriminatory recruitment and promotion within a situation of full employment in an expanding labour market, it does not necessarily cope well with discriminatory redundancy at times of contraction.

EEO is too narrow in its scope to affect long-term patterns of inequality. It does not deal with wider employment policies which have a large impact upon total levels of employment available, or on policies which create more flexible labour markets, even though these may actively undermine the avowed aims of EEO.

Another historical pattern which is outside the scope of EEO is that even when disadvantaged groups have been successful in entering white male-dominated occupations in large numbers, those occupations may then simply lose pay and status. The feminisation of clerical work in the Western world during the present century has been an example of this phenomenon (Walby, 1986).

There are other limits on the scope of EEO. Not all groups of disadvantaged workers are designated as target groups, so that for example, EEO is not capable of dealing with inequality in employment arising from social class, even though class has been identified as a major factor affecting educational attainment and job prospects (Willis, 1977).

Moreover, EEO has, from the outset, tended to be relatively uncritical of current employment structures. Although it has been claimed that EEO is 'more than getting rid of glass doors and ceilings', is a way of 'changing what can be seen through the glass' (McNaughton, 1993, p.2), this has never been a major focus of EEO. Nor has EEO been used greatly to improve pay and extend promotional ladders within occupations currently dominated by the more disadvantaged groups such as clerical, retail, services and manufacturing. In fact, EEO has been found to be ineffective as a means of closing pay gaps, especially between men and women. Instead the main emphasis has been upon bringing members of the 'target groups' into the occupations which already have relatively good pay and promotional prospects and requiring them to adapt to a new environment.

EEO has not covered those who work unpaid in the home or community, although some may receive credit for their past unpaid work experience when applying to be hired or promoted in the paid workforce. Instead it has tended to focus upon practices of hiring, promotion, training, staff development and relations amongst specified target groups within the paid workforce (Wilson, 1988).

Furthermore, because of this somewhat limited focus, EEO does not take real account of ongoing inequality in terms of responsibility for unpaid work. EEO treats women as a major target group and even takes some account of past discrimination, yet does not take sufficient account of the fact that women continue to perform around 70 per cent of unpaid household work (Bittman, 1991), whilst having to compete in the paid labour force with men who are the recipients of wifely services (Delphy, 1984). This is symptomatic of the lack of acknowledgment of much of the work performed by women (Waring, 1988).

It can be seen therefore, that EEO from the outset has been relatively narrow in scope. EEO was never intended to be a 'cure all' for inequality in the workplace.

Having now clarified the limits and boundaries of EEO, the following sections of this chapter examine a little more closely the issues which EEO has come to address during the course of its development.

EEO was originally designed to prevent the direct and indirect discrimination against designated target groups in the workplace and the reduction of occupational segregation. Amongst the most striking features of the labour market are the horizontal divisions which confine disadvantaged groups of workers (usually including all women plus male members of specified ethnic, cultural and racial groups and people with disabilities) to a narrower range of lower status jobs; and vertical divisions which allow able-bodied white males to occupy most of the top positions of occupational hierarchies (OECD, 1985). In addition, sexual harassment has come to be regarded as a form of sex discrimination, and is now seen as an EEO issue.

Pressure for EEO Since World War II

EEO in New Zealand evolved in its own distinct ways, but developed in response to both internal and external pressures. EEO came to New Zealand in modified form from other nations and also via international instruments of the United Nations (UN) and the International Labour Organisation. Its adoption can also be traced partly to demands from target groups.

Different nations responded somewhat differently to the long period of labour shortage affecting Western nations from the 1940s to the 1970s. Some countries, such as Germany, the United Kingdom and

New Zealand, relied heavily on immigrant labour. Other countries, such as Sweden and France, made greater concessions to women to encourage them to become permanent and full members of the workforce. Countries which had adopted equal pay and opportunities programmes then had a vested interest in ensuring that other nations adopted similar strategies. This was the source of at least some of the international pressure for employment equity in the post-war years.

International Agreements on EEO

A number of international agreements about equal opportunities at work have been made since World War II. These have provided impetus for ratifying countries to adopt EEO measures, together with some guidance on how to do so. However, governments in some countries, including Britain and New Zealand, resisted pressure to conform fully to the principles contained in these agreements.

The International Labour Organisation (ILO) Convention No 111 on Discrimination in Employment (1958) required ratifying countries to provide equal opportunities and equal treatment in terms of conditions of employment such as sick leave and pensions. In 1975 the ILO went further and declared that positive action aimed at providing effective equality between the sexes would not be regarded as discriminatory. In 1967 there was a declaration opposing discrimination against women adopted unanimously by the General Assembly of the United Nations.

The 1979 United Nations Convention on the Elimination of All Forms of Discrimination Against Women was signed by New Zealand in 1980. Following pressure from the National Council of Women and the Human Rights Commission, the fourth Labour government ratified the Convention (with three reservations) in December 1984 (Chen, 1989). The Convention contained guidelines on the elimination of the barriers preventing women's participation at all levels of occupations and across the range of jobs, such as eliminating derogatory sex-role stereotyping. However, it also provided for affirmative action, or special temporary measures aimed at overcoming the effects of past discrimination and achieving equality between the sexes more rapidly. For a fuller discussion of New Zealand's progress in implementing this Convention see Judy McGregor's analysis in this volume.

Demands from Target Groups

Policy-makers displayed an awareness of the need to placate the groups who were to become designated as target groups under EEO. In the United States, EEO was born in the 1960s, in the context of racial discord in American cities; whereas in Britain, Australia and New Zealand it became acceptable to policy-makers at the height of second-wave feminist activity of the 1970s and 1980s. However, much of the impetus for EEO as a specific policy appears to have come from within government circles, rather than designated target groups.

EEO was however, demanded by New Zealand feminists, although not as vociferously as pay equity. The women's liberation movement of the 1970s demanded equal pay and equal opportunities in employment and education as two of its first three main aims (Dann, 1985).

The pressure for EEO in New Zealand built up once it became clear that the Equal Pay Act 1972 was of limited effectiveness because equal pay provisions applied only to workers performing essentially the same job. The new law encouraged employers to increase occupational segregation in order to avoid job comparisons. This effectively meant that even more women were confined to low paid 'dead-end' jobs.

The New Zealand Working Women's Charter of 1973 demanded the elimination of discrimination on the basis of sex, race, marital or parental status, sexuality or age. The Charter also demanded equality of opportunity of entry to, and promotion within, occupations and equal access to training. However, the Charter contained no demands for affirmative action. It was not until a decade later, in 1983, that affirmative action and the notion of the entry of women into non-traditional areas became a central focus for feminists in New Zealand. In addition the women's movement also explored different ways of working; including co-operatives, collectives and job-sharing (Dann, 1985).

Voluntarism versus Compulsion

In the 1970s it was accepted by the women's movement that EEO was something that women and others would have to fight to gain. In the 1980s and 1990s attitudes appear to have changed. There is currently a widespread and growing belief that it is in the commercial interests of employers to promote EEO and enjoy the benefits of a diverse workforce. Some writers therefore believe that compulsory EEO is unnecessary, since the old-fashioned employers who discriminate will simply suffer financially for their mistake (New Zealand Employers' Federation, 1985; Knowles, 1993). However, the assumption that employers will become educated simply by observing the benefits of EEO is not supported by historical evidence.

Employers had the opportunity to observe and benefit from women's aptitude at 'men's jobs' during both world wars. Yet employers, trade unions and the state in Britain, the United States and New Zealand actively co-operated in the removal of women workers from occupations such as engineering and the building trades when wartime ended (Walby, 1986), despite the fact that women were employed at significantly lower rates of pay than men.

In the United States during the 1960s it was quickly realised that voluntary affirmative action was ineffective and simply a 'shield for inaction' (Sawer, 1984). Conversely, strong compulsory EEO programmes in which employers were forced to promote workers who had previously been victims of discrimination, were successful in educating employers and managers about the capabilities of women and ethnic minorities.

However, this potential political learning was not transferred to the United Kingdom or New Zealand. During the early 1970s the British Government came to support EEO in principle but was opposed to legislation.

In New Zealand the Employers' Federation stated that it:

> ... wholeheartedly supports the principle of equal opportunity in employment, education and training. It regards the elimination of discrimination as an essential step forward in social progress (1985, p.3).

They were in favour of encouraging member firms to adopt EEO and issued guidelines and check lists on the grounds that:

> ... it is in the best interests of firms to help all their employees develop their full potential in employment, regardless of sex or ethnic grouping (1985, p. 3).

However, when legislation was being framed, employers' organisations were opposed to the proposed EEO laws (Wilson, 1988).

In 1987 the Human Rights Commission had reported to the Royal Commission on Social Policy that ten years of voluntary EEO had produced no measurable results and argued that structural change in the composition of the workforce would only come about if EEO were to be made compulsory (Human Rights Commission, 1987). The 1988 Royal Commission on Social Policy also recommended legislation on EEO covering the private sector (RCSP, 1988, Vol.II, p.385).

In fact there appears to be no evidence that discriminatory hiring and promotion would cease simply because it might be in employers' financial interests to promote a diverse workforce.

New Right commentators such as Ann Knowles (1993) blame 'patriarchal forces' for the continuation of gender divisions at work and assume that the unfettered free market, facilitated by the weakening of male-dominated trade unions, will allow the target groups to negotiate a better deal. Some feminists in the 1980s also argued that white male co-workers' resistance to EEO has played a significant part in the continuation of inequality at work (Walby, 1986; Cockburn, 1991). Obviously there is some truth in the assertion that white male workers have operated occupational closure to exclude other groups from the most desirable jobs, but this is only a part of the picture. There is no evidence to suggest that male workers are in a strong enough position to continually overrule management. Yet employers and managers have continued to recruit and promote 'in their own image', over and over again, except where there has been intervention from outside to force them to alter their practices.

The 'Merit' Principle

The 'merit' principle assumes that free competition between individuals will ensure that the most able and deserving will move into the top decision-making positions irrespective of attributes such as ethnicity, being able-bodied or gender. The merit principle is firmly based upon the notion of equality of opportunity to compete. It therefore contains an implicit assumption that if the target groups do not then move up the occupational hierarchy this is because they lack the aptitude (Jewson and Mason, 1986).

The 'merit' principle has been strongly maintained in EEO programmes, particularly in Britain, Australia and New Zealand. The concept of merit concerns the candidates' actual (rather than supposed) suitability for the job. It is described as including experience, training, demonstrated ability, performance to date and potential for further development (CCH, 1993). However, 'merit' has contained problems for target groups.

Members of target groups who have not had the opportunity to acquire training or experience have not been in a position to demonstrate their ability or potential. Further, the skills which women and ethnic minorities *have* acquired are often not valued objectively and contain gender, cultural and ablest bias. In order to overcome these problems during the 1980s some attempts were made to redefine merit. The aim was to give credit to the skills which women and some cultural groups had gained in the course of unpaid work (Burton, 1988).

Problems with 'merit' have been compounded further because some jobs are rated as more highly skilled simply because men have traditionally performed them (Phillips and Taylor, 1986). Recognition of the 'discriminatory element' in the valuing of women's and men's jobs formed an important part of the argument in favour of equal pay for work of equal value, but has not figured largely in EEO. This is problematic because the target groups have been expected to make themselves acceptable by retraining to compete with men in men's jobs, when in fact they could have stayed where they were and had their existing jobs revalued.

Anti-discrimination Elements in EEO

Initially, EEO was primarily concerned with anti-discrimination measures to remove any formal barriers against the selection and promotion of individuals. Anti-discrimination continues to be a major and basic component of EEO.

Anti-discrimination is derived from an eighteenth and nineteenth century liberal philosophical background, which asserted that all men are born equal. It was gradually extended in principle to women as a result of first and second-wave feminist activity.

In the United States the Civil Rights Act of 1964 forbade discrimination in employment on the grounds of race, colour, religion, sex and national origin (Sutch, 1973). Employers were forbidden from advertising posts in such a way as to suggest that only one sex or ethnic group should apply. Individuals who believed themselves to be victims of unlawful discrimination could bring cases against employers. American employers were obliged to report annually to the Equal Employment Opportunities Commission upon the gender composition of the various grades of workers.

Anti-discrimination EEO measures appeared in law in Britain and New Zealand a decade later than in the United States. In Britain pressure for EEO appeared to come from within the public service and the political system. A 1972 Select Committee report on EEO showed the pervasiveness of sex discrimination in employment, education and training. The public service was the first to accept the recommendations of this report on the conditions of women civil servants.

By 1974 both Labour and Conservative parties were committed to introducing EEO as the general election loomed. Both parties issued remarkably similar documents supporting equal opportunities for men and women. The 1975 Sex Discrimination Act was passed by the incoming Labour government. Under this 1975 Act, which had provisions very similar to the 1964 United States legislation (except that discrimination on the grounds of race was outlawed under separate legislation), employers were obliged to train and promote employees on the basis of their 'individual qualities and qualifications, irrespective of sex or marriage', although there was a number of exemption categories. The emphasis was on the removal of formal barriers and retention of the 'merit' principle.

Preferential recruitment of women was not allowed under the Act. Some acknowledgement was made of the lack of representation of women in many industries by allowing women-only training courses and employers were permitted to encourage women to apply for jobs and promotion. However, there was no real compensation for the effects of past discrimination.

If discrimination occurred, the burden of proof was on the complainant, which was usually extremely difficult. Furthermore, enforcement of the legislation has been almost impossible. Not surprisingly, only a small number of cases have been brought to the tribunals and of these less than one-fifth were successful. In November 1983 the European Court ruled that the 1975 Sex Discrimination Act did not comply with the European Economic Community's Equal Treatment Directive of 1978 (Hansard 6th series, Vol. 50, col.157; Briar, 1987). The UK Equal Opportunities legislation was subsequently amended, but continued to lack effective means of enforcement.

In Australia, central government anti-discrimination EEO measures were adopted somewhat later than in many other nations. The marriage bar in the public service was lifted as late as 1966 and 'men only' and 'women only' job designations finally removed in 1973 (Sawer, 1984). ILO Convention 111 was ratified in 1973, and there followed a series of pieces of legislation, covering discrimination on a variety of grounds, enacted by the various states. However, it was not until 1984 that the federal government's Sex Discrimination Act, covering direct or indirect discrimination on grounds of sex, marital status or pregnancy, was passed.

New Zealand explored the possible introduction of anti-discrimination legislation at the same time as Britain. Between 1973 and 1975 three Bills on women's rights in employment were introduced into Parliament. The 1975 Bill was strikingly similar to the Sex Discrimination Act which was passed in Britain the same year. Those who opposed the legislation claimed they did so on the grounds that it was piecemeal and 'inadequate to deal with a feature of society so entrenched as the traditional differentiation of the sexes'(New Zealand Parliamentary Debates, Vol.401, p.4791).

Instead, a single piece of legislation, the Human Rights Commission Act of 1977 was passed, which prohibited discrimination in employment on the grounds of sex, marital status, race, ethnic origin, and religious or ethical belief. In 1993 this Act was replaced by the Human Rights Act, which brought together the Human Rights Commission Act and the Race Relations Act of 1973 into one piece of legislation. In addition the grounds for discrimination in employment were expanded to include sexual orientation, disability, the presence of organisms capable of causing disease, family status, employment status and political affiliation. Like the British Sex Discrimination Act of 1975 and the New Zealand Human Rights Commission Act, the Human Rights Act provides a complaints-based system to deal with individual cases of discrimination. It does not deal with the discrimination that occurs at a systemic level.

The Labour Relations Act of 1987 also contained a section on discrimination which covered colour, race and ethnicity or national origin, sex, marital status, religious or ethical belief and trade union involvement. These conditions were carried through into the Employment Contracts Act of 1991.

It can be seen that anti-discrimination measures completely overshadowed affirmative action in EEO policies. This was the case for a relatively short period in the United States and in Australia, but for a much longer time in Britain and New Zealand. This type of EEO legislation had an important educative function for employers, many of whom had previously believed that occupational stereotyping was normal and acceptable. However, the heavy emphasis on anti-discrimination posed a number of problems.

First, anti-discrimination alone was firmly based upon the 'merit' principle. So, for example, candidates for jobs and promotion continued to be rejected on the grounds of lacking qualifications which they had been denied the opportunity to acquire.

Second, the measures were individualised and complaints-based. The responsibility to prove that discrimination had occurred was left with the victim of discrimination, who was usually relatively powerless compared with the perpetrator. This considerably limited the effectiveness of the legislation.

Finally, the measures did little to prevent discrimination from occurring. The legislation was reactive, rather than proactive or preventive, in that discrimination had to occur before action could be taken.

Affirmative Action

More recently EEO has tended to contain elements of both anti-discrimination measures and more proactive affirmative action provisions aimed at improving the overall position of disadvantaged groups of workers within the labour force. Affirmative action has contained a number of elements: it is intended to be systematic rather than individualistic; proactive rather than reactive and based upon greater equality of outcomes instead of simply equality of opportunity.

The principle of pursuing greater equality of outcomes has raised the greatest controversy. This principle embodied the notion of 'positive discrimination' which was aimed at temporary additional assistance to disadvantaged groups – for example, by the use of quotas in recruitment into training courses – until they were more fairly represented in the top positions and could compete on an equal footing. However, this was seen by its opponents as undermining the 'merit' principle. Opposition came mainly from white males, although some members of target groups opposed the quota system because they felt patronised and devalued by it. Nevertheless, many members of target groups benefited from an opportunity to 'prove' themselves that they would not otherwise have had.

Affirmative action, which aimed to break down the effects of past discrimination, was first introduced in 1961 and was aimed at assisting black Americans. Feminists campaigned for the legislation to be extended to women, and this was achieved from 1967 (Sawer, 1984). From 1968 in the United States all employers with more than 50 employees were required by law to develop an affirmative action programme. This was reinforced in 1972 with the EEO Act, which allowed for individual complaints of discrimination. This legislation covered all private firms with 15 or more employees, as well as central and local government, trade unions and educational institutions.

In 1974 the American EEO Commission issued guidelines stating that equal opportunity usually required positive affirmative action beyond the establishment of non-discriminatory hiring systems. Where organisations were found to have previously acted in an unlawful and discriminatory manner, preferential hiring and 'fast tracking' of women and blacks could be ordered as a way to compensate the groups who had earlier been denied these benefits. Between 1970 and 1980 there was a marked increase in the number of women in executive, administrative and managerial positions and in areas such as law, computing and engineering. It was this aspect of EEO which received criticism, mainly from white males, who believed that they were now the subjects of discrimination.

Britain, Australia and New Zealand were considerably more cautious in adopting affirmative action into their EEO legislation. In addition, when elements of affirmative action were finally incorporated into their programmes they were generally made less potent than they had been in America.

In Britain the main emphasis was on anti-discrimination legislation, with affirmative action being given little prominence or priority. As a result of Britain having been taken to the European Court because of the inadequacy of its equal opportunities legislation, an amendment was made to the Sex Discrimination Act in 1986, to include elements of affirmative action. However, specific provisions were minimal. For example, the mainstay of the government's affirmative action initiative under the amended Act was the provision of additional part-time employment in the civil service (Briar, 1992).

In Australia the adoption of affirmative action was shaped by competing forces. On one hand there was a concern by the Australian Labour Party to attract women voters by bringing in affirmative action, as opposed to merely anti-discrimination legislation. On the other hand there was concern about the white male Reaganite backlash in the USA to affirmative action, and especially about the quota system, which was out of all proportion to its measurable effects for target groups (Burstein, 1982). Supporters of EEO were concerned to distance themselves from this in order to avoid criticism.

The Australian Affirmative Action (Equal Employment Opportunity for Women) Act of 1986 (which was additional to various state EEO initiatives) extended affirmative action requirements to all private sector employers and higher education institutions employing 100 or more employees. Employers were obliged to implement an affirmative action programme, and submit an annual report on the progress made.

In New Zealand, as in Australia, EEO measures catering for public sector workers had been implemented earlier than those covering the private sector. Section 56 of the 1988 State Sector Act required that chief executives of government departments develop and publish an EEO programme each year that was:

> ... aimed at the identification and elimination of policies, procedures and other institutional barriers that tend to cause or perpetuate inequality in respect of the employment of any persons or groups of persons.

Additionally they were required to ensure compliance with the EEO programme. Thus the programme was to be systematic rather than individual, and proactive, not reactive. However, the Act did not mention positive discrimination, and under section 60 the 'merit' principle was specifically maintained.

Although New Zealand public sector workers now had EEO coverage under the law, it was still voluntary in the private sector. The 1990 Employment Equity Act, which was designed to extend the benefits of EEO legislation covering the public sector to private employment, was to a high degree modelled on the 1986 Australian EEO legislation. The main differences were that the New Zealand legislation covered more target groups – Maori, ethnic minorities and people with disabilities, as well as women – and was to have been applied to firms with 50 or more employees. Employers had a responsibility to develop an EEO package, and firms could be fined up to $5,000 for non-compliance.

The affirmative action intentions of the 1990 Act were plain from the definition of EEO given by the Wilson Committee which shaped the legislation. It was prescriptively seen as:

> ... a systematic, results-oriented set of actions that are directed towards the identification and elimination of discriminatory barriers that cause or perpetuate inequality in the employment of any persons or group of persons; and are further directed to redress the effects of past discrimination so as to bring those disadvantaged groups to the level of the advantaged (Wilson, 1988, p. 10).

In order to reduce opposition to the legislation, the 'merit' principle was retained. Moreover, the legislation was to have been phased in gradually over three years. Despite this, the Act was repealed by the incoming National Government only months after it had become law.

It can be seen that affirmative action remained the junior partner compared with anti-discrimination measures, especially in Britain, but also in Australia and New Zealand.

Not all of the elements of affirmative action outlined at the beginning of the section were given equal priority. In the drive to accommodate affirmative action within the existing anti-discrimination legislation and the 'merit' principle, the systematic, goal-setting elements were made prominent, but the emphasis on producing more equal outcomes via positive discrimination became substantially modified in transition from the United States.

The new emphasis was upon employers attempting to create a less segregated workforce. There were no clearly defined penalties for failure to achieve greater equality of outcomes. However, even this milder form of affirmative action was opposed by a government dedicated to reducing direct state intervention in the labour market.

Was EEO the Way to Go?

This final section assesses whether EEO was the most effective and appropriate means of reducing structural inequality during the years after World War II. This period of full employment, when marginalised workers were recruited into the paid workforce in greater numbers, was a time when there appeared to be scope for greater equality in the workforce.

As we have seen, the main drive of EEO has been towards the removal of barriers against competition by breaking down occupational segregation in the 'top jobs'.

The notion of bringing about reductions in inequality at work by eroding occupational segregation, whilst superficially economical and attractive, has contained many problems. Prominent is the fact that it leads to assimilation and tokenism, in which the target groups, usually remaining a minority, continually aspire to membership of a group to which they can seldom fully belong. This continues to convey a subtle message that the white male-dominated professions and the people who occupy the top positions within them are somehow superior.

Although some members of target groups have benefited from EEO in terms of a career and status in the community, the majority have remained largely unaffected by EEO. Indeed, since the onset of the recession, EEO has served to partially disguise a situation where inequalities within the workforce have been increasing, and the target groups have become generally worse off.

In addition, both anti-discrimination (based on the 'merit' principle) and affirmative action (embodying positive discrimination) have contained problems for target groups. The 'merit' system implicitly assumes that if the target groups do not become represented in top positions relative to their numbers in the population they must have failed (Jewson and Mason, 1986; Burton, 1988). Conversely, however, positive discrimination (and especially quota systems), may suggest to unconvinced stake-holders that members of target groups are second-rate employees.

Moreover, evidence suggests that occupational segregation is diminishing only very slowly. For example, although there are now fewer male-only and female-only occupations than earlier in the century, the vast majority of women continue to work in female-dominated occupations, and the majority of new entrants to the labour force continue to be employed in 'traditional' sex-typed areas (OECD, 1985; Mumford, 1989).

One way of reducing inequality at work, which would have had a stronger effect on reducing pay differentials than equal opportunities in the countries that adopted it, would have been the implementation of equal pay for work of equal value. This would have involved revaluing the work which people already did, to remove the discriminatory element in wage-fixing. Another would have been to reduce pay differentials via more progressive taxation systems.

However, EEO was the preferred option of policy-makers, despite its relative ineffectiveness. For example, overall pay levels were not affected even by strong EEO legislation in the United States. Because of the weak equal pay legislation in the United States, women's hourly pay remained at only two-thirds of men's. This is in contrast with Australia and New Zealand, where equal pay legislation has been responsible for a reduction in the difference in average hourly pay rates between men and women to four-fifths since the mid-1970s, despite weaker EEO legislation.

EEO has been reformist in the sense that it has deflected attention from issues that could have been of greater assistance to the target groups and which might have brought about more radical and permanent changes. It has been recognised as a 'vote catcher' which has helped to improve the image of political parties in the eyes of the target groups (who together form a majority of the population).

However, whenever EEO has threatened to have any major effects upon the status quo, it has caused an outcry from privileged white males who, of all groups, have traditionally had the largest representation in policy-making circles. This may help to explain why states have had the opportunity to make EEO more effective via 'political learning' but instead have actually chosen to use the experience of other nations to make EEO less effective.

EEO has proved highly acceptable to most policy-makers and businesspeople, provided that it is voluntary. However, the more that inequality in the workforce widens, as is happening at present, the more vociferous will be the opposition to genuine equality at work from a privileged and influential minority.

As state intervention in the labour market has diminished and trade unions have been weakened, EEO has come to be regarded by target groups as having the responsibility to compensate for most of the ills in the labour market. The fact that EEO, with limited resources and poor enforcement, has come to be held as a 'cure-all' appears to be a retrograde step. It may well be counter-productive to assign additional functions to EEO which it may be unable to fulfil. In order to make a real difference, EEO and EEO workers require greater material support. It is important to combine this with a realistic assessment of the limits of EEO and recognition of the fact that it can only be truly effective as part of a range of strong and effective policies to reduce inequality at work.

References

Bakker, I. (1988), 'Women's Employment in Comparative Perspective', in J. Jenson, E. Hagen and C. Reddy (eds), *The Feminisation of the Labour Force*, New York: Oxford University Press.

Bittman, M. (1991), *Juggling Time: How Australian Families Use Time*, Canberra: Office of the Status of Women, Department of the Prime Minister and Cabinet.

Briar, C.J. (1987), 'Women in State Employment Policy: a Description and Analysis of Policies Affecting Women's Work in Twentieth Century Britain', unpublished PhD thesis, University of Sheffield.

Briar, C. (1992), 'Part-time Work and the State in Britain, 1941-1987', in L. Lundy, K. Lundy and B. Warme (eds), *Part-time Work : Risk or Opportunity?*, New York: Praeger.

Burstein, P. (1982), 'Equal Employment Opportunity: What We Believe, What We Know and What Research Can Show'. Paper given at the American Sociological Association Annual Meeting, San Francisco, September 6-10.

Burton, C. (1988), *Redefining Merit*, Canberra: Australian Government Publishing Service.

CCH (Australia) Ltd. (1993), *Australian and New Zealand Equal Opportunity Law and Practice*, Sydney: CCH Australia Ltd.

Chen, M.(1989), *Women and Discrimination: New Zealand and the United Nations Convention*, Institute of Policy Studies, Wellington: Victoria University Press.

Cockburn, C. (1991), *In the Way of Women: Men's Resistance to Sex Equality in Organisations*, Basingstoke: Macmillan.

Dann, C. (1985), *Up From Under: Women and Liberation in New Zealand, 1970-1985*, Wellington: Allen and Unwin.

Delphy, C. (1984), *Close to Home: A Materialist Analysis of Women's Oppression*, London: Hutchinson.

Hufton, O. (1985), 'What is Women's History?', *History Today*, 35, 38-40.

Human Rights Commission (1987), 'Affirmative Action for Women in Employment'. Paper submitted to the Royal Commission on Social Policy.

Hunt, S. (1992), 'Equal Employment Opportunities: Valuing Women's Work?'. Unpublished Masters thesis, Massey University, Palmerston North.

Jewson and Mason (1986), 'The Theory and Practice of Equal Opportunities', *Sociological Review*, 34 (22), 314-6.

Knowles, A. (1993), 'Women and Work'. Paper presented at the conference Women at Work: Issues for the 1990s Seminar, held at Victoria University, Wellington, 12 February.

Korndorffer, W. (1992), 'Putting Equal Employment Opportunities into Practice: A Review of Three Years at Victoria University of Wellington', in C. Briar, R. Munford and M. Nash (eds), *Superwoman, Where Are You? Social Policy and Women's Experience*, Palmerston North: Dunmore Press.

McNaughton, T. (1993), 'Where to with EEO?'. Paper presented at the conference, Women at Work: Issues for the 1990s, Victoria University of Wellington, 12 February.

Mumford, K. (1989), *Women Working: Economics and Reality*, Sydney: Allen and Unwin.

New Zealand Employers' Federation (1985), *Positive Action Manual: Implementing Equal Opportunities in the Workplace*, Wellington: New Zealand Employers' Federation.

Organisation for Economic Cooperation and Development (1985), *Equality for Women: a Survey of Ten OECD Countries*, Paris: OECD.

Phillips, A. and Taylor B. (1986), 'Sex and Skill', in Feminist Review (ed.), *Waged Work: A Reader*, London: Virago.

Royal Commission on Social Policy (1988), *The April Report*, Wellington: Government Print.

Sawer, M. (1984), *Towards Equal Opportunity: Women and Employment at the Australian National University*, Canberra: Australian National University.

Sutch, W.B. (1973), *Women with a Cause*, Wellington: New Zealand University Press.

Walby, S. (1986), *Patriarchy at Work*, Cambridge: Polity Press.

Waring, M. (1988), *If Women Counted: A New Feminist Economics*, London: MacMillan.

Willis, P. (1977), *Learning to Labour: How Working-class Kids Get Working-class Jobs*, Farnborough: Saxon House.

Wilson, M.A. (1988), *Report of the Working Group on Equal Employment Opportunities and Equal Pay: Towards Employment Equity*, Wellington: Government Print.

2

Defending a Beachhead: Managerialism and EEO in the Public Sector, 1988 – 1992

Pat Walsh & John Dickson

Introduction

This chapter reflects on progress, or lack of it, in the advancement of equal employment opportunities in the public sector in New Zealand. Its aim is to analyse the development of EEO as a political and industrial issue in the public sector since the early 1980s. The chapter does this by discussing how the issue of EEO unfolded over time, the manner in which it acquired both political and industrial resources and the process by which it lost them. It also addresses the bit in the middle – the programmes which were established in the salad days when EEO appeared to be becoming entrenched in the management of government departments.

The Liberal and Radical Models of EEO

Jewson and Mason (1986) observe that the liberal model of EEO looks for the free and open operation of a competitive labour market in which advancement is dependent only on merit, which is seen, crucially, as an objective and individual attribute. The purpose of an EEO policy is to ensure that impediments to a freely operating labour market are removed, and that individuals compete there equally, with outcomes decided by relative merit.

The radical model emphasises labour market outcomes rather than procedures. To supporters of the radical model, liberal notions of merit as an objective and individual attribute 'contain and conceal a series of value judgements' (Jewson and Mason, 1986, p.315). Merit, in the radical model, is a socially constructed concept, reflecting the ability of powerful groups in the society to define what abilities, skills, and knowledge will be valued over others. The group is the conceptual basis of the radical model. It seeks to remove labour market impediments to the equal advancement of target groups. Thus, for radicals, 'the absence of a fair distribution is, ipso facto, evidence of unfair discrimination' (ibid., p.315) and is itself justification for labour market intervention.

The liberal model takes a positive action approach to the implementation of EEO (Jewson and Mason, 1986). Positive action policies include changes to a wide range of personnel practices, recruitment, selection and promotion, as well as other policy changes such as provision of child-care facilities, EEO awareness training to change workplace attitudes, support for domestic leave and so forth. Radicals favour positive discrimination. This 'entails the deliberate manipulation of employment practices so as to obtain a fair distribution of the deprived or disadvantaged population within the workforce' (ibid., p.322). Positive discrimination policies include specific employment quotas, varying entry requirements or different criteria for performance assessment.

Recent analysis has focused on the limitations of the liberal/radical framework (Cockburn, 1989). Cockburn found little support for the radical prescription of positive discrimination among target groups in her case study. 'Moving the goalposts' was seen as unfair itself, and as likely to divide target groups (and possibly stimulate a conservative backlash). Even more importantly, it was criticised for accepting as given the character of the organisations that generate discrimination and exploitation. She has proposed a transformational model of EEO, which incorporates the liberal and radical agendas, but which also 'brings into view the nature and purpose of institutions and the processes by which the power of some groups over others in institutions is built and renewed ... it also looks for change in the nature of power, in the control ordinary people of diverse kinds have over institutions, a melting away of the white male monoculture' (p.218).

These ideas are discussed in the context of EEO Management Plans later in this chapter, but first it is necessary to acknowledge some external pressures that have impacted on EEO up to and including this period.

EEO in the New Zealand Public Sector

EEO first emerged as an issue in the public sector in the first half of the 1980s. National government politicians did not support EEO, but nor did they oppose it. An informal coalition of supportive managers and trade union officials succeeded in promoting the EEO agenda (Tremaine, 1991).

The dominance of a managerialist restructuring agenda (Boston *et al.*, 1991) in the public sector set limits to what could be achieved with EEO in the second half of the 1980s. Managerialism aimed to reshape the public sector in the image of successful private sector firms and do away with bureaucratic constraints on managerial direction. In contrast, supporters of EEO were proposing new measures to constrain managerial discretion. A compromise was found in the liberal model of EEO. The latter could be made compatible with managerialism by highlighting their common concerns with efficiency. Managerialism looked for the efficient operation of different markets, and if the labour market could be made more efficient by the elimination of discriminatory practices, then managerialism was able to accept EEO.

Thus, the liberal model of EEO predominates in the good employer provisions of the State Sector Act 1988, but is combined somewhat uneasily with elements of the radical model. Liberalism's emphasis on fair dealing based on individual merit is central to the good employer obligation in the Act. The chief executive is enjoined to operate a personnel policy 'containing provisions generally accepted as necessary for the fair and proper treatment of employees'. These include 'the impartial selection of suitably qualified persons for appointment' and an obligation to provide 'opportunities for the enhancement of the abilities of individual employees' (s.56). The Act defines an EEO programme in orthodox liberal terms as 'a programme that is aimed at the identification and elimination of all aspects of policies, procedures, and other institutional barriers that cause or perpetuate, or tend to cause or perpetuate, inequality in respect to the employment of any persons or group of persons' (s.58). But even that definition contains a hint of the radical agenda. The reference to the need to remove 'institutional barriers' that cause inequality arguably goes beyond the individualist and procedural emphasis of the liberal model.

Other provisions of the good employer obligation draw on aspects of the radical model of EEO. The focus on target groups rather than on individuals, which is central to the radical model, is firmly entrenched in the State Sector Act, which identifies Maori, women, ethnic minority groups and persons with disabilities as the subjects of EEO programmes. A statutory obligation upon chief executives to take account not just of the labour market needs of the organisation but of the employment requirements of affirmative action target groups, is a clear departure from managerialist principles and from the previously dominant liberal model of EEO. Similarly, if taken at its word, the Act's requirement that EEO programmes take account of the 'aims and aspirations' of Maori and ethnic minority groups forces upon chief executives a set of considerations from outside the organisation which neither managerialism nor the liberal model of EEO would embrace.

EEO Management Plans under the State Sector Act

In this study, we examined the EEO Management Plans for 1988/89, 1989/90 and 1990/91 for nine government departments, their annual progress reports and the statistical reports provided by each department on the demographic make-up of their employment structure. The content of the Management Plans are discussed below, with objectives categorised by whether they fell into the liberal or radical model of EEO. The analysis does not set out to identify a set of best EEO practices, nor to provide a comparative report card on the fate of EEO. Our interest is in understanding the character of EEO Management Plans, the internal struggle between competing models of EEO which they reflect, and the manner in which the issue of EEO unfolded in the New Zealand public sector over a four-year period. This process is best understood in terms of the location of EEO within a wider institutional context, which created opportunities for the advancement of EEO at the same time as it set limits to what could be achieved.

The Liberal Agenda

The first requirement for the advancement of EEO was to guarantee its status and its resources within departments, and to provide a secure platform for progress. All EEO Management Plans, therefore, concerned themselves with the question of institutional security. This was expressed in aiming for the appointment of EEO Co-ordinators at appropriate levels, reporting to or actually part of senior management and the appointment of EEO liaison staff. A key objective was that all job descriptions for management positions include responsibility for EEO, and that a commitment to EEO be a requirement for management appointments. Many programmes included as an objective the development of a database on advertising, job applicants, appointments, promotion, disciplining, training, dismissals and redundancies for systematic assessment against the principles of the EEO programme.

Common elements in programmes to raise awareness of EEO included publicising the department's commitment to EEO, circulating information packages among employees, banning the use of sexist and racist language in all departmental communications and ensuring that an EEO grievance or complaints process was established and well known. All departments relied upon training as a means of raising awareness.

Human Resource Management Policies and Practices

Undoubtedly the biggest component of all EEO Management Plans dealt specifically with personnel and human resource management policies and practices. The determination to give all individuals of comparable merit a roughly equal chance of being appointed to an organisation and of progressing within it is at the heart of the liberal model of EEO. This concern was expressed in a focus on recruitment, selection, performance appraisal and job evaluation policies. Thus, departments sought to ensure that all their personnel material reflected their EEO policies, that recruitment booklets were multilingual and that recruitment methods were culturally appropriate. This entailed establishing relations with community groups which might be a source of potential job applicants, advertising jobs widely to affirmative action target groups inside and outside the department, noting in all job advertisements the department's commitment to EEO and its desire to receive applications from target group members. Additionally, where appropriate, plans dealt with advertising vacancies in Maori and other languages and including in job advertisements knowledge of Maori and community languages and cultures as part of the criteria for appointment and promotion. The EEO plans aimed for job interview panels with an appropriate gender and cultural balance, and to provide suitable EEO training for all interview panel members to ensure they were free of bias in their questions and evaluations of applicants. All plans permit job applicants to bring whanau or a support group to interviews. Many plans addressed the need for a physical audit of the workplace to assess its suitability for people with disabilities, and to make any provision necessary such as car-parking. In the area of performance appraisal, the plans emphasised the importance of incorporating EEO indicators into any performance appraisal system. The plans called for the review of job descriptions and job evaluation systems to ensure they were gender and culturally neutral, and that they specify appropriate and essential job content, relevant experience and skills. In this regard, there was particular concern not to disqualify workers with disabilities unnecessarily and to identify jobs that could be carried out by workers with disabilities.

The Radical Agenda

Radical provisions in EEO Management Plans involved direct intervention in an effort to alter labour market outcomes for affirmative action target groups. The provision of career development opportunities specifically for target group members was an important example of this approach. This included career counselling with counsellors drawn from target groups where possible. Departments were slow to move towards positive discrimination policies, partly no doubt due to fears of political repercussions, but also because of scepticism about their effectiveness. However, by the third set of plans in 1990/91, there was a visible trend from a liberal to a radical perspective, expressed in quantitative targets for the employment of target group members. Another interventionist or redistributive policy was departmental support for existing State Services Commission management programmes for women, Maori, Pacific Islanders and persons with disabilities.

The Transformational Agenda

However, the approach of liberal and radical agendas do not challenge the structure of the organisation in any fundamental sense. An alternative approach is to accept that the success of EEO policies may require changing the organisation as much as changing its employees. In this vein, most departmental EEO plans included the objective of investigating the possibilities of creating more flexible work patterns. This included numerical flexibility; flexible hours, permanent part-time work, job-sharing, rotation, secondment, special projects or placements in positions of greater responsibility and childcare policy. They also included functional flexibility: occupational reclassification, reskilling target group members into non-traditional areas, new ways of defining and recognising skills, especially those acquired in the home, marae, community work or other non-traditional environments. The plans also included the objective of applying affirmative action policies in selecting workers for training and reskilling opportunities. However, success in these areas was limited.

The Uncertain Fate of EEO in the Public Sector

The tension in the State Sector Act between the liberal and radical versions of EEO was largely resolved in favour of liberalism, with the transformational model subordinated to both of them. As interesting, however, is the manner in which the fate of those plans, once designed, was shaped by the institutional context in which they were implemented. This process is explored in more depth below.

Time and again, departmental progress reports identified restructuring and financial restraint as the key constraints on the achievement of EEO objectives. This was particularly so for policies such as career development and training, which required managers to take a long-term perspective. Few could do this with much confidence. In a period of great job insecurity, personnel policies which seemed to favour particular groups over others aroused opposition. Fiscal constraint made some managers reluctant to allocate scarce and prized resources to what they saw as unnecessary and unproductive activity. The impact of restructuring was most marked in areas drawn from the radical and transformational models. Departments either gave a greater priority to the achievement of objectives from the liberal model, or genuinely found these easier to achieve.

New organisational structures established as part of the restructuring process had a distinctive impact on the fate of EEO. Responsibility for EEO, as for other management functions, was decentralised. It remains a moot point whether direction from the centre under the pre-1988 structure might have achieved more and at a faster rate than working through separate and autonomous departments and divisions. The old structure had essentially one crucial veto point, and a change in the prevailing balance at the centre could have brought progress to a sudden halt. The new structure is more favourable to EEO when a particular department or division is strongly supportive, and can move ahead at its own pace and according to its own judgement. It is less favourable to EEO when the opposite is the case. The creation of a greater number of potential veto points enhances the opportunities for successful resistance to EEO. Decentralisation has also made for greater variation in EEO policies and practices. The range of departmental plans attests to that. But, in the case of some departments with autonomous divisions or service units, the differences among the EEO plans are quite marked, and hence EEO outcomes may be notably uneven within a department.

Conclusion

The promotion and consolidation of EEO prior to 1988 depended upon a particular and favourable balance of political, bureaucratic and industrial coalitions. By the early 1990s, that balance was far less favourable. It became increasingly clear following the National government's repeal of the Employment Equity Act, that EEO was a lower government priority than it had been under Labour. Without political support, and notwithstanding the continuing statutory obligation to be a good employer, the impetus for EEO perceptibly weakened.

The continual process of restructuring made promotion of EEO difficult for government officials, the second party to the EEO alliance. Official responsibility lay with the EEO Unit in the State Services Commission, but the decentralisation of responsibility for EEO reduced its capacity to influence the course of events from the centre. Moreover, despite the State Services Commission's statutory obligation to 'promote, develop and monitor' EEO, an active role for the EEO Unit would have gone beyond the new kind of relationship that was emerging between the central agency and government departments. There was a deliberate effort in general to discard most of the control historically exerted by the Commission, and it was not intended that EEO should be exempt from that.

Public sector union officials, the third party to the EEO alliance, also found it difficult to give EEO the priority it had previously enjoyed. Union officials were increasingly preoccupied with the consequences of restructuring – job losses, redundancies, departmental reorganisations, loss of services and with employer pressure on established conditions of employment. Managerialism had another impact on EEO by making it more difficult to sustain the co-operation between union and government officials which had been so important to the progress of EEO previously.

The loss of momentum from earlier supporters placed a great responsibility upon EEO co-ordinators in government departments. They, however, were also in a difficult situation. They faced the usual difficulties of promoting a relatively new agenda in a bureaucratic setting where possibilities for resistance and opposition abound. In addition, they were required do so amidst a process of managerialist restructuring whose very premises were often hostile to EEO.

EEO co-ordinators are caught in the middle of demands for EEO and expectations from senior management that they will support and promote wider organisational objectives. As Cockburn (1989, p.218) puts it, EEO officers operate as 'an interface between a particular constituency of interests and the management system'. They are like community officers in local authorities:

> If they do the job to the benefit of their constituency they incur the wrath of their employers. If they satisfy their managers they will certainly be blamed for treachery by those they hoped to assist. Both jobs attract progressives and both jobs destroy them.

In such difficult circumstances, where key supporting alliances have been disrupted by wider developments, and where new and potentially effective alliances are not immediately apparent, it is not surprising that a sense of gloom pervades many of the assessments of the fate of EEO in the New Zealand public sector. A different perspective would argue that the promotion of EEO is a long-term project, and that an exclusive preoccupation with current difficulties obscures progress made in the last decade. Most importantly, what matters is the acquisition of resources and the embedding of EEO programmes in government departments, however unevenly and in some cases very tentatively. Defending a beachhead may seem a modest objective for the immediate future, but successful defence offers at least the prospect of progress in the future.

Note

We would like to thank the Faculty of Commerce and Administration and the Internal Research Committee, both of Victoria University of Wellington, for their support for this project. We are grateful also to the nine government departments, and particularly their EEO co-ordinators, who helped us with our research. We have presented this research twice to the EEO co-ordinators Group in the public service, and we appreciate the time that they have taken to discuss it with us. This chapter is a substantially shortened and revised version of *The Emperor's New Clothes: Equal Employment Opportunity in the New Zealand Public Sector, 1988 – 1992*, Working Paper 3/93, Industrial Relations Centre, Victoria University, Wellington.

References

Boston, J., Martin, J., Pallot, J., and Walsh, P. (eds) (1991), *Reshaping the State: New Zealand's Bureaucratic Revolution, 1984-1990*, Auckland: Oxford University Press.

Cockburn, C. (1989), 'Equal Opportunities: the Long and Short Agenda', *Industrial Relations Journal*, 20, (3), 213-225.

Jewson, N. and Mason, D. (1986), 'The Theory and Practice of Equal Opportunities Policies: Liberal and Radical Approaches', *Sociological Review*, 34, (2), 307-334.

Tremaine, M. (1991), 'Equal Employment Opportunity and State Sector Reform', in J. Boston, J. Martin, J. Pallot, and P. Walsh (eds) (1991), *Reshaping the State: New Zealand's Bureaucratic Revolution, 1984-1990*, Auckland: Oxford University Press.

3

Never Turning Back, But Where to Now for People with Disabilities?

Wendy Wicks

This paper is dedicated to the late Joan Stone, with much aroha. Her pursuit of equal employment opportunities, in particular for people with disabilities, was fuelled by passion, sincerity and a truly inspirational vision of justice.

> *Equal opportunities is widely seen as a tool of management that has sanitised and contained the struggle for equality.*
>
> *(Cockburn, 1989, p.213)*

Introduction

The implications of Cockburn's statement for disability EEO (D-EEO), indeed for EEO in general, are challenging. It is a stimulus for analysis of the situation in Aotearoa. To respond to it requires answers to three questions. Is the statement accurate for this context? If so, to what degree? Finally, is there any action which is recommended in its light? It is as a beginning point for inquiry, rather than as a statement of fact, that Cockburn's comment is used.

It has been five years since the 1988 State Sector Act required government departments to have Equal Employment Opportunities (EEO) programmes and people with disabilities were named as one of the target groups. Last year, 1993, human rights legislation coverage was extended to include people with disabilities. That human rights legislation provides employment coverage for people with disabilities by protecting

55

individuals with disabilities from workplace harassment. Considering these events it is appropriate to assess their impact on employment-related programmes and policies for people with disabilities.

In this paper three background sections form the base for subsequent analysis. These are the broad sweep of disability issues, theoretical orientations in disability and the building of a rounded picture of D-EEO and the changes over five years. This background provides context for the analysis section which delineates gaps in our knowledge, assesses its impact and suggests future directions and issues for exploration.

My assessment is less than wholehearted in its acclaim for the impact to date of EEO. I will suggest that now is a good time to form a relationship, based on mutual respect, between theoretical and practical perspectives. I believe that such an action-oriented alliance offers hope for D-EEO and for progress, which in the present situation, has proved elusive.

Three perspectives have influenced me and are relevant to this paper. They are first, the lived reality of disability; second, my work 'at the coalface' as an EEO Co-ordinator; and third, my involvement with social policy at a theoretical level. These perspectives underlie my analysis and are discussed further in the concluding section.

Beginnings

This section examines three areas of theory which are useful in understanding EEO issues in New Zealand. These are Lindquist's five-stage historical typology of the evolution of attitudes regarding people with disabilities; the medical model of disability; and social theories which challenge the medical model of disability and provide alternative ways of understanding disability in society.

To both D-EEO and disability issues more generally, historical currents are important. It is by what has been that we trace patterns in what is happening now. The reminder is consistently given from Maori of the way in which the present and past are interconnected. Further, it is important that people without disabilities, whose power in disability issues is still highly pronounced, are able to form an understanding of the way that history and assumptions about disability impact on laws and policies, visibility and the way lives are lived. Awareness of issues, events and currents of thought is important to the process of analysis.

Bengt Lindquist (1990) provides a useful five-stage historical typology which is used here to illustrate the evolution of attitudes regarding people with disabilities. However, a word of warning about the generalisability of this typology. Although the typology has applicability over much of the world, it cannot be assumed that all parts of the world experience the same stages at the same time. Thousands of people in the third world live in conditions associated with the first stage of isolation, while most of the Western world experiences the fourth stage of normalisation. Nor can it be assumed that the stages follow one another in a start-finish sequence, since they almost inevitably overlap each other.

Lindquist's Typology

The first stage, one of isolation, lasted for a number of centuries. People with disabilities were ignored, neglected, hidden or driven away because of superstitious fears about disability. Survival tended to be marginal.

The second stage was one of care. Care was accompanied by religious charity or humanitarian philanthropy. Initially there was a provision of protection and shelter. Later there developed a mind-set which said that 'they' were best off with others 'of their own kind', usually in some isolated setting. Gradually an understanding was reached that 'they' were educable.

The third stage was one of habilitation. Simple crafts and skills for everyday living began to be taught. As understanding of disability grew, so did the scope of the teaching. People with disabilities were beginning to move to living in the community, although the employment tended to be of the sheltered workshop variety – largely simple, repetitive, and at a lower rate of pay.

The fourth stage, where ideas about normalisation were critical, occurred around the 1950s. Normalisation principles stated that people with disabilities were entitled to a life as normal as possible. This meant life, including work, in community settings. The movement to return people with disabilities from the institutions in which they had been segregated began to gather momentum. As well, trained people with disabilities began to live active lives in the community They began to discover the barriers to their participation in a society not planned for the inclusion of people with disabilities. This, Lindquist suggests, is the stage which most Western countries have come to, but not progressed beyond, since community living, integration and barrier-removal is still being worked on throughout most of the Western world.

Lindquist's fifth and final stage of citizenship talks of the inclusion of people with disabilities in the full range of human activities and an absence of barriers in policies, laws and attitudes. It would be foolish to suggest that this stage has been attained yet, but it is a logical progression from the previous stages and from the theoretical constructions of disability that have emerged from them.

The Medical Model of Disability

The historical progression outlined above illustrates some continuing themes. One that is particularly salient is a paternalism that is exemplified in the medical model. Medical advances from the eighteenth century on have included, notably, a medical concept of disease. This concept is associated with the work of Koch and Pasteur. This concept of disease, allied with technological advances such as stethoscopes and ophthalmoscopes, meant there was now a means of diagnosing disability. The ability to diagnose disability was encouraged and used, as many states saw the advantages in being able to distinguish 'real' disability. The separation out of the deserving from the undeserving became, as Stone (1985) points out, more effective as a result of medicine's tools.

Thus, there was an increase in medical influence on disability, an influence that is still very powerful. Ever more specialised categories of medical diagnosis became a primary focus in this; an individualistic, deficit-centred concept. Medical control was centred upon hospitals, and on medical 'professionals'. Their control has become considerable and it has included such aspects as living arrangements, financial benefits, equipment, reproduction and relationships, educability and the ability to work. The ultimate expression of medical power over people with disabilities lies in right-to-life issues. The power that grew then, still exists now.

This power can also be seen in the prevalence of ideas with which the medical model is associated. There is a focus on the individual's pathology and upon identifying their 'deficits'. Morris (1992) details a comprehensive range of ideas about people with disabilities which are associated with 'inability', 'negativity' and a lack of wholeness or normality. An association of these terms with the medical model is readily discernible.

Selection from List of Beliefs About People with Disabilities

* That we feel ugly, inadequate and ashamed of our disability
* That we crave to be 'normal' and 'whole'
* That we 'never give up hope' of a cure
* That our disability has affected us psychologically, making us bitter and neurotic
* That we don't have, and never have had, any real or significant experiences in the way non-disabled people do
* That we can't actually *do* anything. That we 'sit around' all day 'doing nothing'.

Medical science has helped to construct the stereotype of people with disabilities shown in Morris's list although it has provided many advances which aid the living conditions for people with disabilities. The benefits of relief from suffering are great, and few would suggest that they should be abandoned. But the medical model has had considerable negative effects on people with disabilities. Of particular note, for its continued effect in the employment arena, is the 'grab-bag' of negative attitudes which arise from medical model ideas. The focus on individual pathology and deficits in capabilities contributes to and reinforces the widespread stereotype of people with disabilities as passive, dependent and helpless, deficient in 'normal' abilities, and productive only to a diminished degree (this means an inability to be employed). The mortgage on the advances of medical science has meant high payments for people with disabilities.

Other Perspectives

Over the last 15 to 20 years, alternative constructions of disability have been developed. They have principally arisen from within the disability community and are a challenge to the assumptions of the medical model. There are two particular strands of significance that are explored in this section: the creation of disability theories and human rights theories of disability. While the two understandings have considerable complementarity, it is useful to describe both strands.

In social theory, the vision of an imperfect and incapable individual has been recognised as conceptually flawed. Instead there is an understanding that disability is largely a social creation. The focus in this alternative position is on the disabling effects of society's organisation. This is not only the exclusion from houses, footpaths, public buildings and facilities, but also exclusion from access to goods and services such as the transport systems, policies, regulations, information systems and laws. Social theory traces the links between the external ways this disabled society operates, the attitudes and behaviours of able-bodied people, and the ways that these attitudes and behaviours are translated into social policy. For instance, the belief that disability represents inability, gives rise to laws and policies where workers with disabilities are seen as unable to produce at a 'full' rate (whatever that means) and creates a society where choices and chances are limited for some.

A critique of the ableist society and its effects is well developed by such writers as Finklestein (1980), Oliver (1990), Morris (1991) and Sullivan (1991). But an alternative approach to the manifest disadvantages of social discrimination has not yet been well developed in lived reality.

Human rights theorists emphasise that people with disabilities have an intrinsic humanity which confers on them the same entitlement to basic human rights as all other humans. In common with social creation theorists, they point to the way stereotypes and attitudes are used to create laws and practices which deny people their basic human rights (Hahn, 1987; Gartner and Joe, 1987). Human rights discussions involve fundamental issues of human nature which touch a deep vein of philosophical debate, particularly issues of autonomy, personal self-determination and the intrinsic value of individual privacy. In a recent document from the Australian Privacy Commissioner's Office, Montague comments:

This stems from the fundamental premise that all people have intrinsic value independent of their particular circumstances, and the principle of autonomy is upheld by specific autonomy related rights (1993, pp. 3-4).

This document makes clear the constituent parts of human rights in relation to disability and is recommended to interested readers.

While human rights may be seen as a consequence of attitudes and behaviours, they are also intrinsic entities. An avowal of this, and an insistence on inclusion of all people in the life of their society, presents a challenge to the whole medical model ideology (Pearpoint and Forrest, 1992).

Human rights approaches have strong implicit support from the disability community in general in Aotearoa, as well as more explicit support from writers such as Patson (1993). Human rights legislation has frequently featured as a top issue in D-EEO too, as workers have been well aware of its complementarity to the provisions of EEO legislation, and of the anti-discrimination in employment coverage which they did not have.

In this section some of the consequences of theoretical stances can be seen in the historical stages. Their effect in the lives of people with disabilities has been comprehensive. Among the areas in which effects can be seen are (notably, but not exclusively): health, housing, income, relationships of all varieties, reproduction, language and employment. The global and interconnected nature of disadvantage, with its genesis from a nexus of attitudes transformed into action, should not be forgotten as the focus of this paper moves to employment, EEO and disability.

EEO Beginnings

The growth of the EEO movement arose largely from a public service background. It was closely interlinked with such legislation as the 1971 Race Relations Act, the 1972 Equal Pay Act, the 1973 Industrial Relations Act and the 1977 Human Rights Commission Act. There was concerted pressure for the removal of inequities in the employment practices then current. Pay and job stereotyping were, and still are, inequitable practices at issue. The 1984 EEO policy statement by the State Services Commission (SSC) was followed by the institution of an EEO Unit at the SSC in 1986. This was also the year in which the Employers' Federation issued their EEO policy statement.

When the State Owned Enterprises Act 1986 was introduced, the first legislation to deal with EEO, there was considerable dissatisfaction with a lack of explicit provision for EEO. Pressure intensified, and when the 1988 State Sector Act extensively restructured the public service, considerable struggles followed to ensure EEO provisions were spelled out in far more detail. (The events are decribed in Walsh and Dickson's 1993 paper.) The EEO provisions were, in the end, more comprehensive, but they still gave rise to some controversy. To some, the apparent contradictions in the Act, between the aims of EEO and restructuring, were visible (Wicks, 1989). Others more optimistically noted that there was considerable progressive potential in the EEO provisions (Sullivan, 1991). Walsh and Dickson (1993) however, argue that the impact of EEO in government departments was muted by two interrelated issues. These were first, the managerialist agenda in the drive to reorganise the public sector which was the Act's main thrust, and second, the liberalist focus in both the wording of the EEO section and the translation of the wording into actions. In effect, the EEO provisions seemed to become progressively more difficult to achieve as time went on.

D-EEO: At the Start

The attitudinal disadvantages to people with disabilities in the employment arena have been outlined. Actual barriers were also present. Even before EEO gathered momentum in the early 1980s, expressions of concern for the tangible evidence of disadvantage had come from organisations such as the Rehabilitation League, the Royal New Zealand Foundation for the Blind and the Society for the Intellectually Handicapped. Now the gathering of other data became more systematic. Statistical information identified a high level of unemployment amongst people with disabilities. Jack's 1978 survey for the Wellington Hospital Board indicated an average disability unemployment rate of 33.7 per cent in contrast to a general rate of two per cent. A 1981 rate of 48 per cent was identified in an Auckland survey for the International Year of Disabled Persons.

But there were no systems for recording such data about disability on an ongoing basis as would be needed for the monitoring of EEO, and no governmental collection of data such as census information. An important initial issue, then, was to institute information systems for gathering that data. Two early pieces of work from the EEO Unit provided the basis for this. Both the 1986 review of disability employment in the public sector (Stone, 1986) and the Burns and Gray 1988 survey of disability gave good statistical data.

Stone's report highlighted the scope of employment issues for people with disabilities. For example, the following employment barriers were identified: people with disabilities are generally employed in basic grade jobs in a very limited range of occupations; they have low rates of pay; limited prospects of promotion; limited training prospects; are disadvantaged by the effect of myths and stereotypes and are restricted in their ability to obtain job interviews or, if interviews are obtained at all, enduring discriminatory ones. Burns and Gray's survey put figures to a number of the issues raised in Stone's report and also confirmed Jack's opinion that the situation was considerably worse for women with disabilities than for men with disabilities.

In this survey, where 44.6 per cent were female, 71 per cent of the women earned under $30,000 compared with 41 per cent of the men. Five per cent of the women earned over $40,000 compared with 21 per cent of the men (Burns and Gray, 1988).

A corollary issue to the need for statistical information was its accuracy. Many people with disabilities would not identify as having a disability. This meant that figures from surveys were likely to be somewhat smaller than the reality. While identification is an issue for all target groups, it is particularly so for people with disabilities. There was (and is) widespread concern in the disability community about identifying leading to labelling, negative stereotyping and job or work-place discrimination. There was, in the 1980s, no human rights legislation. The discrimination identified in the 1988 survey included job interviews, transfers, promotion, lack of physical access, harassment, job security, sick leave and negative attitudes.

These problems of non-identification will continue. While the long-anticipated human rights legislation for people with disabilities finally became law in 1993, it is unrealistic to expect the instant disappearance of discrimination or an instant surge of identification.

D-EEO: the Later Picture

The situation for D-EEO that existed with the advent of the 1988 State Sector Act was dissimilar from that for other target groups because disability was not included in any 'official' counting process, nor in human rights legislative cover. The first survey of people with disabilities in the public service was carried out by the EEO Unit in 1988 and was of great benefit in setting a base for future surveys and comparisons. Because of regular reporting of standardised target group statistics in annual reports supplied by government departments to the Unit, comparisons are possible. Figures from the 1991 progress report from the EEO Unit help present a picture of the situation of D-EEO now.

In 1991 the proportion of people with disabilities employed in the public service had dropped from the 1987 level of 20.8 per cent to 14.1 per cent (EEO Unit, 1991). This represents a considerable drop. One optimistic reason advanced for this change is that there is now a more accurate perception of what disability means so this figure represents a more correct self-identification. Another reason advanced is that, in a more stringent employment situation in which redundancy is common, people with disabilities have been heavily affected. That 14 per cent of those leaving the public service in 1991 (reasons include redundancy) had self-identified disabilities would tend to support this hypothesis, as does anecdotal evidence from EEO co-ordinators that more people with disabilities are leaving than are being taken on.

The sex difference in salaries not only remains, but is accentuated. In the 1991 report from the Unit, the proportion of men with disabilities earning under $30,000 had dropped by 35 per cent, from 41 per cent to 26.5 per cent; while for women the proportion under $30,000 had dropped only 17.6 per cent, from 71 per cent to 58.5 per cent. And the proportion of women earning over $40,000 had doubled to 10 per cent while the proportion of men over $40,000 had increased by 57 per cent to 33 per cent.

The statistical information is useful, highlighting as it does that the overall lack of improvement in salary and seniority. For women with disabilities, slipping back in comparison to men with disabilities is indicated. But it would be misleading to imply that it forms a complete picture of D-EEO. The workplace issues and the reality experienced are a major component of the whole picture.

Quite a number of workplace issues are the same as they were in 1986. It has been an ongoing concern that people with disabilities attain Human Rights Act coverage and this was achieved in mid-1993. People with disabilities are still concerned to get employment. In order to get employed they need interview and selection processes to be fair. Once employed they are concerned with promotion, training, and workplace support which includes an accessible work area. Self-esteem is an aspect of career development which is also an ongoing issue.

There is a cluster of issues related to workload levels and they may well be an offshoot of a pared-down public service where fewer workers carry a proportionately increased workload. Issues identified at a 1993 conference for public servants with disabilities were lack of peer support, finding that network sessions were often unsupportive 'gripe sessions' and raised stress levels brought on when unrealistically high expectations of productivity meet the brick wall of reality. In such a situation, where negative stereotypes of capability are little changed, self-esteem is unlikely to improve.

Some additions to the list of issues of concern are elaborations of, or adjuncts to, issues already mentioned. They include the provision of scholarships, job design, performance appraisal, network support, harassment and disability awareness training for staff without disabilities. There is also the addition of disability pride.

Although some of the issues above are of negative concern, the same issue may also have a positive aspect. For instance, there is an increase in self-worth, reflected in the growing willingness of more people with disabilities to speak out on disability issues. The change in wording of the Public Service Disability Pride Month from Public Service Disability Awareness Month has become a clear and powerful focus for self-worth to be recognised. The existence of scholarships and viable disability networks are also positive factors which are strongly supported.

Analysis of Issues

Progress and change may be viewed from the perspective of EEO and what it was intended to do. Although many employment problems identified by people with disabilities have changed little and statistical evidence backed by anecdotal evidence presents a picture that has worsened somewhat, there are areas which show progress. These include disability scholarships, which have had a modest efflorescence; the increased numbers of viable disability networks and the annual marking of Disability Pride Month. However, the positive effects have been more for people with disabilities than organisational culture. Other (and less innovative) change has been largely in the area of physical access. This focus has had, at times, a marked effect. One disability networker commented, 'If I'm told about one more building audit, I'll scream!'. Given the scope of the issues it might be expected that change might more effectively concentrate elsewhere. For instance, change could usefully focus on such issues as recruitment, job design and job evaluation. While job interviewing practices have received a moderate amount of attention, change has been of variable extent, being more observed in guidelines than in practice.

Overall the amount and rate of change is small. One of the major influences on this is attitudes. In attitudinal change there has been little progress, despite great effort. There has been a variety of approaches to disability awareness training. Those trained have participated in simulated experiences of disability, had appeals to their better nature and sense of equity, heard people with disabilities talk about their needs, listened to non-disabled 'experts' on disability needs, role-played job interviews, and considered the benefits to the organisation of diversity as illustrated in the employment of people with disabilities. But, a correlation between awareness training and attitude change, action or behavioural change is hard to trace.

This lack of progress is not unexpected. EEO change cannot happen independent of a context. And in that context, which includes the way legislation is written and then interpreted into policy and practice, the influence of ideologies, or patterns of ideas, is crucial. The connection between ideas and action has already been noted in relation to the medical model and in relation to right-wing economic/liberal models. It may be expected that where a course of action based on one ideology is added onto a structure which operates on a rather different ideology, there will be a 'neutralising' tendency.

Cockburn's assessment of EEO as a tool which has been adapted by management to fit within the existing patterns of thought and action is comprehensible and reasonable in the context of interacting ideologies and systems. D-EEO change has (in common with EEO in general) proceeded on the basis that a change to required standards of behaviours will induce a change to attitudes. I do not believe that this is an accurate summation of the process; it does not give sufficient acknowledgement to the power of ideas. As Charlotte Bunch commented, in relation to the concept of the 'personal is political':

> But we must also recognise that our personal experiences are shaped by the culture, with all its prejudices. We cannot therefore depend on our perception alone as the basis for political analysis and action (1988, p.290).

If we expect to take action to change ideas without addressing the way in which ideas have influenced the arena in which that change must take place and without setting boundaries for the change, it is far less likely that we will stretch beyond those limits to real change.

There has been, I believe, a degree of recognition of the effect ideas have had and continue to have in shaping an organisation's culture. A well developed sense of what change is possible, or is not possible, within an organisation, can be heard from any gathering of EEO co-ordinators and is reflected in the variety of EEO plans. If the recognition becomes more overt, and more systemic, D-EEO change has a chance to shift attitudes and behaviours to a more significant extent.

Suggestions for New Directions

It is tempting to examine the extent of change and, upon deciding that it is less than satisfying, compile a list in which 'more' features largely. I believe that this would be less than productive. Instead I have offered below a strategy which looks at the 'how' of change rather than the tools for it. This strategy is focused on the lived reality (for all people with disabilities, at least some of the time) of disadvantage and discrimination. The strategy is an outline, rather than a detailed blueprint.

- A re-examination of what is being done and on what basis this is being done.
  That is, an overview appraisal. The issue of whether EEO disability is the vehicle for achieving the change that is desired needs to be discussed, since there are always more ways than one to achieve a desired end. For such a reappraisal, workable partnerships between people with disabilities and the able-bodied community would be necessary.

- The formation of alliances.
  These alliances would need to be based on mutual respect. Alliances would need to be between practitioners of EEO, theoreticians, and people with disabilities working in the area and those interested in being involved.

- A choice of tactics.
  These would depend on the outcomes of the alliance discussions. Specific areas, and techniques targeted to the 'audience' may be chosen.

- Partnership research projects with people with disabilities.
  Research is likely to generate creative options. Such projects should be considered independently of the examination of desired ends and how they may be achieved.

Conclusion

At present, progress is less than satisfactory. There is a choice of leaving the situation unchanged, or looking at options to alter it. In short, to change change. This paper has traced a link between ideas and action, and suggested an altered approach to change which involves partnership of theoretically and practically oriented people with those people whose lived reality is disability. Partnerships that are not based on genuine respect and inclusion will merely serve to perpetuate the status quo. A cosy interdepartmental committee which produces a comfortable paper is not what is being recommended!

This chapter, and its conclusions, are not presented from a position of detachment. I acknowledged, in my introduction, three personal perspectives that have informed my analysis. As a former EEO Co-ordinator, I am well aware of the considerable difficulties faced in trying to translate the vision into reality and to maintain, let alone enhance the reality. I believe no co-ordinator has an easy job. The hard, everyday reality of EEO is imperfectly acknowledged.

My second personal perspective is that of theoretical social policy. While I too have felt that my everyday work was being effectively ignored by the theoreticians who analysed and pronounced patronisingly from afar, I have often been dismayed by the lack of theoretical analysis that is used by practitioners in a truly change-oriented way. I am aware of the power of theories to back and shape dreams, and an effective working partnership of these two perspectives based on mutual respect is a most effective path towards change.

A final perspective is the lived experience of disability and this is the perspective that has enabled me to see the potential in partnerships. To belong to a target group is always to be half a heartbeat from structural inequality. This closeness of the political and personal and the actions taken in its light can be highly challenging. But it can also fuel visions of 'the real oil' in EEO issues.

There is potential for equity in disability employment. If D-EEO can be turned in the directions suggested, I believe the change could be more real.

References

Bunch, C. (1988), 'Making Common Cause: Diversity and Coalitions', in C. McEwen and S. Sullivan (eds), *Out the Other Side*, London: Virago.

Burns, J. and Gray, A. (1987), *Results of a Survey for People with Disabilities in the Public Service*, Wellington: State Services Commission.

Cockburn, C. (1989), 'Equal Opportunities: the Long and Short Agenda', *Industrial Relations Journal*, 20 (3), 213-225,

EEO Unit (1991), *Progress in the Public Sector as at June 1991*, Wellington: State Services Commission.

Finklestein, V. (1980), *Attitudes and Disabled People*, New York: World Rehabilitation Fund.

Gartner, A. and Joe, T. (1987), *Images of the Disabled: Disabling Images*, New York: Praeger.

Hahn, H. (1987), 'Civil Rights for Disabled Americans: the Foundations of a Political Agenda', in A. Gartner and T. Joe (eds), *Images of the Disabled: Disabling Images*, New York: Praeger.

Jack, A. (1982), *Physical Disabilities: Results of a Survey in the Wellington Hospital Board Area*, Wellington: Department of Health.

Lindquist, B. (1990), 'A Disability History'. Speech to the Royal New Zealand Foundation for the Blind, Auckland, July 18.

Montague, M. (1993), *Private Lives?*, Australia: Privacy Commissioner.

Morris, J. (1992), *Pride Against Prejudice*, London: Virago.

Oliver, M. (1990), *The Politics of Disablement*, London: Macmillan.

Patson, P. (1993), *Alternatively Speaking*, Wellington: Winston Churchill Trust.

Pearpoint, J. and Forrest, M. (1992), 'Inclusion: the Bigger Picture', *Network*, 2 (1), 6-10.

Planning for Action: Taking the Initiative (1993), EEO Conference for Public Servants with Disabilities, Wellington, August.

State Services Commission (1984), 'EEO Policy Statement', unpublished paper.

Stone, D. (1985), *The Disabled State*, London: Macmillan.

Stone, J. (1986), *Review of Disabled Persons in the Public Service*, Wellington: State Services Commission.

Sullivan, M. (1991), 'From Personal Tragedy to Social Oppression: the Medical Model and Social Theories of Disability', *New Zealand Journal of Industrial Relations*, 16 (3), 225-273.

Walsh, P. and Dickson, J. (1993), *The Emperor's New Clothes: the Fate of EEO in the New Zealand Public Sector*, Working Paper 3/93, Wellington: Industrial Relations Centre, Victoria University.

Wicks, W. (1989), 'Women with Disabilities and Public Sector Employment', unpublished BSW (Hons) thesis, Massey University, Palmerston North.

Wicks, W. (1991), 'Women with Disabilities: Some Aspects of Invisible Lives', *New Zealand Journal of Industrial Relations*, 16 (3), 281-291.

4

Different Ways of Making A Difference: EEO Maori and Tino Rangatiratanga in Public Sector Organisations

Marianne Tremaine

Introduction

Several commentators have made the point that in its pure form, as a concept, Equal Employment Opportunity is seen as something that should evoke a universal response of support and approval. Conceptually speaking, everyone approves of fairness and equity, particularly in New Zealand, a country which has internalised the notion, if not the practice, of egalitarianism. But although concepts may be able to evoke a response untainted with thoughts of everyday realities, the moment those concepts are transferred into real-life situations and have to exist in time, space and even worse within an historical and political context, things change. People begin to realise that to support the concepts may be to support a world-view or a course of action which could compromise their beliefs, their values or their position of advantage.

This kind of compromise is involved for Maori and for Pakeha in reconciling EEO Maori with Article Two of the Treaty of Waitangi. Article Two guarantees the preservation of tino rangatiratanga, full chiefly authority, over all taonga or prized possessions of the Maori. The moral authority of the government to govern and make laws, rests on Article One of the Treaty which gives the Crown kawanatanga or governorship of New Zealand. The right to equal treatment of Maori and Pakeha before the law is enshrined in Article Three which states that Maori will have all the rights and privileges of British citizens.

EEO Maori recognises that Maori have been disadvantaged in employment and is an attempt to change and improve that situation. The Treaty responsibilities of organisations involve all aspects of organisational life, all the functions of the organisation and the way that they relate to the Treaty. This chapter explores the tensions between EEO Maori and the Treaty of Waitangi and explains ways that each could co-exist with the other in organisational settings. One of the problems with the relationship between EEO Maori and Treaty issues is that Maori and Pakeha tend to conceptualise that relationship quite differently. Each sees the context and interlinking of the issues from a very different perspective, taking different considerations into account. Many distinctions which are obvious to Maori are seldom seen by Pakeha.

Difficult Compromise

Organisational life can be very difficult for Maori because of the need to walk a tightrope in conforming to the organisation's values without compromising Maori values. A typical example of this kind of dilemma is the account Joe Doherty gives in his interview (p.261, this volume) of the young Maori woman given the responsibility for organising a hui who chooses a marae as an appropriate venue, but is then told by her manager that the event requires a much more prestigious setting as it is a high-profile occasion.

The messages that she is being given by this exchange are distressing and humiliating. She is being told that a marae is not a prestigious setting, that it is not suited to the dignity and importance of the occasion. Yet a wharenui or meeting-house on a marae is named for an important ancestor of the tribe and is personified as that ancestor. People who go inside the meeting-house are taken into the body of that ancestor and nurtured and protected there. So to be told that a wharenui lacks prestige is a crushing insult.

She is also being told that her judgement is faulty as she did not realise that a marae would be inappropriate, so she did not carry out the task she was given satisfactorily. Yet she is aware that just as she is being judged by her manager for selecting a marae for a gathering of

Maori women, she will be judged also by the participants at the hui if she selects an up-market, Pakeha-style venue such as a big international hotel. Her response is the decision to leave her job in the public service. If she does leave it is quite possible that her manager will be unaware of the reason for her decision, so may not learn anything from losing her.

Better communication could help to prevent situations like this where Maori staff feel compelled to leave their positions because their organisations put them into situations where their values are compromised. If Maori values were better understood in Pakeha organisations or if ways were created for Maori values to be expressed and respected, then much of the frustration that exists for Maori staff and the confusion that exists for Pakeha managers, might be avoided. Opportunities to communicate about organisational policy and practice that affects Maori need to operate on two levels.

One level is concerned mainly with actions and events that take place internally, within the organisation. For the most part EEO Maori takes place on this level inside the organisation. The other level is external to the organisation and concerns the way the organisation interacts with Maori on matters where Maori interests and the interests of the organisation are both involved out in the community. By and large the Treaty responsibilities of the organisation are located in this external area.

Figure 4.1: Model of EEO Maori
and an Organisation's Treaty Responsibilities

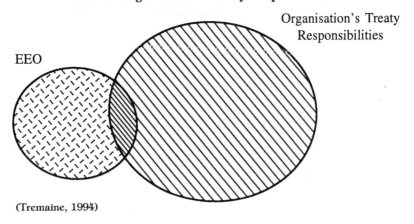

Organisation's Treaty
Responsibilities

EEO

(Tremaine, 1994)

The relationship can be conceptualised by envisaging a small circle and a much larger circle side-by-side and slightly overlapping each other. The smaller circle represents EEO Maori with its sphere of influence limited mainly to activities taking place within the organisation. The larger circle represents the Treaty responsibilities of the organisation which are located for the most part outside the organisation. The segment where the two circles overlap is where EEO Maori and Treaty responsibilities can overlap, in areas such as recruitment, training and resource allocation.

This model of the two overlapping circles may be helpful to consider in the light of the next sections of this chapter which explore the advantages and disadvantages of EEO Maori and Treaty responsiveness as they are practised in organisations in terms of their potential for positive and negative outcomes. EEO Maori has tended to concentrate on attempting to recruit more Maori into organisations and has examined and reformed selection procedures. Another important area where EEO has brought about significant changes is in the recognition of the value of cultural qualifications such as knowledge of tikanga and te reo, knowledge of Maori sources of information and expertise and the ability to be proficient in both cultures, interpreting each to the other.

Advantages and Disadvantages

There is no doubt that EEO has huge advantages for Maori. First of all EEO has legislative support and is a statutory requirement for public sector organisations. Having the backing of legislation which requires organisations to conform to EEO practices means that Maori who are working in the public sector do not need to mount complex arguments for putting more effort into recruiting Maori staff. They are able to point to the legislation as a sufficient reason.

Once there are Maori staff within an organisation, they can support each other, act as contact people for other Maori outside the organisation, gain more skills and come to understand the organisation's processes from the inside. They can have more influence on the organisation's policy-making and decision-making and provide role models for others who may aspire to careers in the public sector. EEO also works through establishing networks, and Maori networks can help to create a more

Maori-friendly environment at work and can create a channel for formulating joint submissions and group proposals on issues affecting Maori within the organisation.

Beyond these practical advantages associated with having legislative support and increasing the numbers of Maori staff, there is also the less tangible advantage that EEO creates a corporate vocabulary which both Maori and the organisation can use to communicate with each other and where, to some extent, the interests of Maori and the organisation can meet. EEO has a degree of understanding and acceptance throughout the organisation. Managers who do not fully understand the organisation's responsibilities under the Treaty of Waitangi, and do not have a clear notion of the influence Article Two of the Treaty should have on the decisions they make at work are usually more familiar with EEO. They are more likely to find the requirement to have an EEO policy and plan, for which they are accountable and which will form part of their performance appraisal, much more comprehensible because that fits more easily into the pattern of their other organisational responsibilities.

However, there are many potential pitfalls or disadvantages associated with EEO Maori particularly in organisations where the understanding of management is limited to the context of EEO without an in-depth knowledge of Treaty responsibilities. First of all, individual Maori staff may be placed in the invidious position of being expected to be an expert and give opinions on all things Maori, even in situations when it would be essential for the local tangata whenua to be consulted. Sometimes advice will be sought at the last minute on important issues which many Maori would feel should be debated by all the people affected at a hui. Then there is the dilemma of wondering whether to make a few partial patchwork improvements or to leave a policy document in an inadequate state which gives no cognisance to Maori issues.

Although there is some understanding that the Maori approach to life and work is a collective one rather than an individualistic one, it is difficult for people used to the culture of Pakeha organisations to take the imaginative leap required to understand what this means. Maori prefer to plan and strategise as a group and to use the different strengths of all group members as part of their strategy. Usually organisations see their people as self-sufficient all-rounders. However, it is much more common in Maori organisations to use the person with the best ability as the negotiator, the person with the best ability as the orator, the person with the best ability as the chairperson, the person with the best ability as the spiritual leader and so on. The group tends to see each individual's skills as belonging to the group in terms of achieving the common group purpose.

The difference can give a Maori who has joined an organisation a feeling of dislocation when abandoned in a separate office or at a separate desk with tasks to achieve that seem to call for a group approach. Some situations can be embarrassing when the assumption is made that any Maori will be an expert on all things Maori. For EEO to be effective in terms of retaining Maori within the organisation, ideally a more Maori-friendly culture is needed where Maori do not have to turn into Pakeha at work and revert to being Maori only when they leave work at the end of the day. To have an EEO policy which focuses on Maori recruitment but ignores the more intricate environmental and cultural problems is understandable given the complexity of changing organisational culture, but it may affect the retention of Maori and limit what they can achieve as Maori in the organisation.

Perhaps the most serious disadvantage of EEO for Maori is that managers who have only a vague idea of what Treaty responsibilities require but are familiar with EEO, may think that their EEO Maori policy is sufficient to deal with the whole area of the organisation's obligations to Maori and ignore Article Two of the Treaty. Waaka deals with this problem in her report on EEO Maori and a bicultural approach to government saying:

> Equal employment opportunities has nothing to do with a bicultural imperative, the unique tangata whenua status of Maori people or the endeavours of the government to redress the socio-economic imbalance that exists for Maori. EEO is exactly what it says; equal employment opportunities for all people with a particular emphasis on those people who are currently under-represented in government organisations; that includes Maori people (Waaka, 1990, p. 2).

The fudging of areas that are concerned with EEO and Maori as one of the designated groups with areas that are involved with the Treaty partnership of Maori tribes and the Crown is a major problem. Many Maori are unenthusiastic about being lumped into the good employer provisions of the state sector legislation as a designated group because it seems to denigrate their tangata whenua status and detracts from their mana. Besides, many would argue that their underrepresentation is closely related to Treaty issues and the fact that their resources were not protected as promised. EEO policy is controlled by the organisation and so cannot be seen as relevant to the much larger national issues which the Crown and Maori tribes are discussing as signatories of the Treaty.

Nevertheless, EEO policies and programmes can make important differences for Maori within organisations, but whether those changes take place or not is completely within the control of the organisation itself. The organisation is the final authority because EEO exists within and is the creation of the organisation and its managers. To see the organisation itself as the final authority for the implementation of its Treaty responsibilities would be to misunderstand the nature and context of those responsibilities. Public organisations are agents of the Crown carrying out the Crown's role in different functional areas. In carrying out their functions on behalf of the Crown, they need to be aware of the Crown's obligation as a Treaty signatory and implement policies that will acknowledge Article Two of the Treaty and preserve the authority of tribes and protect their taonga.

Naturally it has not been left entirely to public sector organisations to determine for themselves the wishes of the Crown or the government in the way that they acknowledge Treaty responsibilities. Many organisations have relevant legislation which gives details of the requirements for observing Treaty responsibilities. For example, the Resource Management Act 1991 imposes a requirement on local authorities to acknowledge the kaitiaki or guardianship role of Maori over natural resources and to protect and preserve waahi tapu or places sacred to Maori.

However, even legislation, which law drafters try to make as unambiguous as possible, is open to interpretation. So organisations' understandings of their Treaty responsibilities are even more likely to differ from organisation to organisation. The major problem in organisations' acknowledgement of the Treaty is their different levels of understanding. Although EEO is entirely different in scope and breadth of impact from Treaty obligations, EEO can provide a climate which can help an organisation towards Treaty responsiveness.

Organisational Models

Public sector organisations have come a long way in terms of gaining knowledge about the Treaty. At first there was recognition of the mistakes of the past and that government policies had attempted in a monocultural way to assimilate Maori. Then there was the struggle to come to terms with whether or not organisations should be bicultural or multicultural. At the 1982 public service conference at Waahi, the bicultural imperative was strongly expressed. One speaker used these words:

> ... we were all saying that at the end of the day the bottom line is about the position of the Maori in New Zealand and the position of Maori people, Maori culture, and the position of Maori women. So I think that in the end we agreed that we would be attacking multiculturalism through what I would call the bicultural imperative. You cannot dodge the bicultural question (1983, p. 22).

Yet the recommendations which emerged from the conference were phrased in terms of New Zealand as a multicultural society.

The theme of biculturalism versus multiculturalism was to keep on being revisited during the eighties in informal discussion, at Treaty training sessions, and in the literature of groups like Project Waitangi, but it would be far too optimistic to claim that it is universally understood by public service managers even in the nineties. Although in hindsight the monoculturalism of past policies can be seen, the inclusiveness of multiculturalism has a wide appeal. However, multiculturalism puts all cultures on an equal footing and ignores the guarantee of tino rangatiratanga in the Treaty.

Although there have been attempts to explain how organisations should observe their Treaty obligations in documents such as *Te Urupare Rangapu* (Department of Maori Affairs, 1988) and in *Government Management* (Treasury, 1987), background documents like these can only give information Involving Maori tribes in policy formulation and decision-making in areas that affect Treaty obligations is a process and it is a process that many organisations found to be fraught with difficulty.

Most organisations could recognise the kinds of issues that were relevant to their Treaty responsibilities but were often mystified about what to do next. There were few bureaucratic rules or precedents for whom to consult or how to consult with people in the Maori world, and the feeling of having a duty to meet Treaty obligations without knowing where to begin was an extremely uncomfortable one for people who had built careers on understanding the correct procedures.

The Justice Department issued a statement on the principles of the Treaty (1989) which attempted to explain the concepts underlying the provisions of the Treaty in a way that would lead to consistency of interpretation in government departments. Many Maori were concerned about the move to concentrate on the principles of the Treaty rather than the words of the Treaty. By this stage there were several different versions of the Treaty's principles including those of the Court of Appeal and the Maori Council.

In 1989 the Responsiveness Unit of the State Services Commission published *Partnership Dialogue, a Maori Consultation Process,* which explained the three articles of the Treaty and that consultation should take place with the 'total Maori community' (p. 11). The document suggested that consultation should take place by classifying issues according to the relevant article of the Treaty. *Partnership Dialogue* also gives practical advice on giving a koha, or donation, when going on to a marae and other suggestions to help people feel more comfortable in a Maori setting.

In 1992 the Parliamentary Commissioner for the Environment produced guidelines for local government consultation with tangata whenua. This publication (p.1) states that local authorities should:

> ... recognise that local government exercises kawanatanga (government) delegated from the Crown, which under the principles of the Treaty of Waitangi should be exercised so as to accommodate tribal rights of tino rangatiratanga (full tribal authority) in managing resources and taonga of the tribe which means the right of tangata whenua to have a direct and meaningful decision-making role.

The guidelines do not leave the way that local authorities decide to carry out this process to chance. They spell out the procedures to follow. First the tangata whenua should be asked what form of consultation suits them best, which issues concern them and their priority for these issues and how tino rangatiratanga should be reconciled with kawanatanga in the local context. Councils should be prepared to give technical and financial assistance to tangata whenua to enable them to compile background documents, and a charter should be drawn up setting out the responsibilities of the local authority and the tangata whenua.

Advice is given about the importance of openmindedness, adequate time and appropriate venues and it is suggested that an ongoing education programme should be established for decision-makers, staff, clients and ratepayers on agency obligations with regard to tangata whenua and the Treaty of Waitangi. The model for interaction between the two parties underlying this document would seem to be partnership rather than biculturalism. Partnership usually entails the devolution or delegation of authority from the Crown partner to the Maori partner, while biculturalism can be either the introduction of Maori values within government agencies or the development of separate Maori institutions to provide for Maori needs (Durie, 1991).

At the local or regional level, this has usually been carried out by either mainstream participation, appointing Maori representatives onto a governing body or Maori advisory board, or by creating partnership links between parallel institutions. As Durie (1991) says, there has not been a great deal of experience with either of these two partnership models and, although recognising the tangata whenua tribes in local matters comes close to the rangatiratanga principle, it has led to criticism from urban Maori groups who may have worked closely with local authorities but are not tribally based and so do not have tangata whenua status and have lost their influence in favour of local iwi. The situation is further complicated by the fact that regional boundaries on maps seldom take account of tribal boundaries so that there may be several tribes in an area who wish to be seen as the Treaty partner.

Although many of the staff working in central and local government have found intellectual and professional interest and excitement in the challenge of absorbing so much new Treaty knowledge and applying it to their field, naturally there is confusion and uncertainty too because ways of working together are still evolving. The distinctions between biculturalism and partnership are not always clear and organisations sometimes tend to shift between one and the other. Ideally organisations need to have some clarity about which model of co-operation they are working towards with their Treaty partner and need to be aware of the implications of the models and structures they choose. Just as partnership can be seen as having two distinct forms, biculturalism also has different interpretations and different ways of being implemented.

In *Justice and the Maori,* Andrew Sharp distinguishes between two distinct types of biculturalism, reformative and distributive. Bicultural reformism is the type of change that takes place when a Pakeha institution adopts some practices that will make it more in tune with Maori requirements, e.g. Taha Maori in schools, whereas bicultural distributivism is redistributing power by putting more autonomy into Maori hands with the establishment of new Maori institutions, e.g. kura kaupapa Maori.

But as far as biculturalism is concerned, no generalisations can be made which will apply to all organisations. There is no set pattern for interaction between an agency of the Crown such as a local authority and Maori tribes and groups. Rather than attempt a vain search for a foolproof way of achieving biculturalism, Mason Durie (1993) suggests that a useful way of acknowledging the complexity of biculturalism is to see it as a continuum in terms of both an organisation's goals and its structures. Organisations can consider where their bicultural goals would fit on a continuum, from goals such as the development of cultural skills and knowledge through to aiming to initiate joint ventures with Maori, at the other end of the continuum. In terms of structure, an organisation may locate itself or one of its sections or departments at one end of the continuum as an unmodified mainstream institution or as an independent Maori institution at the other.

When structures and goals are brought together in a matrix as a bicultural framework (see Figure 4.2), organisations can locate their policies and programmes within the matrix and gain more clarity about purposes, limits and expectations. This bicultural framework allows room for the complexity of bicultural initiatives and for the dynamic nature of bicultural goals and structures which change and develop over time and shift their positions on each continuum and within the matrix.

Figure 4.2:
A Bicultural Framework Showing an Interlinking Range of
Organisational Goals and Structures

Goals / Structures	Cultural skills and knowledge	Improved awareness of Maori positions	Clear focus on Maori issues and Maori networks	Best outcomes for Maori over all activities	Joint ventures
Unmodified mainstream institution					
A Maori perspective					
Active Maori institutions					
Parallel Maori institutions					
Independent Maori institutions					

(Durie, Mason (1993), p.9)

If one attempts to locate the goals of an organisation which follows the guidelines of the Commissioner for the Environment on the continuum, the position on the grid would probably be between 'clear focus on Maori issues and Maori networks' and 'best outcomes for Maori over all activities'. On the structural continuum, such an organisation would probably place itself in the 'active Maori involvement' section of the grid.

To follow on from this example, the relationship between an organisation's EEO policy and its Treaty policies will be considered by examining the Palmerston North City Council's EEO policy for 1993-94 and the same council's document called *Living Up to Our Bicultural Responsibilities, Actions for 1993-94*.

The Council's EEO plan has three objectives: to reinforce the principles and gain commitment to EEO during a time of change; to assist managers and staff to implement EEO; and, to encourage behavioural change in EEO practices. The first commitment objective is to be achieved by compiling and presenting training sessions and discussing EEO results with the management team each quarter. The second implementation objective is to be acted upon by updating pamphlets and procedures and investigating a Maori scholarship programme. The third behavioural change objective is to be actioned by monitoring EEO statistical data and discussing the results with managers, monitoring the implementation of bicultural training and developing appropriate reward systems.

The bicultural document deals with four areas: policy, relationships, resource management and training. In each of the four areas objectives are specified and the person who is to be responsible for meeting the objective is named and any specific tasks are listed. Under the policy area the objectives are to review existing council consultation policies with tangata whenua and review and assess current human resources policies against the requirements of section 119F of the Local Government Act 1994, specifically the recognition of the aims and aspirations of Maori and their employment requirements and greater tangata whenua involvement in local government employment and opportunities for the enhancement of the abilities of individual employees.

In this policy area, the human resources review could have been left within the EEO programme, but it was obviously felt to be more appropriate to locate these issues in the bicultural document so they could be discussed with Rangitane, the tangata whenua.

In the relationships section, the second area covered in *Living Up to Our Bicultural Responsibilities*, the objectives are to renew formal personal contacts with Rangitane and review and agree on the role of the tangata whenua in the Annual Plan consultation process, define council relationships with taura here (other Maori in the city who are not Rangitane) and review the objectives and process established for the use of the Maori Development Fund.

The third area in the bicultural document is resource management. The objectives include identifying and recording Council's statutory obligations in respect of the Treaty of Waitangi as contained in the Resource Management Act, assisting Rangitane in the production of their Iwi Management Plan and involving Rangitane in the preparation of the District Plan as well as information-sharing on resource management issues with Rangitane and establishing consultation with Rangitane on waste management issues.

The fourth section of the bicultural document deals with training. One of the training objectives is to establish priorities and prepare a training schedule for the 1993-94 financial year, including the specific task of conducting Treaty of Waitangi training for non-Maori staff in July and November, 1993. The other objective is to establish the future function of the Bicultural Training Advisory Group and in association with the group ensure Rangitane input to training, establish the next phase of training for elected members and for staff, and the specific task identified is to provide financial support for Maori staff to participate in the 1993 and 1994 Maori in local government hui.

This example of a local authority's EEO programme and bicultural plan demonstrate at least three important issues. EEO Maori and Treaty responsibilities are not the same and cannot be seen as identical, although each does have some links with the other. For example, in this case the Maori scholarship mentioned in the EEO plan could also be discussed with the tangata whenua as part of the bicultural programme and might have some implications for their iwi management plan. A second issue is that Treaty responsibilities are far broader in scope than EEO and require the involvement of the other Treaty partner, the tangata whenua, in policy development and implementation. Finally, to be effective, Treaty responsiveness policies need to have specified objectives which are monitored. Some managers may imagine that if staff are trained in Treaty awareness, that knowledge will inform their approach to work, but a more systematic process is needed to assess achievements. Durie's (1993) bicultural framework could be used to compare differences between EEO Maori and Treaty responsiveness goals and as a basis for organisational discussion. Treaty responsiveness policies are more likely to affect both goals and structures, while EEO Maori policies will tend to affect goals and have little impact on organisational structure.

Conclusion

The relationship between EEO Maori and Treaty responsiveness does not have to be seen in a negative way. Some see EEO Maori as having its place under Article Three of the Treaty which deals with the rights and privileges of individual Maori, while Article Two deals with tino rangatiratanga and the collective rights of tribes and is the basis for the Crown's Treaty responsibilities to tribes. EEO Maori and Treaty responsiveness are both able to accomplish changes which can be valuable for Maori, but they are different in scope and context. They are different ways of working for change in organisations.

References

Department of Maori Affairs (1988), *Te Urupare Rangapu*, Wellington: State Services Commission.

Durie, M. (1991), 'The Treaty of Waitangi in New Zealand Society', Study Guides One, Two and Three, Department of Maori Studies, Massey University, Palmerston North.

Durie, M. (1993), 'Maori and the State: Professional and Ethical Implication for the Public Service'. Paper presented to the Public Service Senior Management Conference, Wellington: State Services Commission.

Justice Department (1989), *Principles of the Treaty of Waitangi*, Wellington: Justice Department.

Office of the Parliamentary Commissioner for the Environment (1992), *Proposed Guidelines for Local Government Consultation with Tangata Whenua*, Wellington: Office of the Parliamentary Commissioner for the Environment.

Palmerston North City Council (1993), *Equal Employment Opportunities Programme for 1993-1994*, Palmerston North: Palmerston North City Council.

Palmerston North City Council (1993), *Living Up to Our Bicultural Responsibilities*, Palmerston North: Palmerston North City Council.

Sharp, A. (1990), *Justice and the Maori*, Auckland: Oxford University Press.

State Services Commission (1983), *Public Service in a Multicultural Society*, Wellington: Government Printer.

State Services Commission (1989), *Partnership Dialogue, a Maori Consultation Process*, Wellington: State Services Commission.

Treasury (1987), *Government Management*, Wellington: Treasury.

Waaka, L. (1990), 'A Report on EEO (Maori) and a Bicultural Approach to Government', Waaka Consultancy, Rotorua.

5

Ambivalence and Autonomy: the Tension Between Biculturalism and EEO

Paul Spoonley

Introduction

This chapter highlights the tensions and contradictions between equal employment opportunity policies and the politics of biculturalism. Equal employment opportunity (EEO) was one legacy of the relatively liberal period which saw political movements push for workplace equity during the 1960s and 1970s, notably feminism, and a concern with the more effective utilisation of diverse skills in the workplace that was central to the management of human resources. But by the late 1980s, elements of EEO were under attack, notably from the neo-liberal politics which prevailed after 1984. But one of the most significant challenges to EEO has come from Maori, whose politics have transformed the national political agenda and whose concerns often stand in direct opposition to EEO imperatives in the workplace. This chapter seeks to identify some of the reasons for this tension and anticipates why it will continue to grow throughout the 1990s.

EEO: A Liberal Legacy

The origins and development of EEO are covered elsewhere in this book, but it is worth highlighting those attempts to include the workplace concerns of Maori within the developing commitment to EEO. The following discussion focuses on the public sector, partly because this history has been more transparent, and partly because there has been an awareness, at least since the 1970s, that equity must address the interests of Maori as much as those of other groups.

This awareness, that Maori were significantly disadvantaged in the workplace, was made manifest by the research which was completed in the early 1970s by a range of social scientists and made an issue by political interest groups. Researchers and interest groups made explicit the 'gatekeeper' role of management and sought to identify the values and behaviours which prevented Maori and others from having a broadly similar spread across industries and occupations and within the specific hierarchies of firms as that of Pakeha. In this period managers were very explicit about their own prejudices, or those of their clients or workers, and how they affected their recruitment and promotion procedures. Research which demonstrated such practices was published in the literature (see Spoonley, 1981) and used to teach in management and business courses. Interested political groups, such as the Auckland Committee on Racism and Discrimination, also conducted research and then used it to publicise the racism that existed as part of a set of protest strategies (see ACORD, 1977; 1983).

The effect was not dramatic, but there was one. By 1978, the State Services Commission, the Department of Maori Affairs and the Public Service Association had formed a working party on race relations and it suggested that advisory officers be appointed in order to support Maori and Pacific Islanders (Tagata Pasifika) who were employed in the public service or who might be its clients. However, the growing interest in workplace equity for Maori was hampered by the internal politics of the public service and the incomplete understanding of what was to become bicultural. This lack of understanding was evident in the 1982 Waihi Conference when those present, in discussing such issues, opted to privilege multiculturalism over biculturalism because the latter was deemed too narrow a focus.

However, the level of sophistication in the response to the challenge of biculturalism increased dramatically during the 1980s. There were a series of critical reviews of government departments and policies including, in 1986, the review of the Maori and Pacific Island Recruitment

Programme (*Evening Post*, 17 October 1987) and the Ministerial Inquiry on a Maori Perspective for the Department of Social Welfare. The latter, which resulted in the report, *Puao-te-atatu* (1986), was very critical of the Department of Social Welfare's internal structures and its failure to serve the interests of Maori clients. Others had also played a role in highlighting the need to address Maori work-related concerns, and the Vocational Training Council used arguments about economic efficiency to get managers to consider new strategies which successfully incorporated Maori and Pacific Islanders into the workplace (Findlay, 1981).

The effect was seen by the late 1980s in the development of new structures and positions, as well as new instructions and guidelines for staff. The State Services Commission (after two-thirds of its own staff had completed a five-month tikanga Maori programme) issued a new set of requirements which specified how biculturalism might be implemented in the public service *(Evening Post,* 17 October 1987). These included advice on such things as interviewing (Maori representation on the interviewing panel, a mihi, whanau support) and justified that advice in terms of 'good employer/manager' requirements as well as the efficiency that accompanies the full participation of Maori. The 1988 State Sector Act further encouraged such considerations and the growth of units that had responsibility for EEO or Treaty-based issues (Lynch and Nichol, 1989). Managers in the public and private sectors by now were able to call upon a range of private companies whose role was to initiate and advise on equity programmes within organisations. Ihi Consultants, as one example, provided what were called 'tangata whenua' courses for top executives.

Employment equity had become something of a touchstone by the late 1980s. It was enshrined in the pay equity and human rights legislation. There were significant landmark decisions, such as the 1988 finding of the Equal Opportunities Tribunal that Air New Zealand had indulged in practices which discriminated against female employees (Human Rights Commission, 1989a). But, if in the 1970s there had been a degree of common ground between Maori and other groups, notably women, who sought workplace equity by promoting EEO, the sense of common purpose had certainly changed by the late 1980s. For reasons which will be discussed below, Maori interests had now become focused on iwi development and tino rangatiratanga and had departed from the specific concerns of EEO. More than that, there was a degree of conflict about the objectives and enactment of equity.

Limitations of EEO

The presence of EEO units or policies will continue in both public and private sectors, and Maori will undoubtedly continue to be employed within such units with responsibility for EEO Maori (to use the Department of Justice's phrase) as the Maori perspective is considered critical to the administration of organisations in the 1990s. Nevertheless for groups such as Maori there have always been inherent problems with EEO.

The first issue is the universality of EEO. Typically, the policy statements which define EEO in the context of a specific organisation and which legitimate EEO tend to be non-ethnic specific. For example, the 1989 employment equity statement provided by the Human Rights Commission refers to the importance of gaining access to all skills and talents in order to obtain the best person for the job, or the importance of diversity amongst the staff, or the need to have practices which assist all employees to develop their potential. It is hard to argue with such generalised principles. And that generality is a significant weakness. What provisions for the specific concerns of Maori are represented in such statements? Frequently, there is a reference to Maori as tangata whenua or the Treaty of Waitangi, but this is under the organisational need to frame a statement and set of policies which are inclusive and which do not invite substantial opposition from employees. Ironically, this inclusivity or universalism tends to marginalise. Because Maori concerns are not central to EEO, the question then arises as to whether EEO can successfully incorporate the particular interests of Maori. Increasingly, the answer has been no. EEO has been seen as inappropriate (and sometimes hostile) to certain excluded groups and other issues and strategies have been sought. More recent management programmes, notably the idea of 'managing diversity', are seen to be based on specific cultural values and therefore a form of neo-racism (see Grice and Humphries, 1993).

The second issue concerning problems for Maori with EEO follows on from the first. EEO has been compromised (with some exceptions) by the need for its acceptance, especially within the organisation concerned. Amongst many on the outside and quite a few on the inside, the justification for EEO is not self-evident. As neo-liberal politics have gained in significance and competitive individualism has been favoured, EEO has been opposed by employees, managers, politicians and activists such as the Business Roundtable who are strong advocates of market competition. Opposition has been expressed in a number of ways, but one of the more interesting is an inversion whereby those groups, such as women or Maori, who might be targeted by EEO policies are seen as especially advantaged by 'reverse discrimination' (see Edwards, 1993, for such arguments). Males and Pakeha are seen as the new 'disadvantaged' by the criteria of programmes such as EEO. The assumption, readily seen in an Alan Duff or Bob Jones column or book, is that competition benefits both individual and organisation, and the adoption of equity as a goal is deemed to subvert market competitiveness.

In this environment, the moral and organisational legitimacy of EEO is undermined, and becomes even more suspect if Maori interests are specified in any way. The assumed tension between EEO policies which support Maori and the value of unrestricted competition has led to major opposition. The issue of cultural safety as a minority component of nursing education and practice offers a dramatic illustration of an individual's perceptions of what is deemed acceptable as opposed to the carefully identified needs of a programme. In other words, EEO which is defined as addressing specific Maori needs, especially those that originate from outside the workplace, is considerably less acceptable than a more generalised EEO policy. Having failed to win over important managerial and political élites for the latter, it is unlikely that the fragile legitimacy which does exist is going to be sacrificed by accommodating Maori concerns more explicitly.

Analysing reasons for the fragile state of support for policies which assist Maori leads on to expose a third weakness of EEO. This weakness can be seen as the failure to establish coalition-building strategies (Weir, 1993). The practitioners of EEO needed to build inter-ethnic coalitions which might have provided it with the constituencies and support which could then enable EEO policies to withstand the robust challenges that have begun to occur in the 1990s. The lack of supportive coalitions and strategies has placed a substantial burden on the advocates and those who have the responsibility for implementing EEO. They are required to continually justify EEO within an organisational culture and, increasingly, in a public sphere. The energy and skills required are such that an EEO framework that successfully incorporates and legitimates Maori interests is beyond the abilities of most.

What has become apparent is the fact that many Maori concerns are not addressed by the practice of EEO. The rhetoric of EEO has discussed strategies which seek to help groups but the practice has been to encourage individual mobility within an organisation (Weir, 1993). Maori communal concerns, including such matters as resource management and ownership, the power of veto within an organisation and the preservation of cultural traditions, are not addressed by encouraging individual mobility. In the case of Maori, many of the issues of most importance to them are largely external and structural matters (i.e. they concern the significant social institutions of society) and require a much broader definition of what constitutes EEO. For their part, organisations and management tend to regard such 'external' issues as the responsibility of the communities involved and not an issue for the workplace. In this sense, EEO is often regarded as marginal to Maori interests and tends to be seen as silent or irrelevant when it comes to such issues. Without a common cause, inter-ethnic coalitions have not been initiated or maintained.

EEO or Biculturalism?

This final section places the tension between EEO and biculturalism in its current context and argues that, for a variety of reasons, the difference between the two strategies will become even more pronounced in the future. In essence, EEO seeks to address equity matters within the workplace and its ability to do so is governed by the willingness of both management and the workforce to take such matters seriously and to align EEO ambitions with those of the institution or organisation. Biculturalism, or more properly, tino rangatiratanga, is having an increasingly important influence on workplace relations but it is driven by broader political and cultural imperatives and the effect is most likely to be seen in those sectors of the economy where Maori have some control. Equity is an issue but in a wider social and economic sense. The primary reasons for the importance of the social and economic context are identified below.

The first reason is the Maori resurgence which dates from the late 1960s. The central issues of concern to Maori did not change in this period but the strategies and key players did. A new urban-born, often tertiary-educated generation adopted high-profile protest strategies throughout the 1970s and early 1980s in order to fight for Maori political and cultural interests, including reparation for lost resources and the maintenance of cultural practices and language (see Walker, 1990; Ihimaera, 1993). They created a sense of urgency and frustration which saw these new generations of 'activists' align with traditional iwi groupings by the 1980s to provide a powerful political movement (or more accurately, movements) which gained in political influence. It is significant that at the time of the Royal Commission on Social Policy (1988), and via major state-initiated reviews such as *Puao-te-atatu,* a new set of concepts were introduced to represent these new political initiatives.

The early generation included words such as 'partnership' and 'biculturalism', but these were replaced by the language of the Treaty of Waitangi (tino rangatiratanga) and Maori political history (mana motuhake). It was also made clear that the language and arguments of EEO were inappropriate to iwi concerns and ambitions, and the equity of the workplace was contrasted with justice and sovereignty for iwi. By the late 1980s, at Maori insistence, major public documents and policies made a clear distinction between EEO and tino rangatiratanga.

There is a second reason for the breadth of the social and political agenda of Maori which takes it far beyond the scope of EEO. Their political resurgence has been reflected in state policies and in legislation. Under a Labour government, recognition was given to reparative justice for Maori. The 1985 amendment to the Waitangi Act, followed by a recognition of the Treaty in the State Owned Enterprises Act in 1986, provided an opportunity for iwi to seek a resolution to past breaches of the Treaty and to make claim on a variety of resources, including land, coal and fisheries. Something of a legal revolution took place, at least between 1985 and 1988, and the Treaty was given a new constitutional status. This new status was recognised by the courts in a series of significant decisions which found in favour of Maori complainants. While the government and the courts retreated from this quite radical position after the Waitangi Tribunal's recommendations on the Muriwhenua fisheries claim in 1987 (see Kelsey, 1993), the framework within which New Zealanders would understand Maori concerns had been changed irrevocably. In the 1990s, iwi have continued to negotiate on the use and ownership of resources and the undertakings of the Treaty have become a touchstone which cannot be ignored by governments. Whatever the setting, whether it be local or national government, schools, government departments or social services, an acknowledgement of the Treaty for workplace practices and the importance of meeting client or customer needs is now considered to be a standard requirement.

Ironically, a third reason is that the neo-liberal restructuring of New Zealand has also helped privilege biculturalism/tino rangatiratanga. The move to a deregulated, market-driven economy and society has encouraged the devolution of the management of a variety of services. As the state has minimalised its role, it has encouraged the transfer of responsibility from state-funded and state-provided services to a much more complex contractual, privately-funded set of arrangements. In the language of the new managerialism, 'accountability', 'client-centred services', 'performance appraisal' and market-led initiatives have become a central part of the cultural revolution which has taken place within organisations. There are important differences between the traditional private sector and those who have taken over the provision of traditional public sector services, but what is significant is the contrast between Maori and non-Maori in their relationship with the latter groups. The growing emphasis on the private purchase of goods such as health or education and the decline of interest groups such as trade unions has tended to fragment the workplace and those involved in the provision and the purchase of services.

Maori, given the politics described above and their communal interests and organisations, have exercised more and more power as they are able to negotiate collectively in a way that few others are able to do. Their bargaining power in certain areas has noticeably increased and they are able to specify what they require from a particular organisation. For instance, the move to Crown Health Enterprises has provided iwi in a number of localities with the opportunity to establish their own health services or to be an important contractor of services from a traditional medical provider. Maori are not simply clients or patients, they are managers or 'purchasers' of the service. In terms of such public services, their involvement in specifying what they require has given a new importance to tino rangatiratanga and issues such as cultural safety, as opposed to EEO.

A fourth and related reason is that these issues of Maori self-determination have become more urgent by virtue of the position of Maori in a collapsing labour market. Since the late 1980s, unemployment and under-employment have increased dramatically as the labour market has become deregulated. Lowering of wages has been a major strategy in cost containment and the state has declined as a significant employer. Maori have been particularly affected. Many of the Maori who had migrated to the urban-industrial centres in the post-war period found themselves mid-career and without a job. Redundancies meant that one-fifth of the Maori workforce lost their jobs in the two years between March 1987 and March 1989 (see Spoonley *et al.*, 1993). Multi-skilling or up-skilling were largely meaningless for these generations of Maori, although there were some significant career moves into particular occupations and sectors such as teaching and community work. Younger generations simply did not make the transition from education to paid work. In 1986, 20 per cent of Maori in the age group 15 to 24 years were unemployed. Five years later in 1991, the figure was 35.5 per cent, a jump in excess of 15 per cent. The same figures for non-Maori were 8 per cent for 1986 and 17 per cent for 1991, an increase of 9 per cent, which is bad enough but considerably less than the figures for Maori. For all age groups in 1991, the Maori unemployed rate was 23 per cent as compared with 8.5 per cent for non-Maori (Spoonley *et al.*, 1993).

The workplace concerns, as well as education and training requirements, tend to be different for Maori by virtue of the much greater disadvantages experienced and the focus on developing economic independence. The loss of paid employment in the late 1980s and early 1990s has created a crisis situation for Maori, and one which will continue to have major repercussions for a long time to come. One response has been to try and establish a separate economic base, Maori owned and managed, which reflects the communal concerns of Maori (mauritangata). The results can be seen in the growth of Maori-directed training and educational programmes, areas such as tourism (whale-watching in Kaikoura is one example) or horticultural and forestry ventures, or a growing Maori ownership in the private sphere (i.e. in a company such as Deka.) Again, Maori interests in workplace issues are given a quite different focus because of the problems that have arisen since the late 1980s, how they have been perceived by the community concerned and the initiatives that have been taken by iwi in order to address these problems.

The demographics of Maori also demand an interest in tino rangatiratanga. Maori are a much younger population than Pakeha, with 37.5 per cent of the Maori population less than 15 years of age compared with 21 per cent of non-Maori in 1991. Throughout this decade, the numbers of the school-age population who are Maori (by self-identification) will grow and it is estimated that in 2011, about 19 per cent of New Zealand's population will be Maori. This is to be contrasted with the Pakeha population which will tend to age and have a larger proportion of its population in the older age groups. Already, nearly 20 per cent of non-Maori are over the age of 60 compared with only four per cent for Maori. The requirements of the two populations will be quite different with one concerned about the needs of its large younger population, and the issues of education, employment and the problems associated with the 'at risk' teenage years. The other population's requirements will be more concerned with the issues of the middle-aged and older person: retirement income, job security, law and order, etc. The need to address the quite specific cohort and generational concerns of Maori will help reinforce the importance of those initiatives which establish iwi independence. On this the neo-liberal politicians, those who manage the minimalist state and iwi are agreed.

Conclusion

The argument of this chapter is a relatively straightforward one. The events of the 1980s and early 1990s have encouraged the development of tino rangatiratanga for Maori communities, partly as the natural outcome of an evolving concern with cultural identity and economic autonomy, and partly as a response to problems that have been created by neo-liberalism in New Zealand. Tino rangatiratanga reflects a broad set of political, economic and cultural concerns, and is firmly community-focused. Maori self-determination has become part of the national political agenda and, for the reasons identified above, will gain in importance throughout the 1990s. In contrast, EEO lacks the breadth of power and influence of such politics. By its very nature Equal Employment Opportunity is workplace-focused and unable to adequately encompass the wider labour market and cultural issues that are central to biculturalism or tino rangatiratanga. As Weir (1993, p.106) has noted:

> Such approaches require the ability to understand economic issues
> in terms other than the individual; neither the liberal approach of
> the 1960s nor the conservative market economics... provide such
> a perspective.

If the two approaches can be reconciled, it can only be in quite minor ways. Given the events that have taken place since the late 1980s, it would seem that EEO will remain irrelevant for most Maori.

References

ACORD (1977), 'Equality of Opportunity – the Myth, Affirmative Action – the Answer'. Address to a Public Service Association Seminar on Race Relations, June.

ACORD (1983), *The Racism of Economics and the Economics of Racism*, Auckland: Auckland Committee on Racism and Discrimination.

Edwards, B. (1993), 'A Cup of Cold Sick', *Metro*, May, 133-134.

Findlay, K. (1981), 'Narrowing the White Collar Gap', *New Zealand Listener*, 9 May, 34-36.

Grice, S. and Humphries, M. (1993), 'Managing Diversity: a Wolf in Sheep's Clothing?'. Paper to the Confronting Racism Conference, University of Technology, Sydney, December.

Human Rights Commission (1989a), *Proceedings Commissioner versus Air New Zealand, Equal Opportunities Tribunal*, 1/87, Wellington: Human Rights Commission.

Human Rights Commission (1989b), *HRC Newsbrief*, March.

Ihimaera, W. (ed.) (1993), *Te Ao Marama 2, Regaining Aotearoa: Maori Writers Speak Out*, Auckland: Reed Books.

Kelsey, J. (1993), *Rolling Back the State*, Auckland: Oxford University Press.

Lynch, J. and Nichol, R. (1989), 'The Job Equality Industry', *Dominion*, 20 November, 13.

Ministerial Advisory Committee on a Maori Perspective for the Department of Social Welfare (1986), *Puao-te-atatu*, Wellington: Government Print.

Royal Commission on Social Policy (1988), *April Report*, Wellington: Royal Commission on Social Policy.

Spoonley, P. (1981), 'The Politics of the Disadvantaged: Observations on Work, Race and the Polynesian in New Zealand', *New Zealand Journal of Industrial Relations*, 6 (2), 73-77.

Spoonley, P., Teariki, C., Newell, J. and Taiwhenua o Heretaunga (1993), *Mahi Awatea*, Palmerston North: Department of Sociology, Massey University.

Walker, R. (1990), *Ka Whawhai Tonu Matou, The Struggle Goes On*, Auckland: Penguin.

Weir, M. (1993), 'From Equal Opportunity to "the New Social Contract". Race and the Politics of the American "Underclass"', in M. Cross and M. Keith (eds), *Racism, the City and the State*, London: Routledge.

6

Breaching the Convention: New Zealand's International Obligations

Judy McGregor

A Question of Honour?

How well does New Zealand honour its international obligations in relation to equal employment opportunities? The question needs to be examined in the light of the conventional wisdom nurtured by popular reporting of Suffrage Centennial Year which acknowledged women's achievements, that New Zealand is a leader in fostering equal employment opportunities. This chapter explores New Zealand's implementation of its international obligations, particularly the 1979 United Nations Convention on the Elimination of All Forms of Discrimination Against Women as it relates to employment. It concludes that while New Zealand has made some progress in recent years to honour its international obligations, this country is in breach of the Convention and falls fundamentally short of its obligations in the area of pay equity.

New Zealand's international obligations in relation to equal employment opportunities are outlined in the 1979 United Nations Convention on the Elimination of All Forms of Discrimination Against Women. The Convention has been described by Chen (1989, p.5) as 'the major document for women's advancement in New Zealand'. And the *Status of New Zealand Women 1992* report states, 'the Convention is considered to be a major human rights instrument, as important as the International Covenants on Civil and Political, and Economic, Social and Cultural Rights and the International Convention on the Elimination of all forms of Racial Discriminations'(p.5). The *Women in New Zealand* (1990) report states that:

> New Zealand's ratification of this Convention in December 1984 gives international backing to efforts to improve the status of women in this country, and a standard against which to measure progress towards de facto as well as de jure, equality (p.29).

A major component of this international instrument prescribing women's rights concerns employment. The chapter also discusses the reservations entered by New Zealand with respect to the Convention on women in combat and maternity leave with pay.

New Zealand is obliged to present progress reports every four years on its implementation of the Convention. These reports are made to the Committee on the Elimination of Discrimination Against Women (CEDAW). At the time of ratification New Zealand entered three reservations which will be discussed later. The first progress report to CEDAW was presented in 1988. As this chapter was being written a spokeswoman for the Ministry of External Relations and Trade indicated that New Zealand's second progress report would be presented in January 1994.

This second periodic report, *Status of New Zealand Women 1992* was prepared by the Ministry of Women's Affairs. The report in general is of good quality and is candid about many aspects of the contemporary status of women in New Zealand society. In relation to employment the report covers statistical material on women in the paid workforce, looks at the right to work, developments in equal employment opportunities, the choice of profession and employment, equal remuneration, social security benefits, occupational health and safety, discrimination on the grounds of pregnancy and marital status, maternity and parental leave, childcare and early childhood education.

Despite the quality of the report, a critical analysis of its content raises questions about whether New Zealand is fulfilling its international obligations. Such scrutiny is important in the process of raising the profile of New Zealand's international obligations. For as Chen (1989 p.5) notes:

> ... very little has been heard about the Convention in New Zealand since its ratification, and this low level of awareness was not significantly heightened during the presentation of New Zealand's first report to CEDAW

The second periodic report is also likely to be a low key affair. In addition to the anticipated low media profile of New Zealand's progress in eliminating discrimination against women, the publicity focus on Suffrage Year activities during 1993 has helped divert attention from New Zealand's lack of progress in tackling structural inequalities. Individual achievement was highlighted during the celebrations which was a worthwhile consciousness-raising activity in itself. But while such activities as the Electricorp-sponsored television advertisements featuring women achievers in work were a fitting acknowledgement of female strength and success, attention needs to be given to fundamental employment issues concerning New Zealand women. The celebratory tenor of Suffrage Year activity was most appropriate during 1993 but life after Suffrage Year will be a continuation for women of the struggle against fundamental and historical inequalities inherent in our society without the hoopla.

Raising Public Awareness

The possibility of a Suffrage Year 'backlash' and the resumption of complacent attitudes by policy-makers towards women at work emphasise the need for a better knowledge of the Convention. Women's groups could use the Convention on the Elimination of All Forms of Discrimination Against Women to pressure policy-makers to make significant changes. But no one will use the Convention in this way unless they know about it. As Chen (ibid., p.6) states:

> The Convention needs to be brought back into the public consciousness so that New Zealanders can use it to pressure the government to keep its promises to women and to encourage the

government to initiate measures against sex discrimination to achieve *de jure* and *de facto* equality for women.

This chapter hopes to help raise awareness of New Zealand's breach of the Convention in respect of pay equity.

Pay Equity Requirement

Article 11(1)(d) of the Convention specifically obliges New Zealand, as an adhering state, to take 'all appropriate measures' to provide women with, *the right to equal remuneration, including benefits, and to equal treatment in respect of work of equal value, as well as equality of treatment in the evaluation of the quality of work.* This article goes beyond equal pay for equal work and requires New Zealand to give women pay equity and also the same rewards for work of equal value.

New Zealand did not enter a reservation against Article 11(1)(d) allowing it to suspend or avoid its obligations with respect to employment equity. In addition, New Zealand has ratified the International Labour Organisation Convention No. 100 which concerns Equal Remuneration for Women and Men Workers for Work of Equal Value. The ILO convention stresses the importance of the adoption and implementation of job evaluation systems based on gender-neutral criteria allowing comparison of the value of female-dominated jobs with male-dominated jobs.

The fight, won and lost, for pay equity in New Zealand has been comprehensively described by one of the architects of the shortlived pay equity legislation, Margaret Wilson (1992). She describes how women worked during the years 1984-1990 to become a political lobby which effected a change in the legal and economic status of women through employment equity legislation.

The legislation was no mean achievement in view of a lack of wholehearted support from government, virulent opposition from employer groups and covert and overt manoeuvres by some government departments. The opposition to pay equity and the concept of compulsory equal employment opportunities programmes embodied in the legislation rested on assumptions they were contrary to the notion of a free market and to *laissez faire* economic policies.

Comparable Worth Provisions

The Employment Equity Act 1990 provided that an employer, union or twenty women workers in a female occupation, could apply to the Employment Equity Commissioner to make a pay equity assessment of their particular occupation (Wilson, 1992).

The Act stated the claimant when making the application must specify two male occupations (occupations in which 60 per cent or more of the workers were male) with which female occupations could be compared for the purposes of assessment. The Commissioner determined the occupational classes for assessment after comparing a number of factors including skills, effort and responsibility, rates of pay and so on (Wilson, 1992).

One of the first acts of the 1990 National government was to repeal the Employment Equity Act. As a result New Zealand is in breach of its international obligations, both the ILO Convention 100 and the Convention on the Elimination of All Forms of Discrimination Against Women.

The low profile domestically of New Zealand's international obligations, particularly with respect to the Convention, is apparent in an analysis of the parliamentary debates on the repeal of the employment equity legislation at the end of 1990. Not one Labour Opposition speaker in a vigorous debate raised the Convention as an issue. The Member of Parliament for Mangere, David Lange, raised the consequences of repeal in relation to the New Zealand Bill of Rights Act, 1990. And while four Labour Members of Parliament, Liz Tennet (Island Bay), Larry Sutherland (Avon), Sonja Davies (Pencarrow) and Whetu Tirikatene-Sullivan (Southern Maori) noted the repeal flew in the face of the New Zealand Government's ratification of ILO Convention 100, there was no mention that it breached S 11(1)(d) of the Convention on the Elimination of All Forms of Discrimination Against Women (NZ Parliamentary Debates, 28 November-19 December, 1990). The failure of politicians to cite the Convention in debate provides further confirmation that the international instrument needs a higher profile if it is to be used by women to press for policy changes.

The government is likely to continue to downplay the Convention and New Zealand's performance in future. New Zealand's manner of reporting on employment equity to CEDAW in 1994 is heralded in the *Status of New Zealand Women 1992* report which will form the basis of New Zealand's summary of its progress. The report neither explicitly acknowledges employment equity as a breach of the Convention nor places any emphasis on it. The report is written in a way that minimises, if not obscures, New Zealand's lack of progress in the employment pay equity issue. New Zealand will be coy indeed about the repeal of pay equity.

New Zealand's current absence of pay equity legislation is glossed over. Early on the report states that pay equity was introduced, then later in a throwaway half sentence states it was repealed. The first mention of employment equity in the *Status of New Zealand Women 1992* report comes in the section talking about the advancement of women, in which New Zealand under the Convention is asked to:

> ... describe the means used to promote and ensure the full development and advancement of women for the purpose of guaranteeing them the exercise and enjoyment of human rights and fundamental freedoms in all fields on a basis of equality with men (p.7).

The report talks about the work of non-governmental organisations and in particular the work of women's groups working to change social prejudices and practices. The report states that:

> ... typical issues raised by women's groups during the period included:
> *   *equal pay for work of equal value* which resulted in the passage of legislation on pay equity (p.9).

It is only later in the report, however, that New Zealand acknowledges to CEDAW that the legislation was shortlived and was repealed so that New Zealand no longer enjoys pay equity.

In the section on employment the *Status of New Zealand Women 1992* report states:

In the 1980s, some test cases under the Equal Pay Act confirmed that the courts interpreted the provisions of the Act to apply only where men and women were doing the same or substantially similar work. Many groups recognised the need for wider legislation to cover pay equity or equal pay for work of equal value, and to address the differing pay rates of women and men in predominantly 'single sex' occupations such as nursing and police work, which many considered carried equal levels of remuneration.

The campaign for *pay equity* was strengthened during the reporting period by the formation of CEVEP, the Coalition for Equal Value Equal Pay, a coalition of unions, women's groups and individuals. The government convened a Working Group on Equal Pay and Equal Employment Opportunities. The report of this group chaired by Margaret Wilson, recommended pay equity legislation and the setting up of a Commission for Employment Equity which would cover both pay equity and EEO. The Employment Equity Act was passed in 1990.

The Act was constructed within the industrial relations framework prevailing at that time.

After the repeal of the Employment Equity Act, in December 1990 the government established the Working Party on Equity in Employment which recommended that legislation be enacted requiring large employers to establish EEO programmes, and that government establish a joint private/ public sector trust to promote EEO in the private sector. *On the issue of pay equity, the Working Party concluded that they did not see it as the function of an outside body to carry out comparable worth exercises either across or within organisations* (p.40) (My emphasis added.)

The report appears to minimise pay equity as an issue despite New Zealand's obligations under the Convention. Continuing to breach the Convention in relation to employment equity looks set to be government policy. Chen (1989) notes that when New Zealand's first report was reviewed CEDAW asked 164 questions concerning the Convention's impact on New Zealand. She states (p.5) that:

Apart from comments concerning the inadequacy of the report and the regrettable adoption of three reservations, the questions covered the structure and role of the Ministry of Women's Affairs and non-governmental organisations (NGOs); the feminist movement; family planning and abortion facilities; the position of Maori women; women's situation in politics, education, health and employment; violence against women; rural women; childcare; sex-role stereotyping and affirmative action.

CEDAW is likely to consider the *Status of New Zealand Women 1992* report inadequate in relation to its reporting of employment equity. Chen (1989) states that some of the major shortcomings of adhering states' reports to CEDAW include such things as; a tendency to be self-congratulatory as opposed to being self-critical, the failure of reports to provide material on the extent to which the Convention's provisions have been implemented, the report's coverage of only some areas of the Convention, avoiding those areas that are controversial or have not been implemented by the adhering states (p.75).

While the *Status of New Zealand Women 1992* report is acknowledged as an improved report and certainly superior to those provided by some other states, it will require vigilance of interpretation by CEDAW. Only a punctilious reader would note from the report that the early promise on page nine which talked of the passage of pay equity legislation does not match the brief acknowledgement later in the document on page forty that the legislation was repealed, and that government policy is opposed to legislating for employment equity.

The area of pay equity provides daily tangible experiences of inequality for New Zealand working women. As this chapter was being written one of the debates which had emerged from controversy over health reforms in 1993 was a pay equity row involving midwives. An increase in base rate maternity fees was recommended by the Maternity Benefits Tribunal. The *Dominion* (27 April 1993, p.3), reported:

One of the main issues facing the tribunal had been whether doctors and midwives should be paid the same rate for antenatal care and for delivery of babies.

The Medical Association had argued that the work of midwives and medical practitioners was not of equal value. General practitioner obstetricians could deal with complications or emergencies and should be paid a higher fee for their skills and qualifications.

Midwives and the department said they provided the same or a similar service, and should be paid the same fees.

General practitioners involved in the delivery of babies had recommended to government that they receive a pay increase to over $160 an hour, while recommending midwives be paid less than $60 an hour for work of equal value. Government resolved a rate of about $90 an hour but doctors were preparing (as this chapter was being written) to seek a judicial review of the decision of the Minister of Health, Mr Birch. The dispute is just one of the contemporary pay equity issues affecting New Zealand women.

Wilson (1992) in her useful review says it is impossible to assess how the equity legislation would have worked in practice because while it came into force on October 1990 it had been repealed by the end of the same year and was in effect for a few months only. She also states that government policy on pay equity mirrors that of various employers' groups and the Business Roundtable, that women can best achieve equality in employment through the operation of the free market. But, as Wilson notes, on the available evidence, women have been disadvantaged by the restructuring of the labour market.

The disadvantage to women is confirmed by Sayers (1992) who states the Employment Contracts Act and labour flexibility strategies of government and management are contributing to the marginalisation of women's work in both the paid and unpaid spheres. Opposition employment spokeswoman Liz Tennet also points to women as one of several groups disadvantaged by the Employment Contracts Act. She told a Women in Management suffrage year conference held in Wellington in July 1993 that although the Employment Tribunal did not collect figures on ethnicity or gender, anecdotal evidence 'showed the people most exploited under the Employment Contracts Act were women, Maoris and Pacific Islanders and the young' (*Dominion*, 15 July, p.7).

Revitalising a political campaign over pay equity may also be difficult. The combination of economic recession and the sweep of market liberalism will hinder building a climate of opinion which embraces employment equity. Wilson (1992) is pessimistic about the future. She states that:

> It is difficult to see progress being made by women towards gaining equity in paid employment now that the legislation has been repealed. It may also be difficult for women to mount such an effective political campaign in the foreseeable future, although the experience gained should provide a base for any future campaign to influence public policy. Such a campaign will be necessary if women are to obtain employment equity (p.130).

It is hoped CEDAW's response to the inadequacy of New Zealand's report on its breach of its international obligations in relation to employment equity will provide an impetus for a renewed struggle by New Zealand women. But this depends in part on an improved public awareness of New Zealand's international obligations for equal employment opportunities and the fact that we lag behind other more progressive countries. The *Status of New Zealand Women 1992* report is a worthwhile document and as Jenny Shipley, the Minister of Women's Affairs, states in the foreword, 'This document represents the most definitive piece of work to date on the status of women'. But its tenor and tone also exude an air of false optimism about New Zealand's progress in eliminating discrimination for women at work at a time when women are facing the consequences of a 'roll back' in pay equity and in terms of the status and protection of their work.

Holding the Fort: New Zealand's Reservations.

New Zealand has a practice of ratifying international conventions only when the provisions are substantially implemented in New Zealand law and practice, except for those areas which are the subject of reservations, according to the *Status of New Zealand Women 1992* report. Generally reservations are entered at the time of ratification and in this instance New Zealand entered three relating to women working in underground mines, women in combat, and concerning maternity leave with pay.

When New Zealand's report is received by CEDAW the Committee will note progress with respect to two of the three initial reservations.

The reservation concerning the employment of women in underground work in mines has been withdrawn. And there has been progress in relation to the recruitment of women into active combat roles and as aircraft or ship crew in the armed forces.

In 1990 the *Report of the Working Party on Women in Combat* made a majority recommendation as a government working party, that women should be able to volunteer for combat roles in the armed forces on the same merit basis as men. The *Status of New Zealand Women 1992* report states that government has yet to make a decision on whether to implement the recommendations of the working party.

> However, since August 1988, women have been allowed to perform all combat roles in the Royal New Zealand Air Force in peacetime. In 1992 the New Zealand Army announced it would undertake a trial, to last two to three years, which will give some women the opportunity to train in combat roles (p.5).

And in May 1993 it was reported by New Zealand Press Association that women were to be posted to a New Zealand warship for the first time, to fill mainly administrative, radio and cooking jobs. Separate accommodation , toilet and ablutions had not previously been available on frigates, but reduced manning on the frigate *Southland* had allowed separate sleeping quarters for a dozen women. The frigate *Wellington* would also take women, according to the Navy (*Evening Standard*, 8 May, 1993, p.2).

From these changes it appears that the recommendations of the working party have been substantially implemented and progress towards equality has been achieved, although this has not been enshrined in statute. New Zealand's armed forces should be monitored with respect to equity issues.

A far-reaching reservation in which no progress has been made concerns the issue of paid maternity leave. S 11(2)(b) states that:

> State Parties shall take appropriate measures to introduce maternity leave with pay or with comparable social benefits without loss of former employment, seniority or social allowances.

When the Convention was ratified New Zealand entered a reservation to this obligation and the *Status of New Zealand Women 1992* report states, 'New Zealand's reservation concerning maternity leave with pay still stands' (p.5).

Elsewhere the report describes the Parental Leave and Employment Protection Act 1987 which prohibits dismissal by reason of pregnancy, or because an employee is taking or wishes to take parental leave. The parental leave legislation allows for mothers and fathers to take leave at the time of the birth or adoption of a baby if the parent-to-be has been working for the same employer for a year before the baby's arrival and has been employed for at least 10 hours a week.

But in relation to the paid maternity leave required by the Convention, New Zealand appears unflinching. The *Status of New Zealand Women 1992* report states unequivocally:

> Maternity and parental leave on pay is not part of New Zealand law or practice, and it is not the intention of the government to introduce this requirement (p.42).

Many other industrialised nations have moved in recent years to offer at least partially paid maternity leave or related benefits as a positive acknowledgement of working women who have children.

Yet New Zealand is signalling clearly that it does not intend to adopt a progressive stance on paid maternity leave.

Using the usual language of United Nations diplomacy, it can be expected that CEDAW will note the continued adoption of reservations by New Zealand with regret. The predicted bland reaction raises the whole issue of the means of enforcement of the Convention by adhering states. The system of periodic reports which is the major enforcement system is beset by delays and is limited as an effective enforcement mechanism. Reports have to be submitted every four years, but in fact the *Status of New Zealand Women 1992* report will be at least two years old before it is presented in 1994. This will mean the second periodic report will not be received and reviewed until six years after New Zealand's first progress report on the implementation of the Convention in 1988. Not only are some member states tardy in furnishing reports but CEDAW also has a huge backlog of reports yet to be reviewed.

Conclusion

The notion of enforcement through a system of periodic reporting is based on the concept of sanction by public criticism. Reports from adhering states are reviewed by an international forum and commented on publicly and the notion is that no state is immune from criticism and comment which emerges from such a process. But if this reporting becomes sporadic rather than periodic and the reviews are based on outdated statistical data and information, then enforcement by state reporting has limited effect. The concept of CEDAW measuring New Zealand's progress and comparing it with other adhering states by periodic reporting is also undermined. All of the available reports may be so out-of-date that there is no means of making realistic comparisons or using international peer group pressure effectively.

Similarly it is difficult to raise public awareness about the Convention when CEDAW's comments on review relate to past years. Politicians and policy-makers are deeply rooted in the present. They are proficient at deflecting criticism on the basis that real and apparent improvements have been made in the period between submission and review. If the Convention is considered to be the major human rights instrument with respect to the women's struggle, then it must be seen to be relevant. The long time-lags and unwieldy reporting structures need to change. Effective mechanisms are needed for making a country's non- performance visible. Only when the reports reflect current reality and are well publicised both internationally and domestically can they be used to lobby politicians in adhering nations to face up to that same reality. Only then is the Convention likely to become a more powerful instrument for change.

References

Chen, M. (1989), *Women and Discrimination: New Zealand and the UN Convention*, Institute of Policy Studies, Wellington: Victoria University Press.

Department of Statistics (1990), *Women in New Zealand*, Wellington: Department of Statistics.

'Inequality in public service lamented', *Dominion,* 15 July, 1993, p.7.

'Maternity fees unlikely to increase 26pc – Birch', *Dominion, 21* April, 1993, p.3.

Ministry of Women's Affairs (1992), *Status of New Zealand Women Second Periodic Report on the Convention on the Elimination of all Forms of Discrimination Against Women,* Wellington: New Zealand Parliamentary Debates, 28 November – 19 December 1990.

Sayers, J. (1992), *Women, the Employment Contracts Act and Labour Flexibility,* Department of Human Resource Management Working Paper Series, 92/7, Palmerston North: Massey University.

Wilson, M. (1992), 'Employment Equity Act 1990: A Case Study in Women's Political Influence', in J. Deeks and N. Perry (eds), *Controlling Interests: Business, the State and Society in New Zealand,* Auckland: Auckland University Press.

'Women to get frigate duty', *Evening Standard,* 8 May, 1993, p.2.

7

Making the Connections: An Analysis of Equal Employment Opportunity Theory

Janet Sayers

Introduction

Equal employment opportunity (EEO) is consistently identified by writers as a major issue in human resource management. There is an evolving body of theory which has been developed in order to help facilitate understanding of EEO. The present chapter aims to introduce the reader to some of this theory and to suggest that there are deficiencies in the current theoretical constructs used to try and understand EEO.

Much of the literature discusses EEO policies in the contexts of liberal and radical strategies (Jewson and Mason, 1986; Webb and Liff, 1988; Dickson and Walsh, 1993). However, conceptualising EEO as involving either liberal or radical strategies is problematic. In particular, the positioning of 'liberal' and 'radical' strategies as mutually exclusive and ideologically antithetical, as much of the literature implies, does not help facilitate understanding of the practice of EEO or help to unravel its complexities. For example, an EEO strategy such as providing scholarships for Maori can be categorised as 'radical' because it is 'interventionist'. However, such a policy is mainly used within a broad 'liberal' human resource strategy. This chapter argues that research needs to be conducted on EEO-related activities across a broad range of issues in both the private and public sectors in order to locate the practice of EEO within a framework which appreciates the complexities of its practice. Any theoretical analysis needs to be able to interrelate the broad range of 'isms' which form the backbone of EEO (racism, sexism, ableism, the analysis of capitalism) as well as get beyond the dichotomy implicit in the notion of liberal and radical policies.

In addition to analysing EEO theory, the present chapter presents a model of EEO. The model is an attempt to illustrate the relationship between EEO and human resource management, as well as the perspectives of various EEO groups such as women, Maori and people with disabilities. The model uses a short-term pluralistic human resource management (HRM) perspective and a long-term radical perspective based on Cockburn's (1989) conceptualisation of liberal and radical EEO agendas. The long-term perspective has many features in common with workplace reform objectives. This long-term perspective argues that for there to be more equitable work places, organisations need to adopt more democratic and participative styles and forms. The short-term perspective is based on a strategic human resource management perspective which argues that EEO should be integrated into core business objectives.

This chapter also argues that pluralism, and other related theoretical areas such as discourse theory, offer fertile ground for the analysis of EEO. The aims and aspirations of various EEO groups are different. For example, the long-term agenda for Maori may be economic and political self-development; for women it may be equal representation in all spheres of work activity; for people with disabilities it may be self-empowerment. Pluralism is a useful concept with which to illustrate the differences between stake-holders, but also to depict the inter-connectedness between them. Additionally, pluralism enables the fluid and mutable nature of the relationship between groups to be depicted.

This chapter is structured as follows: first, it briefly describes some current trends in EEO policy development; second, it discusses typical perspectives of EEO, HRM, women and Maori; third, it discusses the concept of pluralism which this paper argues is a useful theoretical construct with which to analyse and understand EEO; and finally, this chapter attempts to synthesise these perspectives into a model.

EEO in the 1990s

EEO in the 1990s is a different phenomenon than it was in the 1980s. The political and economic climate in New Zealand now favours a voluntary approach to EEO. This is in contrast to the predominant influences of the 1980s which favoured a more interventionist approach to both EEO and labour market policy.

It is clear that legislative compulsion to implement EEO in the public service has been critical to the success of EEO implementation in this sector in comparison with the private sector where no such legislation exists (Commission for Employment Equity, 1991). However, despite the continued presence of EEO provisions in the State Sector Act 1988, the public sector is having to find reasons beyond legislative compulsion to implement EEO. In particular we have seen four legislative changes that have directly influenced the environment in which EEO operates: the introduction of the Public Finance Act 1989; the introduction of the State Sector Act 1988; the repealing of the Employment Equity Act 1990; and the introduction of the Employment Contracts Act 1991. The deregulationist approach to labour market policy, signalled by these policy initiatives, ushered in a new era in employment relations in New Zealand. In particular, employment practices and policies became more firm-specific and market-driven than they had been in the recent past.

The new approach of non-intervention in the labour market has created something of a crisis for EEO in New Zealand. Reliance on legislation to compel EEO adherence was clearly no longer appropriate. In order to respond to this challenge the practice of EEO underwent a metamorphosis. EEO in the state sector became more market-oriented. Many state sector managers looked for business reasons to implement EEO despite the implicit acceptance of fairness and equity values in their guiding statutes.

EEO protagonists in the private sector also continued to draw upon market-oriented strategies in order to 'spread the message' of EEO. EEO consultants in the private sector often studiously avoid the term 'EEO' even though their practices are very similar in nature to those in the public sector. A sample of private sector services could include managing diversity programmes, change management programmes, cultural auditing, career development training courses and employee empowerment programmes. However, the practice of EEO in both the private and public sectors involves processes that are planned, systematic and include accountability and monitoring mechanisms (see for example Ross and Schneider, 1992).

In this more market-oriented environment, EEO, in both the public and private sectors, has moved towards concerns with 'family-friendly' work practices, integrating EEO into Total Quality Management programmes, performance assessment, job evaluation, service and business-oriented EEO strategies, the impact of organisational restructuring on EEO, integrating EEO into employment contracts, cultural auditing, and human resource accounting (*Report of the EEO Practitioners' Conference*, 1992).

These concerns are arguably more 'acceptable' to the mainstream business community and less 'challenging' to the status quo than issues relating to monitoring and compliance to legislation. However, several writers have suggested that EEO may be appropriating too closely the rhetoric of the new wave of 'managerialism' and liberalism (Lewis, 1992; Sayers, 1992). This suspicion of managerialism is hardly surprising considering the personal backgrounds of many EEO activists in social movements such as feminism and trade unions. EEO has evolved out of a 'bottom-up' movement, a ground-swell of opinion that has argued the reasons for inequality lie in patriarchy, capitalism, racism and ableism. EEO has attempted to straddle this diverse range of 'isms' and work within the system as well.

The economic and political environment has exacerbated these tensions in EEO theory and practice and so it is particularly important that the future directions of EEO are debated and articulated by stake-holders. Clearly, as this paper argues, EEO has a role to play within the 'system'. However, EEO theory has not developed to the extent where it can adequately explain the role of EEO in the workplace.

Who Says What and Why? Theoretical Perspectives on EEO

In this section I discuss EEO and human resource management theory. I then go on to discuss the perspectives of two main EEO groups – women and Maori. In doing so my aim is to illustrate four issues: the interconnectedness of EEO with HRM; the limitations of existing EEO theory; the differences between the perspectives of the EEO groups; and the similarities between their views regarding the role of EEO in organisations.

EEO Theory

One of the most important studies regarding EEO was conducted by Jewson and Mason (1986). Their study has been the subject of debate and has formed the basis of subsequent analysis. They described differences between 'liberal' and 'radical' approaches to EEO. In their view the aims of the two types of policies are as follows:

> ... the aim of liberal equal opportunities policies is the removal of unfair distortions to the operation of the labour market by means of institutionalising fair procedures in every aspect of work and employment.... . The radical approach is very different. It seeks to intervene directly in workplace practices in order to achieve fair distribution of rewards among employees, as measured by some criterion of moral value and worth. Thus the radical view is concerned primarily with the outcome of the contest rather than the rules of the game, with the fairness of the distribution of rewards rather than the fairness of procedures (p. 315).

These differences are represented diagrammatically in Table 7.1:

Table 7.1:
Liberal and Radical Conceptions of Equal Opportunity Policies

Elements of Equal Opportunities Policies	Conceptions of Equal Opportunities	
	Liberal	Radical
Principles	Fair procedures	Fair distribution of rewards
Implementation	Bureaucratisation of decision-making	Politicisation of decision-making
Effectiveness	Positive action	Positive discrimination
Perceptions	Justice seen to be done	Consciousness raising (e.g. training)

(Jewson and Mason, 1986, p.312)

Having identified two approaches characteristic of equal opportunity processes, Jewson and Mason go on to argue that in practice these two approaches are routinely confused. In particular the preferred procedures of the liberal approach are widely assumed to result in the preferred outcomes of the radical approach. They argue that 'policy-makers thus evolved their beliefs and negotiating stances out of a fluid and paradoxical amalgamation of philosophically antithetical positions' (p. 308).

There is at least one main problem with this analysis: it places liberal and radical policies in contradiction to one another. Cockburn (1989) argues that:

> ... this dichotomous schema [of liberal and radical policies] is a straitjacket we need to escape if we are to understand the equal opportunities movement and its potential place in contemporary politics (p.215).

Cockburn proposes the replacement of the liberal/radical dichotomy with the notion of an EEO agenda of greater or shorter length. The shorter agenda entails the modification of personnel and HRM policies that are essential to the liberal model. The longer agenda entails a project of transformation that incorporates the radical agenda of fair outcomes for target groups. This longer agenda also recommends the critical examination of the nature and purpose of institutions and the processes by which the power of some groups over others in institutions is built and renewed. Cockburn's model advocates a change in the nature of power. More specifically she argues for a reorganisation of work structures so that diverse people can exert more control over their institutions.

Cockburn, like Jewson and Mason, regards liberal and radical agendas as distinct and to some extent antithetical and so her analysis suffers the same limitation. However, her analysis is useful because it explains how we might amalgamate the radical agenda of social activism with the practicalities of everyday business practice. This combination of the two aims of EEO, social activism and business practice, is also discussed by Boxall (1991) in the context of being a 'good employer'. This concept is discussed in the next section.

Human Resource Management

The dilemma of EEO regarding the managerialist/equity debate has some parallels with debates within human resource management. HRM writers have been concerned with similar ambiguities although the focus has tended to be on the humanitarian versus the scientific management schools of thought. Boxall summarises:

> [HRM] writers typically review the tensions which emerged in the historical development of specialised personnel departments; on the one hand, specialists were hired to humanise the workplace (the 'welfare' and 'human relations' traditions) and, on the other, they were hired to improve labour productivity and react to trade union organisation (the scientific management and IR [industrial relations] management traditions) (1991, p.238).

HRM has been concerned with unitarist and pluralistic models in much the same way that EEO has been concerned with the managerialist/ equity debate. HRM writers have argued that the 'top down' approach of unitarist views does not take employee concerns into consideration. However, a pluralistic view of HRM, where the interests of employees are seen as legitimate and valid, is seen by many HRM writers as both a more adequate reflection of the practice of HRM and an attitude that should be encouraged if healthy work and social relationships are to be developed.

It is clear that EEO and HRM are strongly interlinked in practice. Burton (1991, p.7) for instance, has commented on the relevance of a human resource management perspective for EEO:

> The changing profile of the workforce requires that agencies plan their human resource programs to accommodate this change, which means collecting and maintaining EEO data and using it effectively in the overall strategic planning contexts.

Boxall (1991) has also attempted to link EEO into HRM strategy through his attempts to define the concept of a 'good employer'. His guidelines for good employer practice are useful in envisaging how EEO may fit into an HRM strategy. Underlying his discussion is the conviction that employees' values and concerns are legitimate. In particular, a 'good employer' would: seek to understand the interests of employees; recognise the rights of employees to choose how to express their interests; seek to maximise employers' common interests with employees; seek to resolve conflict of interest with employees in ways that are compatible with enterprise effectiveness and (as far as possible) the advancement of employees' interests; and, seek to take a long-term strategic approach to employment relations which is expressed in a consistent set of policy signals. Boxall also gives a number of process implications of such a philosophy which includes merit-based decision-making and the 'partnership response' amongst others.

An organisation can only be a 'good employer' if it is in business. That is, a business must be viable, in whatever way it measures its productivity, so that it can remain as an entity and employ people. For instance, to remain in business employers may, from time to time, make difficult economic decisions regarding cutting wages, down-sizing or relocation of the enterprise. Such decisions must limit our notion of an employer's 'goodness' because the employer is not acting in the employees' best interests. So, the notion of 'goodness' is bounded by what makes practical business sense.

In the contexts of EEO this notion of 'goodness' is useful because it allows us to understand how an EEO policy might operate within a pluralistic HRM perspective. The business agenda is retained, so is the concern for employee well-being which is at the heart of EEO, and EEO is linked to a wider human resource management philosophy.

The Perspectives of Two EEO 'Groups'

Different perspectives on EEO centre themselves in the particular experiences and backgrounds of the protagonists in the debate. For example, the perspective of people with disabilities is uniquely centred around an historical and social analysis based on the experiences of having a disability (Cahill, 1991). For Maori the Treaty of Waitangi and the meanings attached to self-development, biculturalism and partnership help define how Maori perceive EEO. Feminist thinkers have grappled on many levels with questions relating to inequality between the genders, particularly regarding the gendered nature of workplace relations. The following discussion briefly outlines characteristic perspectives of two groups about EEO; women and Maori.

Women

Two typical perspectives on the causes of inequality in the workplace are described and discussed; liberal and radical feminist perspectives.

Liberal feminist perspectives often focus on issues associated with the individual rather than looking at structural reasons for inequality. In line with this perspective the liberal feminist view of EEO is that it can be achieved if equal numbers of women and men are represented at all levels of an organisation. This view implies that the existing structures are legitimate and valid and there is no need to alter them (Wieneke, 1991).

Radical feminist views look at underlying structural reasons for the inequalities in the position of men and women. A common view is that existing social and organisational structures are patriarchal and capitalist and by their nature incompatible with the notion of equity and social justice. Existing institutional structures are perceived to serve the interests of men. The exclusion of women is necessary to preserve patriarchal structures and so while there may be some concessions to include a few women who do not challenge the dominant culture there is no possibility of equal participation. Achieving equity, according to this perspective, is only possible when the existing structures are broken down and power redistributed among all the groups (Weineke, 1991). A more radical view would argue that there is no hope of restructuring existing organisations because of their inherently patriarchal nature and that women can only be free to participate fully and effectively if they set up their own organisations (Weineke, 1991).

More radical perspectives have been debated in New Zealand, especially over the effectiveness of legislation in achieving the outcome of equity that is desired. Lewis (1991) questioned the likely effectiveness of the Employment Equity Act and argued, based on overseas evidence and a lack of real movement towards equity in New Zealand, in support of quota systems and numerical goals embodied in affirmative action compliance programmes.

This description of two women's perspectives does not do justice to the sophisticated and complex body of feminist thought on gendered relations in the workplace. However, in the contexts of this paper they illustrate two main perspectives of EEO's role in the workplace: the predominantly liberal view related to issues of representation, and the more radical view concerning restructuring workplace power relationships and the limitations of a liberal model in achieving this objective.

Maori

There has been a confusion as to the meaning of biculturalism and the Treaty in the contexts of EEO. This confusion has been heightened because the State Sector Act 1988 made Maori a target group along with people with disabilities, women and ethnic groups. Several Maori commentators have attempted to clarify the relationship between Maori and EEO.

Waaka (1991) argued that EEO was not an appropriate mechanism for dealing with bi-cultural issues in government departments. Waaka argued that Maori who understand EEO Maori see organisations using EEO as an excuse to avoid issues of tangata whenua status and the Treaty of Waitangi. Most Maori, she argues, believe that employment initiatives for Maori should be centralised within a Maori co-ordinating body and not through an EEO co-ordinator in organisations. Waaka argues that:

> The development of Maori people hinges on the restructuring of power relations. Future directions for government organisations will be influenced by Maori directions .... Unless the structures and power relationships within organisations alter, then Maori development will be limited and inequality will continue (1991, p.2).

In this view Maori are considered to be inappropriately 'lumped' in with other EEO target groups, thereby obscuring their real concerns which relate to their status as tangata whenua. However, EEO is seen, in Waaka's view, as an important ally that should facilitate the selection and advancement of Maori in organisations along with other target groups.

Other views also underscore the self-determination theme implicit in Waaka's paper and the usefulness of EEO in helping achieve limited, but significant, progress towards these aims. For instance, *Maori at Work* (1991) argues that 'if the costs of EEO policies are kept low, they can be seen as a useful tool in helping to slowly improve the position of Maori in the labour market' (1991, p.65).

It is clear that the long-term objective for Maori is a restructuring of power relationships in society. It also appears clear that EEO has a role to play in facilitating this objective.

Liberal feminist views and two Maori perspectives allow a short-term role to EEO in facilitating opportunities for groups of women and Maori workers. Furthermore, the long-term visions of both groups entail a restructuring of power relations in society. It is beyond the scope of this paper to compare these short-term and long-term aims in detail. However, the following discussion of 'pluralism' may help illustrate the interconnectedness of long-term perspectives.

Pluralism

An alternative model of EEO to the liberal/radical dichotomy can be found in a pluralistic perspective. A pluralistic model recognises that different groups have valid stakes in the employment relationship and that they are interrelated. McClennan (1989, p.18) describes two of the main features of conventional pluralism as being:

* A sociology of competing interest groups;
* A conception of the state as a political mechanism responsive to the balance of societal demands.

Pluralism has been discussed to some extent in the previous section on human resource management. However, pluralism may also be a useful theoretical tool with which to analyse the relationship between competing groups within EEO including 'target' groups, other workers and managers, as well as the role of the state in responding to demands of interest groups and setting policy regarding EEO. For instance, the following diagram illustrates how distinct 'target groups' may interrelate with each other through an EEO strategy.

Figure 7.1:
A Pluralistic Model of EEO

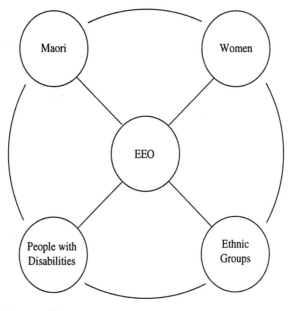

(Sayers, 1994)

Using such a perspective highlights the distinct nature of each group's aims, aspirations and strategies, but also allows us to portray EEO's role. We can also explore such issues as the dangers of adopting a strategy that assumes 'unity' of purpose such as that which may occur with a rigid strategic human resource strategy. However, areas of commonality and 'unity' between groups can be examined while retaining a sense of varying employee values.

A Model of EEO

There are distinctions between the two approaches of liberal and radical strategies. Liberal versions of EEO can be strategies such as redefining merit, family-friendly employment policies, and managing diversity strategies that do not seriously challenge the operation of 'pure market forces'. Radical versions of EEO may be strategies such as quotas, mainstreaming programmes and other interventionist strategies that are more structural in their approach. However, as I have argued in this paper, the simplicity of such a conceptualisation of the issues belies the complexity involved. For example, I have argued previously that the act of 'redefining merit' may cause renegotiation of the value of 'women's worth' in the workplace (Sayers, 1992).

A more sophisticated approach based on Cockburn's (1989) idea of short-term and long-term agendas can be illustrated as follows:

Figure 7.2:
Short-Term Human Resource Management
Approach and a Long-Term Radical Approach.

	Short-term HRM agenda		Long-term radical agenda

No
EEO
	- integrating EEO
	  into TQM
	
	- developing diversity
	
	- redefining merit
	
	- managing change
		Full
		
		EEO
			- full participation of
			  people with disabilities –
			  being valued for ability
			
			- workplace change
			  (democratisation,
			  autonomy, participation)

	- 'catch' up
	  scholarships
	
	- numerical targets
	
	- mainstreaming
	- targeting
			- partnership Maori-Pakeha
			
			- equal representation of
			  women, recognition of
			  women's worth, equal pay

(Sayers (1994), adapted from Cockburn, 1989)

This model describes a continuum. At the beginning of the continuum is a 'no EEO' state where an organisation does not recognise EEO and has not done anything to try and achieve it. In the middle of the continuum are a range of HRM strategies that can be used to implement short-term EEO goals. These policies can also be divided using Jewson and Mason's (1986) distinction of 'radical' policies (below the continuum line) and 'liberal' policies (above the continuum line). At the end of the continuum is the full implementation of EEO, the desired end state for all EEO groups. The model shows that the long-term aims for groups are quite distinct and different. This is not to say this difference is necessarily the case, as the discussion of pluralism above has illustrated. The model also describes the various HRM techniques that may be used to achieve EEO in the workplace.

In addition to the perspectives of EEO groups the long-term aim specifies workplace democratisation as being an important objective. This long-term perspective argues that for there to be more equitable work places, organisations need to be informed by more democratic and participative styles and forms. The short-term aim is based on a strategic human resource management perspective which argues that EEO should be integrated firmly into core business objectives.

This model integrates EEO, HRM and the agendas of the various groups into a whole that provides a useful framework for conceptualising EEO. The issues of EEO implementation that relate to HRM perspectives can be shown to be relevant to business objectives. In addition the similarities and differences between the aims and aspirations of groups and the power relationships between them (including management and employees) can be usefully illustrated with a pluralistic approach.

Conclusion

This paper has argued that the practice of EEO in New Zealand has changed considerably during the last ten years. These changes have meant EEO needs to consider its relationships to business strategy, human resource management strategies and workplace reform initiatives. It is clear that for EEO to maintain its relevance in the current economic climate its usefulness to organisations must be clearly demonstrated. The business imperative then, is strong. But, as Burton has argued:

EEO programmes are having, and will continue to have, limited success in delivering equitable employment practices and outcomes, without a radical restructuring of social institutional arrangements (cited in Weineke, 1991, p.2).

EEO is, and continues to be, fundamentally concerned with humanising workplaces and promoting the objectives of disadvantaged groups at work. Any theoretical model needs to represent the range of 'isms' that have attempted to understand power and the ways it is acted out in organisational settings. However, a reassessment of the liberal/radical dichotomy is needed as it is probably too crude a division to realistically reflect the practice of EEO in the workplace. Pluralism and the notion of being a 'good employer' appear to be more fruitful avenues of exploration for those interested in modelling the practice and theory of equal employment opportunities.

Note

This chapter was previously published as Sayers, J. (1993), *An Analysis of Equal Employment Opportunity Theory,* Working Paper 93/3, Palmerston North: Department of Human Resource Management, Massey University.

References

Boxall, P. (1991), 'Would the Good Employer Please Step Forward? A Discussion of the "Good Employer" Concept in the State Sector Act 1988', *New Zealand Journal of Industrial Relations*, 16, 211-231.

Burton, C. (1991), 'Equal Employment Opportunity: Where to Now?'. Paper presented to Human Resource Management in the Public Sector Conference, Sydney, 27-28 May.

Cahill, M. (1991), *Exploring the Experience of Disability*, Wellington: Health Services Equal Employment Opportunity Development Unit.

Cockburn, C. (1989), 'Equal Opportunities: the Short and Long Agenda, *Industrial Relations Journal*, 20 (3), 213-225.

Commission for Employment Equity (1991), *Into the '90s. Equal Employment Opportunities in New Zealand. A Report from the Commission for Employment Equity*, Wellington: Department of Labour

Jewson, N. and Mason, D. (1986), 'The Theory and Practice of Equal Opportunities Policies: Liberal and Radical Approaches', *Sociological Review,* 34 (2), 307-334.

Lewis, N.C. (1991), 'Prospects for Equal Opportunity: A Woman's Choice?', *Sites*, 22 (Autumn), 123-141.

McClennan, G. (1989), *Marxism, Pluralism and Beyond*, London: Polity Press.

Report of the EEO Practitioners' Conference (1992), Wellington: EEO Practitioners' Association.

Ross, R. and Schneider, R. (1992), *From Equality to Diversity: a Business Case for Equal Opportunities*, London: Pitman.

Sayers, J.G. (1992), 'Equal Employment Opportunities: Directions for the Future?', in Celia Briar, Robyn Munford, Mary Nash (eds), *Superwomen Where Are You? Social Policy and Women's Experience*, Palmerston North: Dunmore Press, 141-155.

Walsh, P. and Dickson, J. (1993), *The Emperor's New Clothes: Equal Employment Opportunities in the New Zealand Public Sector 1988-92.* Working Paper 3/93, Wellington: Industrial Relations Centre, Victoria University.

Waaka, L. (1990), 'A Report on EEO Maori and a Bi-cultural Approach to Government', prepared for the Manager, Equal Opportunities Unit, State Services Commission, Wellington by The Waaka Consultancy, Rotorua.

Webb, J. and Liff, S. (1988), 'Play the White Man: the Social Construction of Fairness and Competition in Equal Opportunity Policies', *Sociological Review*, 36 (3), 532-551.

Weineke, C. (1991), 'EEO in Australia: A Practitioner's Perspective'. *Equal Opportunity International*, 10 (1), 1-10.

Part Two

The Practice and Theory of Equal Employment Opportunity

8

A Strategic Approach to Human Resource Development: A New Opportunity for EEO?

Janice Burns

Introduction

EO practitioners have lived with the frustration of having EEO viewed as an extra, a peripheral add-on located out to the side of the core business of the organisation. The add-on view of EEO limits its potential to feed into the central purpose of the organisation. However, a strategic approach to human resource development (SHRD) offers new hope. EEO practitioners have strongly advocated SHRD, seeing it as a way of developing EEO as an integral part of the human resource strategy in the same way that the human resource strategy is central to the business strategy of the organisation.

This chapter attempts to explore the possibilities and the limitations of linking EEO to strategic human resource development and draws mainly on the experience of working with public sector organisations, an analysis of the literature and discussion with colleagues.

Defining Strategic Human Resource Development

There have been many attempts to define SHRD, but all involve some linking of the business direction or strategy of the organisation with the way in which the work of staff is organised, managed and rewarded. For example, Wright and McMahan (1992, p.298) define it as 'the pattern of planned human resource deployments and activities intended to enable an organisation to achieve its goals', and Gunnigle (1991, p.23) says that:

> The basic premise of strategic HRM is that organisations incorporate human resource considerations into strategic decision making, establish a corporate human resource philosophy and develop personnel strategies and policies which complement business strategy and maximise human resource utilisation.

Thus SHRD has potential to radically change the role and orientation of the human resource function and tie its performance into the overall performance of the organisation.

In the 1980s a major shift began in the way organisations across all sectors thought about their business, much of it provoked by developments in their operating environment. Huge changes were taking place in the domestic economy and there was an increasing sense that the economy in Aotearoa/New Zealand was linked to the global economy. Technological changes, predicted future demographic trends, changes in our industrial relations frameworks, changes in the way work was organised, an increased focus on quality and customer satisfaction and the need to respond to increased competition, all required organisations to attempt to position themselves in this new marketplace and design strategies not only to get there, but to stay there. The public service also had to face these changes and looked at issues such as accountability to their customers or clients and the cost-effectiveness of their business. Indeed, the whole nature and structure of the public service was radically altered by the passing of the State Sector Act 1988 and the Public Finance Act 1989. Miles and Snow (1984) have defined the response to such changes as 'a dynamic search that seeks to align the organisation with its environment and to arrange resources internally in support of that alignment' (cited in Dunphy and Stace, 1990, p.40).

In the public service the last five years have seen an increased emphasis on business planning, with environmental scanning as one of the variables contributing to that planning. A consciousness of the interface of the business with its environment and the key importance of skilled and committed employees has been seen as essential to survival and development. In fact, Dunphy and Stace (1990) believe it is the change strategy that organisations develop to position or reposition themselves in the marketplace which has the major influence on the human resource strategy adopted. They say it is:

> ... a systematic logic that leads from the development of the business strategies, to an assessment of the scope of the change and leadership style needed to reposition the organisation and then to the determination of the kind of human resource management strategy needed to make the change strategy work (p.132).

Hendry and Pettigrew (1992) believe that human resource management itself involves the management of this change and that, 'this includes the continuing process of adjusting personnel systems to organisational needs, and also the complex processes that integrate strategy – structure – culture change' (p.138).

EEO and Strategic Human Resource Development

So what was the basis of optimism for the achievement of EEO within this new conceptual and business framework? EEO has been seen, and to some extent promoted in the early days of its development, as a sort of equity product tacked on to other functions or practices. For example, organisations could provide a scholarship for a Maori student without examining the ways in which their human resource practices disadvantaged their existing Maori staff. This approach, coupled with the inherent reluctance of organisations to change their structures and systems, has resulted in a somewhat constrained and limited amount of EEO progress being achieved. Within the public service, many organisations have achieved changes in areas such as school holiday programmes, women on interview panels and the creation of networks which, while 'sweetening' the environment are not reaching to the heart of organisational business or creating any real changes for EEO groups. In fact, it could be argued that we may have reached the limit of what it is possible to change unless the relationship of EEO to the root of the organisation is radically altered.

Until recently there has been little discussion in the public sector of the linkage of EEO to the business of the organisation or of the way that the nature and vision of the business could influence the EEO agenda and method of implementation. An increased focus on understanding the nature of the business and the repositioning of the general human resource function as a full partner in the strategic planning process, potentially offers an enlarged and more integrated role for EEO to create a more holistic approach to people management. The new view of the importance of human resources has also offered the opportunity to redefine the value of EEO in assisting the achievement of business goals and place this objective alongside the legal and social justice rationale for implementing EEO.

The 1992 report *EEO Progress in the Public Service as at June 1992* identified three important changes in departmental thinking about the way EEO is marketed and practised. Probably the most important of these is that many organisations are beginning to see EEO as part of their strategy to meet their business goals. The report concludes that 'organisations which adopt this approach and apply it consistently across the organisation, are likely to become leaders in the EEO field' (p.29). Ideally, this integrated approach would also offer the organisation the opportunity to revalue the skills of the EEO practitioner as someone who is familiar with the concepts and practice of strategic planning and the methods it requires, e.g. environmental scanning, risk assessment and monitoring outcomes. I have written before that I believe one of the reasons for the unpopularity of EEO (and sometimes of the practitioner) is that EEO has often been the only rigorous process within human resource practice and so it has demanded a standard of organisational behaviour in terms of planning and monitoring that put other practices to shame (Burns, 1992). In some public sector organisations, EEO has pioneered planning and strategic thinking.

Potentially in the public service, the move to a more strategic approach to an EEO agenda that is closely tied to the business of the organisation, means that we are likely to see some diversification in the practice of EEO between organisations as they seek to find and implement their own custom-built version. This sense of business 'ownership' of EEO may serve to increase its acceptability and encourage a more creative approach to its implementation.

The development of a mission or vision for the organisation is the first task in defining the business strategy. Incorporating EEO principles as part of this vision offers the possibility of some consistency between what the organisation says it is trying to achieve and the way it goes about achieving it. A reflection of this vision should be seen at the most basic level in the approach or values inherent in the human resource practices. For example, if the vision of the organisation includes the development of committed and skilled staff, does the policy on the use of sick leave start from a basis of believing staff to be committed to the organisation and honest in their dealings with it (as in allowing them the amount of sick leave they need) or is it designed to deal with the occasional potential for abuse (as in penalising people for being sick on a Friday and a Monday)?

The preface to the Harvard Business Review's early (1993) text on strategic management says that it is, 'the way of managing a company whereby the overall strategy and purposes of the firm dominate decisions at all levels and in all functions of the company'. Strategic management offers the potential for congruence between EEO and the business, and the chance for EEO to have a wider and deeper influence.

However, researchers studying the literature on SHRD would have difficulty in finding any discussion of the potential for EEO within a context of strategic human resource management and development. Much of the literature on SHRD is either silent on the issue of equity or pays it scant attention.

Some of the literature appears to veer almost towards a kind of 'strategic determinism' in that attempts have been made to determine prescriptively the kind of business strategy which best fits a particular set of environmental imperatives, the sort of leadership which could best implement it and the sort of human resource strategies which could best fulfil the goal (Millar, 1991).

In some cases the discussion of SHRD in the literature becomes almost stereotypically prescriptive. For example, Millar (1991, p.31) presents a chart headed, 'matching managers to strategy' in which he suggests that if the objective of the business is growth, the chief executive should be 'young, ambitious, aggressive'!

Other research has developed models to assist organisations in repositioning themselves based on an analysis of how companies either presently or previously have made changes and maintained a market advantage (Dunphy and Stace, 1990). The problem with this is that it includes only the experiences of those who have traditionally been in a position to lead or develop strategy. The potential for a range of quite different but equally effective responses does not appear to have been built in.

Strategic human resource development is a management-driven model. 'In most organisations "strategic flow" is top down' (Millar, 1991, p.25). While this does not necessarily mean that the development of the strategy will be completely without the influence of people lower down the organisation, it does raise questions about how the voices of women, Maori, people of the Pacific Islands, staff who belong to ethnic groups and those with a disability will be heard. In the public service, the 'voice' of EEO networks has been able to exert influence on some human resource practices such as the way interviews are conducted. But the influence of networks has been from the bottom up. How much will the particular concerns of these groups influence the development of the business strategy? What role will they have in the development of the resulting human resource strategy? Unless these views are legitimised and required as part of the scanning of the internal environment that precedes the development of the vision and the strategy, the SHRD process may not have a place for them.

A strategic approach to business and to human resource practice stresses the importance of the contribution of managers. The literature (Garavan, 1991; Gunnigle, 1991) emphasises the need for the organisation to have skilled and effective leaders. These chief executives may adopt a variety of leadership styles depending on the task at hand, but all are seen to be pivotal in the development and maintenance of the business vision and direction. Other senior managers are also likely to play a very influential role in the direction and structure of the organisation. The recently released report on EEO progress in the public service highlights the key role chief executives and managers play in the successful implementation of EEO. The report highlights the continued need for managers to be held responsible for EEO implementation and progress through their contracts and performance agreements and to be trained in the skills to carry out these roles with knowledge, sensitivity and confidence. For strategic human resource development to hold any promise for EEO, those developing the strategies must have a commitment to EEO and a relatively sophisticated understanding of its operation.

There is a somewhat evangelical ring to the discussions that happen around strategic human resource management. As Cooke and Armstrong (1990, p.31) argue, 'Everyone is in favour of strategic human resource management, just as they are in favour of virtue'. It is as if the intellectual satisfaction with such an holistic concept can, in itself, provide the guarantee of its success. Those who have a concern for equitable outcomes cannot afford to leave such things to an act of faith.

Some of the old problems remain even in this new context. For example, human resource technologies such as job evaluation systems, performance appraisal systems, and selection tests are often imperfect from an EEO perspective; pay structures are influenced by perceptions of 'value' or 'worth' that particularly affect the work traditionally done by women and stereotyped views of what constitutes 'merit' persist. Policies and practices that relate to recruitment, reward and career development have often operated independently of each other as if pursuing different corporate agendas. An integrated approach to human resource practice should deal with this fragmentation. However, it also provides an opportunity to include the requirement that all the technologies have EEO compatible processes and outcomes and that there is a commitment to develop a plan to tackle those barriers of a more stubborn ilk. A strategic approach to human resources will not by definition provide for equity concerns as the silence in the literature would seem to imply.

Conclusion

A strategic human resource process that has been developed alongside, and in response to, the business goals of the organisation, does indeed offer some new opportunities for EEO to increase the breadth and depth of its influence on an organisation. This is not a one-way street. A commitment to the integrated practice of EEO at all levels of the business actually ensures that the strategic human resource policy is more likely to be successful – a point missing in any discussion of the advantages of having the business and human resource strategies linked. We need to push for the opportunities but also apply the same EEO scrutiny and analysis to the strategic human resource models that are being offered to organisations. The concern is two-fold. Will a more strategic and integrated approach deal with existing EEO concerns within the organisation and will it generate new ones? There is a need to reform current practice and at the same time anticipate the consequential outcomes of any reform. An EEO practitioner's work is a continuous cycle of exploiting the benefits and threats of any changes in their effect on equity concerns. To be an EEO practitioner requires optimism, scepticism and constant vigilance.

Note

The views expressed in this chapter are those of the author and not necessarily those of the State Services Commission.

References

Burns, J. (1992), 'Radical Changes – Same Outcomes?'. Paper presented to the EEO Practitioners Conference, Wellington, September.

Cooke, R. and Armstrong, M. (1990), 'The Search for Strategic HRM', *Personnel Management*, December.

Dunphy, D. and Stace, D. (1990), *Under New Management: Australian Organisations in Transition,* Sydney: Philip Alexander.

EEO Progress in the Public Service as at June 1992. Strategic Human Resource Development Branch, State Services Commission, October 1993.

Garavan, T.N. (1991), 'Strategic Human Resource Development', *International Journal of Manpower*, 12 (6), 21-34.

Gunnigle, P. (1991), 'Personnel Policy Choice: the Context for Human Resource Development', *Journal of European Industrial Training*, 15 (3), 22-31.

Harvard Business Review (1983), *Strategic Management,* New York: John Wiley and Sons.

Hendry, C. and Pettigrew, A. (1992), 'Patterns of Strategic Change in the Development of Human Resource Management', *British Journal of Management*, 3, 137-156.

Millar, P. (1991), 'Strategic Human Resource Management: an Assessment of Progress', *Human Resource Management Journal*, Summer, 23-39.

Wright, P.M. and McMahan, G.C. (1992), 'Theoretical Perspectives for Strategic Human Resource Management', *Journal of Management*, 18, 295-319.

9

EEO and the Invisible Family

Heather McDonald

My public and private worlds can be distinguished, but they also interpenetrate, feed on one another, are mutually influential, and exist at times in tension (Novitz, 1987, p.23).

Introduction

In the 1950s most families in New Zealand included a full-time homemaker and a full-time breadwinner. Today in the majority of two-parent families, both parents have paid jobs. The paid workforce is also more female than it has ever been with a majority of women, and in fact a majority of mothers, now employed outside the home. Increasingly, women are the primary income earners in families. Along with these changes, the number of workers with elder and other adult care responsibilities is growing. These demographic trends have enormous implications for the human resource management policies of New Zealand organisations.

Effective managers of the future will have to manage their staff as whole people, recognising they have work and non-work responsibilities. In this chapter I will outline the key reasons workplaces will want to respond to the diverse non-work responsibilities of their employees. Second, I will outline insights gained from the Work/Family Phone-In held over two days in May 1993. The information gained showed how family responsibilities impact on the workplace and some of the solutions that do, or could, work well in New Zealand (Ministry of Women's Affairs, 1993).

The Work/Family Split

Typical attitudes within the workplace have been that employees' family problems should not intrude on the working day. Family and work are seen as entirely separate and during work hours, work has priority. But the culture of the workplace is having to adapt. The increasingly female workforce, with all its associated family care responsibilities, is only beginning to be seen as a challenge businesses should respond to. This is not just to be non-discriminatory, but is necessary if businesses wish to recruit from the broadest workforce pool, retain their experienced staff and maximise productivity.

The Phone-In demonstrated that women are more likely to be concerned about, or respond to work/family pressures than men. There were nine female callers for every male caller. The balancing of work and family responsibilities has been seen as the domain of women. Women have worked hard to ensure personal family situations impact as little as possible on their ability to carry out their jobs. But family issues are not solely a 'woman's problem'.

Men's family responsibilities are likely to affect their working lives more in the future. Fewer men will have the full-time support of a family 'caregiver', and their workplaces too will experience the results of work/family conflict. There is also evidence of an increased desire by both men and women to share care responsibilities more equally and have their employers recognise and facilitate this need (Van den Heuvel, 1993a; Ministry of Women's Affairs, 1993).

At some stage in their working lives, all employees are likely to experience some conflict between their employment and family responsibilities. It may be when they become pregnant or a parent, when their child has an accident or extended illness, or when a family member dies or needs extensive care. Very few people have no family connections. There are workplaces in New Zealand which are beginning to respond to the childcare needs of their employees. The issue of eldercare is relatively new, but the impact of these demands will be increasingly felt in our workplaces. Writing in the United States, Friedman (1991, p.31) says, 'more employees will have dependent elders in the twenty-first century than dependent children'.

But why should these problems become those of the employer? The reality is they already are. Work/family problems affect the ability of companies to be effective and efficient. There is a growing awareness world-wide of the cost entailed in not providing arrangements to ease work/family conflict. Some of the costs we understand intuitively. For example, if a person cannot find or maintain childcare, or is unable to balance work and personal responsibilities, this is likely to affect their productivity in the long run. Most companies who have introduced work/family programmes, in the United States at least, have done so because they are convinced that doing something is less costly than doing nothing (Johnson, 1993, p.6). The key areas where work/family problems are a cost to companies are recruitment and retention of staff, absenteeism and productivity. Some recent evaluation research in the areas of recruitment, retention, absenteeism and productivity, suggest costs may have been undervalued in the past. Each of these areas is considered in detail below.

Recruitment and Retention

It is widely accepted that for companies to be successful they need to attract and keep the best staff. To do this they must, in the first instance, attract staff from the widest pool of possible applicants. There is evidence suggesting a large pool of talent is being lost to recruiters, particularly because of a lack of childcare.

Primary caregivers, who are usually women, are continuing to increase their participation in the paid workforce. Mothers with youngest children aged one to four increased participation in the labour force from 25.3 per cent to 37.5 per cent between 1981 and 1991. But the age of a woman's youngest child still has the single most important impact on her labour market activity (Department of Statistics, 1993; Department of Statistics and Ministry of Women's Affairs, 1990).

Between 1987 and 1993 the Household Labour Force Survey consistently identified one in eight women as available for work but not seeking it because of a lack of childcare (Statistics New Zealand, 1993). Problems with childcare are not over when children start school. A 1990 Ministry of Education survey of parents of primary school-age children, found 25 per cent of parents said a household member was unable to accept a job or take up training because of childcare responsibilities (Slyfield *et al.*, 1990).

The bottom-line is that if female primary caregivers are unable to find or afford childcare for their children, they are unavailable to the labour market. Bowen Hospital in Wellington recognised this as having an impact on their ability to provide the service they wanted. They opened an on-site childcare centre to attract nurses from the surrounding suburbs back to the workforce, enabling the hospital to offer increased theatre operation (Rose, 1993).

The research literature supports the importance of childcare to availability for employment. Kossek and Nichol (1992) for example, found childcare assistance was likely to significantly affect employee attitudes and behaviours such as recruitment and retention. However, it is clear companies are excluding a large number of women with young children from consideration when recruiting staff and so are not drawing from the complete pool of talent available.

Retention of staff is just as important. According to Marie Wilson (Young, 1993, p.12), of the Graduate School of Business at Auckland University:

> ... the financial impact of employee turnover is enormous. Turnover is too much any time you're losing people you want to stay. Even if it is just one person, you've got a turnover problem.

Even in times of high unemployment the costs of staff turnover harm companies. For all positions there is the investment in staff training, the time and cost of recruiting new staff and the disruption caused by staff leaving. American studies consistently confirm turnover costs of between 70 per cent and 150 per cent of salary, depending on the skill level of the position and the availability of the required employee (Johnson, 1993).

New or on-going care responsibilities for children or adults causing continual strain for the primary carer is one reason staff leave their jobs.

Several studies confirm significant reductions in the number of workers leaving firms once some form of childcare assistance had been introduced (Friedman, 1984; Office for the Status of Women, 1989). The need for employees to leave their jobs to care for elderly relatives is likely to have an even greater impact than the need to care for children. People leaving to care for elderly relatives will have been in the workforce longer, have significant levels of experience and the time of absence may be longer and less predictable.

Absenteeism

As family responsibilities change over the course of each employee's life, related absences will fluctuate. The cost to businesses of absenteeism are easily identified in lost days. Staff and their families will always have some bouts of illness and emergency situations requiring their attention. However, we are seeing some shift in traditional patterns of women/mothers attending to all family emergencies. A Canadian study, for example, found gender explained less than one per cent of the sum of all causes of work absences (job satisfaction explained four per cent and true illness explained 33 per cent) (Friedman, 1991). American studies also show absence rates for men and women move in different directions over the course of their working years; increasing for women during the childbearing years (18 to 44) and decreasing for men during these years. The studies also repeatedly confirm that absenteeism is related less to gender than to workers' economic status and role in the family (Friedman, 1991).

More than two-thirds of the parents questioned in a 1993 Australian study had missed some work over the course of a year for reasons related to the care of their children. This was usually to care for a sick child (52 per cent of mothers, 31 per cent of fathers). The second most common reason was to provide care during school holidays. One in three parents took time off to be with children in the school holidays. In this study it was only when a child was sick that mothers were more likely than fathers to take time off. For a child's other needs, mothers and fathers were likely to share the caring responsibilities. Males and females were also equally as likely to take time off work to care for another family member (Van den Heuvel, 1993a).

As part of this study, analysis was also done to determine which factors were significantly related to the likelihood of parents missing work for the care of sick children. Those mothers who felt their employer was sympathetic to workers' family responsibilities were less likely to miss work to care for sick children. The reasons may be that they had access to flexible work options for getting their work done or that they had access to alternative care arrangements (Van den Heuvel, 1993b).

Productivity

Available research suggests family problems that cause worry at work can result in a loss of concentration and reduced ability of the employee to perform up to par. In eight American company surveys about half of the women and a third of the men contend that childcare responsibilities affect work to some degree (Friedman, 1991). A study of 33 companies in Oregon, America, found that a third of employees with adult dependants work less effectively due to worry about their elders (Friedman, 1991).

A groundbreaking 1993 study at Fel-Pro Inc. (Lambert, 1993), a manufacturing company employing 2,000 workers in Illinois, America, addressed the issue of how family-responsive policies are related to worker performance. In addition to examining more traditional types of work performance (e.g. absenteeism, performance ratings, turnover figures), the study looked at aspects of performance essential to the successful implementation of total quality initiatives (e.g. participation in team problem-solving, submission of suggestions for product and process improvement, organisational commitment and openness to change). The study found that the more benefits workers use, the more they appreciated those benefits and:

- the more committed they were to Fel-Pro;
- the greater their corporate citizenship behaviour, i.e. the more they reported helping out co-workers and their supervisor, volunteering for work and showing initiative;
- they offered twice as many suggestions for product and process improvement than other workers.

These links between benefit use and appreciation and support for quality improvement were supported regardless of workers' race, gender, marital status, job characteristics and length of employment (Lambert, 1993). While the study warns that policies cannot fully compensate for unchallenging, stressful jobs, insensitive supervisors or unsupportive co-workers, the results are nevertheless startling. Employers are clearly reaping benefit from providing and ensuring the use of supportive programmes.

Key Workforce Issues in New Zealand

The key staffing issues in any workplace are recruiting the best staff for the job, keeping those staff, having them turn up every day and maximising their productivity. Ignoring these issues places unnecessary cost on employers. Employers cannot afford to ignore demographic and workforce changes if they are to continue to operate effectively and efficiently. All employees will at some time have family responsibilities of one sort or another. Recognising this, ensuring effective policies and programmes are available, and then recouping the gains for such forethought can increase employee loyalty and the company's profit.

What are the initiatives and policies that are working now in New Zealand workplaces? How well are they working and where might we go in the future? These are some of the questions the Ministry of Women's Affairs considered before running its national Work/Family Phone-In during May 1993.

The Phone-In was not a representative survey but, rather, aimed to raise awareness about work/family issues and to gather information and ideas about how people manage their work and family responsibilities. To gain publicity for the event, 65,000 leaflets and posters were distributed, and the Phone-In organisers were interviewed on over 20 radio and television programmes. The Phone-In was an information-gathering exercise on a grand scale. Phone-In staff completed semi-structured questionnaires for 804 callers (764 employees and 50 employers) and over 2,000 calls were recorded by Telecom during the two days.

In addition, self-completed questionnaires were sent to 100 employers, most of whom were members of the Equal Employment Opportunities Trust. Written questionnaires were used to ensure a good response from employers as they were considered to be less likely to call the Phone-In. These employers were also asked to distribute up to ten questionnaires to their employees. Fifty-six employer and 279 employee questionnaires were returned. In total 1,043 employees and 106 employers responded to the Work/Family project.

Of the 1,043 employees who responded, just under half were responsible for children under five, over 40 per cent had children aged between five and nine, while a third had children aged between ten and 14. Almost a third cared for children in more than one age group. One in ten employees cared for an elderly relative and 4.5 per cent cared for someone with a disability or chronic illness. One in six employees were responsible for a child or children and an adult relative. This was a day-to-day responsibility for nearly one in twelve people.

More than half the employees were employed in professional or managerial positions (53 per cent). Although a special effort was made to attract calls from Maori, and from the sales, service and production sectors, there was a low response rate in these areas.

The number of people managed by employers who responded to the survey was 60,000. Worksites ranged in size from two to 6,500 workers. One in every eight employers had over 1,000 employees, while one third had less than ten employees (Ministry of Women's Affairs, 1993). The largest group of employers worked in the community, social and personal services industries (41.5 per cent).

The Work/Family Overlap

Many of the suggestions from employees who took part in the Work/Family Phone-In would improve the 'family-friendliness' of their workplaces for little cost and modest effort. The Work/Family Phone-In identified a range of workplace practices which could and do assist those with family responsibilities. Three broad themes emerged from the 1,000 employee responses: managing the balance is stressful, it is women who carry most of the load, and there is an occupationally-based variation in the supports available to employees.

There was agreement that managing the balance between home and work was difficult. Some callers were concerned, too, at the stress that their children experience from this process.

Women, regardless of their occupation or work hours, carry the vast bulk of the day-to-day responsibility for meeting the care needs of the family. A number of the men who called also made the point that working women had this dual role.

We also heard from men and women who wanted to see changes: recognition at work that men have families too, men taking leave to care for sick family members and effective policies for both men and women to achieve more of a balance between work and family.

The support organisations gave employees regarding their family responsibilities varied according to the occupational group to which they belonged. In general, professional and managerial employees reported having far greater levels of flexibility and control over their work situations.

Clerical workers have much less control over their work and fewer financial resources. Some clerical workers expressed concern for their jobs if they asked for time off too often. On the positive side, many said they worked in predominantly female workplaces where there was a degree of informal covering for each other and sometimes more formal backup.

Service, sales and production workers had the least access to telephones when they needed them and felt considerable threat to their jobs from fulfilling family responsibilities. Furthermore they had less leave available and a generally less supportive environment. For example, one employee stated that there was a telephone at work but she could spend her entire break standing in line to make a call. A number of respondents in this category also reported that they worked only because of financial necessity. Some were the only earners in the family.

The Ministry collected information from employees in three main areas spanning the relationship between family and work. These were:

- what happens in an emergency or unplanned situation;
- what are employees' usual arrangements at work and how do these help them manage work and family;
- what is the impact of the general workplace atmosphere and culture?

In each of these three areas there was a great deal of similarity in what respondents said made a difference for them.

Emergency and Unplanned Situations

In the first instance, employees should be able to be reached at work when a family emergency occurs. Some employees have easy access to telephones, others need messages taken and delivered quickly. One employee stated that at her workplace calls from children of staff are given priority. The telephonist has the names of all the children and ensures calls and messages reach people fast. Just the knowledge that there is a system that works well will give peace of mind.

An overwhelming number of callers talked of the need to have someone to cover for them in an emergency so they could deal with the situation without the stress of finding a back-up or returning to a huge back-log of work. Those in teamwork situations commented on how well that works for them. They get the back-up when they need it and they, in turn, can cover for others. Job-sharing was seen as another way of dealing effectively with this issue. The problem of ensuring work is done can then be dealt with by the job-sharers rather than the supervisor. Having a list of staff who can work casually was offered as one suggestion for ensuring back-up.

A large number of employees noted the importance for them of having family/domestic leave separate from their own sick leave entitlement. In particular, workers with only five days sick/domestic leave a year noted significant problems. Many would take leave to care for children or other family members and have no option but to go to work sick themselves. As well, separate leave could enable parents to attend special school meetings or occasions legitimately. Some commented that it may be fairer for this leave to be without pay; 'what mattered was the principle that family responsibilities were seen as important'.

A number of additional practices and suggestions included encouraging men to take leave to care for sick children, employers assisting with transport in emergency situations (e.g. taxi chits or dropping the employee home), the ability to bring children to work if need be in an emergency, taking work home, being able to take sick leave in two-hour blocks rather than a whole day at a time, help from personnel staff, and that doctors' certificates should be required only after two to three day's absence. The cost and inconvenience of providing them for just one day was significant.

Work Arrangements to Manage Work and Family

As might be expected, respondents commented extensively about childcare issues. Many thought their employer should consider providing childcare, be it for preschoolers or those needing after school and holiday care. Concerns were expressed about the reliability of care, its quality, its availability for the hours needed and its cost. Others indicated that having information about what care was available and whether it was reliable and safe would help them. Those who worked shifts identified the need for some negotiation and flexibility, so they could manage childcare arrangements.

A number of parents noted they had not expected finding care for their school-age children would be so much harder than finding preschool childcare. Care for school-age children after school and in the holidays is a significant concern. Jobs cannot always be completed in the school day and even two-parent families find it difficult to cover 12 weeks of school holidays a year. In some cases children go to their parents' workplace after school, where space to sit and do their homework is provided.

Working part-time or having some flexibility about the hours/days/ shifts were all mentioned as features helping employees manage their home and work. As well as needing access to telephone calls in emergencies, staff also need to be able to make and receive calls to check in on family. Respondents made comments like 'my kids need to talk to me occasionally' and 'if Mum's not well, it's too long to go all day without checking how she is'.

Those able to take some time during work hours to attend appointments valued this flexibility. Some said they worked outside normal hours on a regular basis so they could 'gain time' to attend to family and personal needs.

Workplace Atmosphere/Culture

Many employees commented positively about how a supportive workplace impacts on them. Some of these comments are shown in Figure 9.1.

Figure 9.1
Comments About the Importance of a Supportive Workplace From Employees Who Responded to the Phone-In.

It's one less stress.

I know I'm valued; that helps me feel less guilty if I have to take time off.

Being given a little leeway encourages me to put in the extra effort at work.

It adds to my job satisfaction and I feel more committed to my employer.

It's great just knowing that I can negotiate if things aren't going well.

My workmates are all women with older children so they are really good to me if anything happens with my girls.

I couldn't work if they weren't good. It's really hard if you're the only parent.

The general theme emerging from comments is that where employees feel valued and able to talk with their supervisors about what is happening for them and the supervisor takes a problem-solving approach, then usually the needs of both company and employee can be satisfied.

Some respondents, particularly men, commented that their workmates and supervisors judged them harshly for having and expecting to meet family responsibilities. Men need and value support in these circumstances, just as women do. For example, when one's wife or another family member is severely ill, having support and acceptance from work makes a huge difference.

Employer Responses

Many businesses provide a variety of policies and programmes that assist their staff. Employer responses to the Work/Family Phone-In provided an indication of the sorts of initiatives progressive employers were using.

Close to three in five of all employer respondents said they provided some staff flexibility over start and finish times; they had part-time employees and they allowed time off during the day for family tasks and appointments. Ten companies provided some childcare assistance; preschool childcare, school age children's holiday programmes or childcare subsidies. A similar number indicated they had a period of paid parental leave.

Of the 56 employers who returned written questionnaires, 53 said their staff had access to make and receive calls in an emergency. Employers' responses to the need for immediate time off in emergencies varied. Some noted that the employer's reaction depended on the situation and the amount of time needed. Responses included time off with and without pay, time off to be made up later, and time offset against sick leave or annual leave.

Employers who responded stated they were the main initiators of family supportive practices and they indicated that overall these practices worked well for them. Employers commented on the practices they operated in three main areas:

* flexible work arrangements
* extended parental leave/childcare assistance
* emergency arrangements.

Under each of these areas, over 60 per cent stated their policy worked well for them. Around ten per cent said they had experienced some problems with their policy.

The Phone-In questionnaire also sought employers' comments on whether they saw any benefit in employing staff who have family responsibilities. Some of the comments are included in Figure 9.2.

Figure 9.2:
Employers' Comments on Employing Staff
Who Have Family Responsibilities

Those with family responsibilities are more stable and committed to their jobs; they bring a sense of balance and that helps ground the workplace and make it seem more real and less separate from life in general.

They're a bloody nuisance actually. People with young families are very disruptive and yet we need their skills and they need the money. It's a Catch 22 situation.

People with family responsibilities often have a broader view of life, are aware of the employment needs of their colleagues/staff and possess better management skills.

Establishing a Family/Friendly Workplace

How can an organisation know what it needs to do to establish a family-friendly workplace? Companies asking this question will want to know what the specific workforce issues are for them. The first step is to gather information. Information about the crucial work/family issues experienced by staff in the company will need to be matched against the key workforce concerns in that company. For example, information may be gathered on such issues as: the number of women not returning after parental leave or leaving when their children are young (for example, see Glendining, 1992); difficulties in attracting and retaining high-calibre staff; small numbers of applicants or only male applicants for jobs and the number of staff given extensive training who leave after only a short time.

Workplace assessment can consist of anything from an informal discussion with staff through focus groups and formal consultations to written questionnaires. The important thing is to clearly identify any problems impacting on employees' ability to participate fully at work. It is important to be cautious about the phrasing of questions and interpreting the information which is gathered. Most employees will be reluctant to identify problems affecting their performance.

One example of a thorough industry-based analysis done in Australia was reported in Gatfield and Griffin (1990). The Queensland Nurses' Union initiated research because nurses, as shift workers, needed more flexible childcare services than most childcare centres offered. This study sought to:

• identify existing childcare arrangements and their adequacy;
• assess the effect of inadequate childcare on desired levels of labour force participation;
• assess current and future demand for preferred forms of childcare.

Through the responses to questionnaires, the under-employment of health workers was identified and criticised as: 'economically inconsistent and irrational, given the state investment in education and training' (Gatfield and Griffin, 1990, p.xiii). Clearly childcare developments needed to reflect the unpredictable shift patterns of the health workers and incorporate a high level of flexibility.

Some companies may be reluctant to assess the need for family-friendly initiatives without first determining the costs and benefits to be gained. However, companies feeling the impact of work/family conflict in even minor ways, may find it costs them money to do nothing.

Where To From Here?

The reconciliation of work and family responsibilities involves contributions from government, employers and employees. Creating the family-friendly workplace also involves a range of other agencies including crèches, school-age care programmes and daycare for elderly people. Callers to the Phone-In proposed ways to minimise the stress they experience from holding all the pieces together: that schools form a nucleus for care services, employers work together to come up with comprehensive help and that childcare be as close to work and as highly valued as carparks. In the future we may see an increase in the number of community partnerships of parties such as employers, local authorities and other agencies (McDonald, 1993).

Few companies in New Zealand are likely to have taken a comprehensive look at how work/family conflict is reflected in their workforce. Further research is clearly necessary to convince other than the trailblazers. This includes both the development and analysis of workplace assessments, and more empirical research clarifying what makes a difference for families, employees and business in the New Zealand context.

As our population ages and the total labour pool shrinks in the decades to come, employers will need to take a comprehensive assessment of what is happening in their workforce and respond with an equally comprehensive life cycle approach to work/family conflict. The issue of eldercare is relatively new but workplaces will increasingly experience the impact of workers with these responsibilities (Friedman, 1991, p.31).

We are likely to see development in the area of staff training. Supervisors need to know clearly what company policy is and how to implement it effectively. Negotiation will often be required. Ultimately the extent to which work/family initiatives achieve the desired outcomes for business and the employee depends on the individuals who are negotiating the arrangement. Achieving the balance will always require an understanding within the company of the employee's contribution to the company and the company's need to maintain that contribution. There will be a need for a flexible approach to achieve effective solutions. Employees, too, need to know what is possible and that they are valued. If a family-friendly policy is initiated, supervisors and managers need to know what the company has to gain from recognising employees' needs and stress that employees' lives do not stop at the workplace door. They also need the skills to implement this philosophy.

Some of the greatest benefits to business from being a 'family-friendly' company cost nothing more than some goodwill, open communication and trust. For example, the telephonist can keep a list of the names of employees' children, sick leave could be available in two-hourly blocks, and staff could bring children to work for short periods in an emergency, and all employees could be given easy access to a telephone.

Some employers and their staff are unconvinced the benefits of even modest efforts are worth the cost or bother to them, particularly for those occupations seen as lower-skilled. As research is undertaken we learn more about the explicit costs and benefits of ensuring the worlds of employment and family can be balanced and managed well. As long as women bear a large proportion of family caring responsibilities, employers who are not providing family-friendly workplaces, are likely to be discriminating against women. This means women are losing out on opportunities, but workplaces will also be losing out on the contribution women could make to their productivity.

Our society has changed dramatically in the last two decades. International trends are already signalling the choices we have in managing the continuing changes. Ultimately in workplaces the choice hinges on our ability to provide opportunities for people, and then assist them to utilise those opportunities effectively. The spin-offs from making workplaces family-friendly will be felt far into the future.

References

Department of Statistics and Ministry of Women's Affairs (1990), *Women in New Zealand*, Wellington : Department of Statistics and Ministry of Women's Affairs.

Department of Statistics (1993), *1991 New Zealand Census of Populations and Dwellings – New Zealanders at Home*, Wellington : Department of Statistics.

Friedman, D.E. (1984), 'The Challenge of Employer-Supported Child Care: Meeting Parent Needs', in L.G. Katz (ed.), *Current Topics in Early Childhood Education: Volume 5*, New Jersey: Ablex Publishing.

Friedman, D.E. (1991), *Linking Work-Family Issues to the Bottom Line*, New York: The Conference Board.

Gatfield, R. and Griffin, V. (1990), *Shift Workers and Childcare: a Study of the Needs of Queensland Nurses*, Women's Research and Employment Initiatives Programme, Department of Employment, Education and Training, Canberra: Australian Government Publishing Services.

Glendining, D. (1992), *This Motherhood Lark! The Report of the Study of Parental Leave taken from Te Mana Arai o Aotearoa*, The NZ Customs Department, 1987-1992, Wellington: Department of Customs.

Johnson, A. (1993), 'Work and Family: 1993', *Seminar Proceedings – Make Your Workplace Family Friendly*, Wellington: Ministry of Women's Affairs.

Kossek, F. F. and Nichol, V. (1992), "The Effects of On-site Child Care on Employee Attitudes and Performance', *Personnel Psychology*, (3) 485-509.

Lambert, S.J. (ed.) (1993), 'Added Benefits: the Link Between Family-Responsive Policies and Work Performance at Fel-Pro Incorporated', unpublished report, School of Social Service Administration, University of Chicago.

McDonald, H. (1993), 'Combining Employment and Family: How Are We Doing in New Zealand?', *Seminar Proceedings – Make Your Workplace Family Friendly*, Wellington: Ministry of Women's Affairs.

Ministry of Women's Affairs (1993), *Ringing the Changes – Report of the National Work/Family Phone-In Held 23 and 24 May 1993*, Wellington: Ministry of Women's Affairs.

Novitz, R. (1987), 'Bridging the Gap: Paid and Unpaid Work', in S. Cox (ed.), *Public and Private Worlds: Women in Contemporary New Zealand*, Wellington: Allen and Unwin/Port Nicholson Press.

Office for the Status of Women (1989), *Childcare in the Workplace*, Canberra: Australian Government.

Rose, R. (1993), 'Make Your Workplace Family Friendly', *Management*, August, 44-48.

Slyfield, H., Culling, C. and Parkin, M. (1990), *Out of School Care – Provision and Demand*, Wellington: Ministry of Education.

Statistics New Zealand (1993), *Household Labour Force Survey* [from INFOS], Wellington: Department of Statistics.

Van den Heuvel, A. (1993a), *When Roles Overlap: Workers with Family Responsibilities*, AIFS Monograph No.14, Melbourne : Australian Institute of Family Studies, with the Work and Family Unit, Department of Industrial Relations.

Van den Heuvel, A. (1993b), 'Missing Work to Care for Sick Children', *Family Matters* (34).

Young, C. (1993), 'Star Performers – How to Keep Them', *NZ Business*, May, 12-18.

10

Job Evaluation: Who's Worth What?

Bev Marshall

In an ideal world people would all be paid what they were worth. In principle everyone believes that there should be 'a fair day's pay for a fair day's work'. But who decides what is fair? Naturally everyone will have a different idea of which job is more important based on personal experience and subjective impressions. Each person judges the worth of a job on different criteria.

To try to calculate the worth of an individual job to society as a whole by aggregating everyone's opinions would be difficult if not impossible. Should we attempt to do these calculations there would be considerable controversy over the relative value of certain occupations. Some would argue that a doctor is more valuable than a teacher and others that a poet is more valuable than either a doctor or a teacher. Still others might contend that politicians or day care workers are more valuable to the growth and well-being of society.

While it would seem an impossible task to gain agreement on the relative importance of different occupations to society, it is not such a daunting task for organisations to rank the value of the jobs performed by their employees. The overall strategic plan or the structure of an organisation will show the comparative importance of different kinds of work within the context of that organisation and jobs can be rewarded accordingly. This type of process of comparing jobs within an organisation for the purpose of creating a pay structure is known as job evaluation.

Job evaluation has become a focus of attention for EEO practitioners because of the potential that job evaluation systems have for disadvantaging women in particular, as well as ethnic groups and people with disabilities. As a prerequisite to understanding the problems of job evaluation for these groups, it is necessary to have a clear understanding of the evaluation process, so this chapter begins with a discussion of job evaluation, looking at both the structure of the job evaluation system and the process itself. An understanding of job evaluation is important in terms of equal employment opportunity issues because of the potential for bias to enter the system and these sources of bias are discussed. The chapter concludes with a look at current New Zealand trends in job evaluation and considers the relevance of the technique in the light of workplace reform.

What is Job Evaluation?

Job evaluation is carried out in response to a number of situations. One kind of situation where job evaluation is often used is when a major organisational change, like restructuring, has meant that the current remuneration levels and structures need to be re-examined.

In the evaluation process the content of jobs is assessed so that they can be placed in rank order. This ranking gives a hierarchy of the importance of jobs to the organisation. The results of the evaluation can then be used to design a pay structure. Jobs are evaluated as to their perceived worth and rewarded accordingly.

In 1960 the International Labour Organisation (ILO) defined job evaluation as:

> ... an attempt to determine and compare the demands which the normal performance of particular jobs makes on normal workers without taking account of the individual abilities or performance of the workers concerned (ILO, 1960, p. 8).

The typical rationale given by developers and users of the technique is that it is the job which is evaluated, not the person doing the job; so the particular skills, abilities, personal characteristics and qualifications of the current incumbent are only relevant if they are those the job requires. For example, if the person doing the job has a university degree, but normal performance of the job does not require that level of qualification, then the degree is irrelevant to the position and therefore irrelevant to the evaluation.

Evaluation Systems

There are various methods for carrying out job evaluation, but it is usually carried out in two stages – classification of jobs and then assessment of compensation. The methods themselves fall into two categories: qualitative and quantitative.

Qualitative methods are those which do not break the job down into components but adopt an holistic approach in comparing one job to another. These are not analytical approaches but grade jobs according to their overall size. These grades are broadly described in line with the duties, responsibilities and skill requirements of the positions within them. Qualitative methods are seldom used: they lack any systematic basis for job comparisons and are likely to be discriminatory. The lack of established criteria leaves the evaluation open to considerable bias, as evaluators have no real standard basis other than the traditional value of the job and their own value judgements.

By comparison, quantitative methods break jobs down into components or factors and analyse each factor separately. Two quantitative techniques are the ranking method and the classification method. The ranking method compares one job to another and ranks them. The classification method allocates jobs a grade in predetermined classes (similar jobs) or grades (similar in difficulty but different in content).

Quantitative methods of job evaluation are widely used and the most popular of them, the points factor system (a ranking method), has been around since the Second World War. This technique is an analytical method that breaks jobs down into a set of compensable factors (aspects considered to contribute to the overall value of the job (Treiman, 1979)) and assigns scores for each job on each factor. The factor scores are then added to give the job an overall rating in relation to other jobs in the organisation. This particular method, the points factor system, is used widely in New Zealand.

In short, the process involves collecting information about the jobs people do, assigning points to aspects of the jobs and then adding up the points and ranking the jobs in relation to each other.

Compensable factors are the fundamental elements of a job which are worthy of reward or compensation, such as:

* skill
* mental or physical effort required
* responsibility involved
* working conditions.

Each of these factors is usually broken down into a number of subdivisions. Anything from about ten to twenty sub factors may be used in the evaluation process. For example, *Equity at Work* (Burns and Coleman, 1991) has several separate factors that come under the four headings of knowledge and skill, effort, responsibility and working conditions (see figure 10.1).

Table 10.1:
Factors and Subfactors for *Equity at Work* (1991)

Knowledge and skill	Effort
• knowledge and understanding • physical skills • mental skills • communication skills • human relations skills	• physical demands • mental demands • emotional demands
Responsibility	Working Conditions
• responsibility for information and material resources • responsibility for supervision • responsibility for well-being • responsibility for planning, organisation and development	• hazards • environment

(Adapted from Burns and Coleman, 1991)

Most points rating methods allocate weightings to each of the factors according to their relative importance, and each factor has steps or levels attached to it. These levels reflect degrees of complexity or importance within the factor. For example, in *Equity at Work* the sub-factor 'responsibility for supervision' has five levels. These are set out in Table 10.2 and have been abbreviated in part. Usually the lower steps have fewer points and the points increase in increments up the scale. Factors with more weight will usually have more points, which reflects their importance.

Table 10.2:
Levels Within the Factor 'Responsibility for Supervision'
Equity at Work (1991).

Level 1	No responsibility other than to demonstrate job functions or give advice to new job holders
Level 2	Some responsibility for supervision, such as periodically allocating work to other staff, checking that work. May include on-the-job training for small groups
Level 3	Moderate levels of responsibility for supervision. Requires allocation of work, evaluation of that work, direction of staff including on-the-job training. May advise on performance appraisal, discipline or other personnel matters
Level 4	High level of responsibility for supervision. Substantial requirements for controlling and directing staff (including training). Responsibility for decisions on personnel matters but may only advise or make recommendations on major personnel decisions
Level 5	High level of responsibility for supervision. Final responsibility for review and evaluation of work of other staff. Major personnel decisions.

(Adapted from Burns and Coleman, 1991)

The Evaluation Process

The process of carrying out job evaluation usually runs along the following lines, although this is a brief description and there will be variations. What is described here is what will occur ideally, rather than what always happens. As there is often a time constraint the process is frequently compressed.

Once the decision is made to carry out job evaluation a steering committee is set up to oversee the process. Ideally this committee will have senior organisational members, a liaison person from the evaluation committee and a facilitator who oversees the project.

An evaluation committee comprising a representative range of employees from all work groups and levels of the organisation is also established. It is the task of this committee to make decisions relating to the information they receive about the jobs, and then again in awarding points to the job. In decision-making, the evaluation committee will usually work to consensus or agreed majority (for example, in a committee of eight, six must agree).

The first step is to identify benchmark jobs in the organisation. Benchmark jobs are those considered to be typical of a grade or group of jobs and are selected to provide a standard against which other jobs can be assessed. Any one-off positions, for example an industrial nurse, are also included in the benchmarking exercise. The number of benchmark positions is contingent on the size of the organisation, but it is important that all types of work at all levels are represented.

The positions of the benchmark jobs are evaluated. Information is gathered in any one of a number of ways. The current incumbent may be interviewed about the job, or will fill in a detailed evaluation form. Sometimes an existing job description may be used.

The evaluation committee uses the information gathered to assess the jobs. Jobs will be ranked at levels within sub-factors (according to the complexity or difficulty of the tasks). The factors are weighted according to their importance. Their weighting should be consistent with the importance of the factors to the organisation, but more often than not they are pre-weighted. A mathematical process will give the jobs a final numbered value, and jobs can then be ranked according to their points value.

Potential Problems

There are a number of potential problems associated with job evaluation for EEO as bias can be introduced directly or indirectly.

Off-the-Shelf Systems

As has been stated, the points factor method has been around since the Second World War. Initially this may seem to be an excellent recommendation for a particular system, but when you think about the demographics of the work force in the 1940s as opposed to the 1990s, the problems become clear. The cultural assumptions about the nature of 'women's work' and the persistent wage gap between the earnings of women and men are embedded in these early job evaluation systems. As Steinberg points out, 'even after conceptions about gender have changed, job evaluation systems of earlier eras may transport outdated criteria into the new labor market contexts' (1992, p. 388).

In her examination of the Hay Guide Chart-Profile Method, Steinberg (1992) found that although the factor descriptions changed from 1958 to 1982, the similarity between the descriptions, the factor levels and factor weightings remained strikingly similar. Steinberg contends that the system has a 'managerial bias' which:

> ... has a pronounced gender effect, both because managerial and administrative jobs have been disproportionately male and because the types of jobs typically held by women involve job content that is not captured in evaluation systems conceptualised in terms of the organisational hierarchy (p. 394).

As a result of her analysis of this system, Steinberg concludes that the application of factors that have remained virtually unchanged, perpetuates discrimination against women.

Many off-the-shelf schemes (those that are predesigned and not structured for the organisation) have their roots in systems that were developed many years ago. Steinberg's (1992) analysis highlights the point that while systems may have updated their language, the potential user must look well beyond this to ensure that the factors reflect the content of all levels and types of jobs.

Vested Interests

It is essential to remember that the scheme will achieve the aims of those who design it, and in some cases it may be in their best interests to preserve the existing hierarchy. Steinberg (1992) describes the situation of a hospital in Toronto where the management had selected and administered a job evaluation system for just such a reason:

> Specifically, the shortage of registered nurses, physiotherapists, respiratory therapists, and others drove up their salaries relative to health administrators. One major objective of the job evaluation exercise was to raise the wages of administrators relative to the health professionals (p. 418).

Subjectivity and Bias

There is no such thing as an objective job evaluation system, as the process relies on evaluators making judgments. One must accept that the process is unavoidably subjective. Any sex role preconceptions that the evaluator (male or female) has can enter into the evaluation process. Personal prejudice can affect both the process of gathering information about the job and discussions within the evaluation committee. As already mentioned, information about jobs can be gathered from a variety of sources. If existing job descriptions are used, then the information they provide may be biased already. Job descriptions will have been written from a job analysis. When the person carrying out the analysis recalls information, occupational sex typing can occur. The value systems of analysts will affect their perceptions and different analysts will place different emphasis on different information.

Unless the evaluation committee receives training in avoiding gender bias, it is more than likely bias will affect the decisions. In the evaluation discussions, the job must not be discussed in gender specific terms, as knowledge of the gender of the job holder may introduce bias. It is also important that no single representative dominates the evaluation process and that every committee member makes an equal contribution. To this end the position of chairperson should rotate among committee members.

Undervaluing Women's Work

There is evidence to support the contention that, in general, women tend to be self deprecating and undervalue their contribution. So in the interview/information-gathering process they may devalue their work (Arvey, 1986; Major, 1989). Studies have found that women will work longer and pay themselves less than males for the same work (Arvey, 1986). This difference may be because women use different comparison standards to evaluate what they deserve (Major, 1989). Inequalities in the social structure (such as gender segregation of work, underpayment of women and of female-dominated jobs, and the inequity in opportunities for women) lead to sex differences in comparison standards. This in turn leads to a perception of reduced entitlement, as women compare themselves with other women who also receive less and perceive they are worth less.

While women undervalue their worth in the job evaluation procedure, men are inclined to inflate the value of their contribution (Major, 1989; McArthur, 1985). Anecdotal evidence is consistent with this research. Esther Livingston (1993), a remuneration consultant with PA Consulting Group, says that women frequently describe what they do using phrases such as 'I only do ...' or 'but that doesn't really count', and it is necessary for the interviewer to question the job holder carefully to ensure that all the relevant information is obtained. If full information is not gathered, the ultimate consequence is a devaluation of women's work and the introduction of bias into the process.

Often there are different titles for the jobs of men and women who are carrying out essentially the same duties. For example, assistant manager as opposed to manager's assistant, or chef instead of cook. Sometimes these titles apply to basically different jobs, but when there is no difference in job content between the two positions, the title often denotes a status differential. This difference in status is then reflected in a pay difference based on sex discrimination.

Choice and Weighting of Factors

Factors used in job evaluation are generally based on existing pay rates and therefore reflect existing pay discrimination. The choice of compensable factors may reflect a male bias as paid employment is historically a male domain. Qualities and skills inherent in female-dominated jobs are frequently overlooked by evaluators (Hegtvedt, 1989).

For example, working conditions and physical strength are usually included in job evaluation methods for manual workers, whereas manual dexterity and caring skills (factors associated with female-dominated jobs) are not. Janice Burns (1993), who is with the EEO Unit at the State Services Commission, says that many of the existing schemes have addressed this by adding words or vocabulary to existing factors so that they appear to cover work that involves for example, caring. However, the overall effect is lost if there is no consistency in including these dimensions across factors, or if the factor does not receive sufficient weighting.

The weighting of factors is very important as this will determine the eventual ranking of the jobs. Discrimination can occur if extreme weights (high or low) are allocated to factors found exclusively in jobs performed predominantly by one sex. For example, physical effort may be weighted more highly than mental effort. As Treiman has pointed out, 'one set of factors and factor weights may produce a particular ordering of jobs while a different set of factors or different weighting of factors may produce quite a different ordering' (1979, p. 6).

A particular problem with off-the-shelf systems is that the factors do not necessarily reflect what the organisation considers important. The job evaluation system should reflect what the organisation values and wants to reinforce as appropriate to its goals. For example, a standard system may give a higher weighting to following set procedures, when the organisation values innovation or creative problem-solving.

Introducing Outside Bias

Job evaluation may be only part of the process when it comes to setting pay rates within the organisation. When the ranking is complete, organisations will frequently validate their internal system against the outside labour market. Even if the most stringent controls have been in effect to prevent bias in the job evaluation system, it is possible to reintroduce the bias that exists in the outside market. The outside market may be influenced by traditional relativities between jobs and the deflated evaluations for jobs that are held predominantly by women.

The New Zealand Experience

In New Zealand there seems to be a growing interest in job evaluation systems. Industry consultants report that there is an increasing demand for the service. An informal survey of some of the larger consultancies providing remuneration consultation (PA Consulting Group, Hay, Wyatt, Price Waterhouse, KPMG Peat Marwick) reveals almost all use some form of off-the-shelf system. Many of the larger international consulting groups (for example, Hay, PA Consulting Group, Price Waterhouse) use systems that they have developed as the result of extensive overseas research. Some consultancies have more than one system. For example, Esther Livingston (1993) of PA Consulting Group explains that they use three different systems – basic, oriented and tailored. The basic system uses off-the-shelf factors, factor definitions and weightings. The tailored approach appraises the culture of the organisation, the behaviours and values that are relevant to that organisation and then builds the factors and scales around these. There is also an oriented system which falls between the other two: the behaviours and values that the organisation seeks to reinforce are identified and then a standard set of factors that reinforce that orientation are used.

It is possible for an organisation to design and develop its own job evaluation system and Beuhring (1989) describes this process as it was carried out by the University of Minnesota. However it is a time-consuming and expensive process and consequently off-the-shelf systems are popular with both consultants and their client organisations.

As noted, many of the international consulting companies use systems that they have developed. This usually means developed outside New Zealand. However, a considerable amount of effort has gone into developing a generic approach to gender-neutral job evaluation in New Zealand.

In 1990 the Commission for Employment Equity was set up as a direct result of the passing into law of the Employment Equity Act 1990. One of the tasks of the Commission was to develop technology to enable comparison between jobs and to investigate methods of measuring jobs for the purpose of pay equity. In November of 1990 there was a change in government and one of the first tasks of the incumbent National government was to repeal the Act. However, the Minister for Employment decided that the work begun by the Commission on the design of a gender-neutral scheme of job evaluation for use in the state sector should continue. This decision enabled Martha Coleman of the Department of Labour and Janice Burns of the State Services Commission to continue their research and development, leading to the publication of *Equity at Work: An Approach to Gender Neutral Job Evaluation* in 1991.

The developers of *Equity at Work* had a keen interest in writing a system that was grounded in the principles of EEO. Consequently, the system reflects human relations qualities that are usually overlooked as factors for evaluation. Among the skills and abilities included in the system are knowledge and understanding of more than one culture, the requirement to communicate in other languages (including braille or sign language), and the requirement to interact with iwi or similar groups. The handbook that is part of the system offers advice on how to evaluate any position that may have been modified for an employee with a disability.

Janice Burns (1993) states that aside from providing a fairer instrument for use in job evaluation, they had two main aims in designing *Equity at Work*. The first was to demystify the process. Burns believes there is a certain mystique associated with job evaluation. She says this is partly because there has been no real history of custom-built job evaluation in New Zealand, and also because it has been the domain of consultants and not something an organisation believes it can do for itself. The reason for this, in part, is that organisations with their current lean structures, do not have the personnel to do it. The second aim was to provide a do-it-yourself generic system that people could pick up and modify for use in their organisations.

No consultancy service was developed around *Equity at Work*, and as it was designed to empower people to use it themselves it is difficult to find out how widely it is being used in New Zealand, although Janice Burns says there are 300 copies 'out there somewhere'. There is some anecdotal information that *Equity at Work* is being used by some organisations to help them make changes to systems they are already using. However, the *Equity at Work* system is being used in Finland, and has been translated for use in Sweden. The system is also being examined in the United Kingdom. Ironically, it would seem that the system is being used more widely overseas than it is in New Zealand.

Job Evaluation and Workplace Reform

There are some questions to be asked with regard to the place of job evaluation in light of current trends in workplace reform. There is a growing focus on multiskilling and work force flexibility, so that employees are skilled in a number of areas and are able to work across a range of jobs. Employees may work as members of a team in which they take responsibility for a range of activities that perhaps previously a supervisor would have controlled. The leadership of that team may rotate throughout the group. Janice Burns (1993) says she has to wonder whether or not job evaluation may have had its day. She says that our way of thinking about work has changed and the way we define a job has also changed. It used to be that 'a job was a job was a job', but the boundaries of jobs have changed and this begs the question of whether or not the static nature of job evaluation is able to capture these moving boundaries. Esther Livingston (1993) believes that job evaluation can still meet these changes. She considers that job evaluation is a process not an end and as such it does not matter how the work is structured as the job evaluation should be built to reflect that structure. Both agree that once job evaluation is done it should not be left to lie. It must be revisited and adapted as the nature of the organisation and its strategy change.

Conclusion

It is a truism to say that we live in a changing world. However, it is undeniable that the pace of change has quickened in recent decades. As society changes, organisations too must change to meet the needs of the external environment. In the past 100 years the nature of work and the characteristics of the people who make up the workforce have changed dramatically. The most dramatic change in the composition of the labour force since the Second World War has been the increase in the number of women in the paid workforce. In March 1990, women comprised 43 per cent of the total labour force (Department of Statistics, 1990). A snapshot of a typical New Zealand business office even thirty years ago would have been dominated by white males. In 1993 that photo would not only show roughly equal numbers of men and women, but also that many of those men and women are Maori, Pacific Island and Asian people and that some of those people will have disabilities.

The changing nature of the workforce means that organisational policies and human resource strategies must take into account the diverse contributions and needs of employees. Part of this is a remuneration structure which rewards people fairly and in a way that is consistent with the overall mission of the organisation. Job evaluation is a technique that can help an organisation achieve this aim, but the system must be one that is designed to assess all contributions fairly and equitably.

References

Arvey, R.D. (1986), 'Sex Bias in Job Evaluation Procedures', *Personnel Psychology*, 39, 315-335.

Beuhring, T. (1989), 'Incorporating Employee Values in Job Evaluation', *Journal of Social Issues*, 45 (4), 169-189.

Burns, J. (1993), Personal Communication.

Burns, J. and Coleman, M. (1991), *Equity at Work: an Approach to Gender Neutral Job Evaluation*, Wellington: Department of Labour and State Services Commission.

Department of Statistics (1990), *Women in New Zealand*, Wellington: Department of Statistics.

Hegtvedt, K.A. (1989), 'Fairness Conceptualisations and Comparable Worth', *Journal of Social Issues*, 45 (4), 81-97.

International Labour Organisation (1960), *Job Evaluation*, Geneva: International Labour Office.

Livingston, E.M. (1993), Personal Communication.

Major, B. (1989), 'Gender Differences in Comparisons and Entitlement: Implications for Comparative Worth', *Journal of Social Issues*, 45 (4), 99-115.

McArthur, L.Z. (1985), 'Social Judgement Biases in Comparable Worth Analysis', in H.I. Hartmann (ed.), *Comparable Worth: New Directions for Research*, Washington: National Academy Press.

Steinberg, R.J. (1992), 'Gendered Instructions: Cultural Lag and Gender Bias in the Hay System of Job Evaluation', *Work and Occupations*, 19, 387-423.

Treiman, D.J. (1979), *Job Evaluation: An Analytic Review*, Washington: National Academy of Sciences.

11

Talking About Equal Employment Opportunity

Deborah Jones

Introduction

What happens when people working in the Equal Employment Opportunity (EEO) area talk about 'managing diversity' rather than about 'equal opportunity'? Are we giving away the project of equality, or are we simply framing it in language we believe senior managers will find more convincing? If senior managers do find such language more persuasive, will the outcomes of programmes framed in 'diversity' terms be the same as those framed as leading to 'equality'?

Current debates about EEO strategy in government organisations have highlighted the language of EEO as a critical area. These debates centre around the strategic use of language to achieve the goals of EEO practitioners in a public service where the metaphor of 'the market' dominates all others.

I have two aims in this chapter. First, I introduce key themes raised by practitioners, as they reflect on the part played by communication in their EEO work. EEO practitioners are generally highly sophisticated communication strategists, who are extremely conscious of the need to adopt effective rhetoric to achieve their goals. For instance, one practitioner described herself as having to be 'multilingual' in the different communication styles she drew upon in her work with different audiences.

In considering their communication strategies, practitioners highlight key contradictions and changes in the creation of EEO policies and practices.

My second aim is to suggest ways in which discourse theory can be useful for students and practitioners of EEO, by providing some new perspectives on issues that we usually frame in ethical or strategic terms. I assume that readers will be unfamiliar with discourse theory, and so this chapter could be used as an introduction to aspects of discourse theory in the context of a familiar topic, EEO. The use of discourse theory opens up a range of questions about EEO to consider, and I aim to leave these questions open, not come to conclusions[1].

In this chapter I draw primarily upon interviews carried out with practitioners working in various aspects of EEO in government organisations during early 1993. My focus is on the intersections of gender and cultural/ethnic issues, rather than the whole range of EEO issues. I have talked with people who deal particularly with these issues, mainly in various EEO units, but also in 'cultural development' positions of various kinds. I have also talked with people who have been in these jobs in the past, to members of 'target group' networks, to researchers who have been involved in EEO related projects, and to some trade union workers who have been involved with EEO in the public and private sectors. My intention has not been to gather a 'representative sample' of views in the scientific sense, but rather to create an account which presents a range of voices articulating their positions on EEO. I have attended especially to the conflicts and changes in these positions over the last few years.

Discourses of EEO

The field of EEO in government – its policies, documents, practices and debates – can be seen as a 'discourse'. What does it mean to call EEO a field of 'discourse'? My discussion of discourse draws upon the work of French philosopher Michel Foucault, whose concept of discourse has been used widely by feminists, although they have at the same time questioned many of the political implications of his work (e.g. Diamond and Quinby, 1988; Game, 1991; Sawicki, 1991; McNay, 1992). Discourse theory, as I use the term in this chapter, is focused on the idea that language is the core of our subjectivity – our sense of self – and our social world. Rather than being a way of describing a pre-existing reality 'out there', language is seen to create or construct our 'reality'. From this point of view, the distinction between 'reality' and the representation of reality is collapsed. From a feminist perspective, another key point is the idea that power relations are always implicated in the way that we construct our reality in language. For instance, in this chapter I will raise questions about the political implications of choosing to represent key EEO issues in a particular way.

Before I explain the theory of 'discourse' in more detail, I want to explain why I think it provides valuable perspectives on EEO. For me its value is in the new perspectives it offers on the process of social change, allowing feminists to reconsider some of what we might see as our political failures and successes in areas such as EEO. It allows us to reconsider some of the concepts and categories that we take as 'givens' such as gender, cultural difference, and equality, so that we can see how they are constructed, and can therefore be changed. For instance, I discuss below the use of the category 'women', and raise some questions about the ways we talk about gender and ethnic or cultural identity in the context of EEO. Discourse theory puts language and communication at the centre of its agenda, and so allows us to study political processes through the study of communication.

The term 'discourse' has been used in the past to refer in a general sense to language or communication, often with an emphasis on speech. However, 'discourse' is used differently in the literature which draws on Foucault's work. Here, discourse is seen as not only a set of communication acts or strategies, but as 'a process of creating social meaning' (Eagleton, 1983, p.115). Society is seen as the site of many discourses, often in conflict with each other. A given discourse regulates what is known and what can be known, what is done and said and what can be done and said, our sense of self, and the particular identities that it takes the form of, and the power issues that permeate all these social practices (Weedon, 1987, p.108). Medical discourse is a good example. It has its own rules about what 'truth' is and can be, and about who is 'qualified' to speak on medical matters. Foucault showed how medical discourse has created certain possible 'selves', categories of 'madness' and of 'sexual identity', that, while socially constructed are represented as descriptions of objective truths (Foucault, 1965; 1978). Within this discourse, certain types of sanity or sexual normality are possible, and some are not. Foucault has emphasised how these regimes of truth are produced by – and perpetuate – certain power relations. However, these power relations are masked by claims of 'truth' and 'objectivity'.

Like medical discourse, EEO discourse creates and regulates its own categories and practices. When asked to define EEO, many practitioners sought to establish their view of what it truly 'is', as against other accounts which they represented as incorrect descriptions, what EEO 'is not'. By contrast, if EEO is seen as a discursive formation, it has no essential definition. Its meanings, often conflicting, are constructed in our language and power relations.

If we see EEO as a discourse, we can analyse the way that EEO policy creates the categories of 'target groups' or 'EEO groups'. I raise some questions below about the political implications of thinking in terms of these categories. I will also consider the ways in which it is useful to see EEO as consisting of a number of discursive fields, often in conflict with others, such as feminism, state bureaucracy, biculturalism, human resource management and liberalism. Each of these discourses represents a different account of EEO issues. From the point of view of discourse theory, each account is not necessarily more or less 'true' than others, but serves to advance the interests of a particular group. Each EEO practitioner is located in one or more of these discursive fields.

EEO Discourse and the EEO Practitioner

One of the central concerns of discourse theory is subjectivity – the sense of self. From this perspective there is no essential self, no true 'me' which can be separated from my discursive context. Instead, the self is seen as *constituted* in discourse. We are, in fact, the discourses we are part of. To explore how this idea might work, I asked EEO practitioners to reflect on where they come from and where they feel they 'belong'. These reflections could suggest the patterns of a kind of 'discursive biography'. For instance, EEO practitioners may describe themselves as 'coming from' the women's movement, Maori community work, human resource management, trade unionism, or the public service. Their sense of 'self' may derive from one or more of these discursive positions, or may have moved from one to another.

This idea of the self as located in one or more discursive fields raises radical questions about individualism, 'free will' or agency, about ethics and strategy. For instance, many practitioners talk about 'using' certain language – such as the language of 'business' – in a strategic way. They see this use of language as separate from their 'real' selves, and from their 'real' commitment to EEO as social justice. But discourse theory challenges the separation of the self from the language we use. Can we 'use' discourse as if it were a strategic tool, or does discourse in a sense 'use' us? In 'using' the discourse of 'business' and of 'market forces', are we not also creating a new subjectivity? Are we not, in a sense, becoming a new 'person'?

Perhaps this is what is happening when someone who identifies herself as a feminist change agent, entering EEO work to bring about social change, comes also – or instead – to see herself as a human resources consultant. In the eyes of some feminists she may be seen as 'selling out', judged in ethical terms. She may in turn defend her position as strategically more effective than one located in a feminist discourse, a discourse that has little or no persuasive power in her organisational context.

Discourse theory raises the question of whether we can evaluate EEO work strategically or ethically from any single perspective. Instead we can ask how different discursive positions can come to be created and maintained, and whose interests they may serve. We can recognise that each of us might occupy positions in a number of often conflicting discourses, and ask how we handle these conflicts both 'within' ourselves and 'between' ourselves and others. Instead of trying to establish universally valid positions, we can ask instead how the process of discourse creation and change works to create outcomes that we may or may not expect or want. One way to do this is to explore some examples of the language of EEO and its political implications.

EEO 'Rhetoric' and 'Reality'

When people talk about the 'rhetoric' of EEO, they frequently use the word in opposition to the 'reality' of EEO. 'Rhetoric' implies 'just words', while the 'reality' is the actual practice. The practice is often seen to contradict the words. The concept of discourse, though, breaks down the distinction between language, or 'rhetoric' and other social practices. For instance, an organisation may maintain the 'rhetoric' of equality in written EEO policies, in employing 'token' members of EEO groups, and in slightly amending its cultural practices. However, the inequalities of EEO groups may remain in terms of indicators such as promotion and retention. Some people would describe this as a gap between 'rhetoric' and 'reality'. On the other hand, others might say that even a token gesture to EEO opens the door for change or even represents an important and legitimate change in itself. It can also be argued that giving a rhetorical impression of change can actually prevent change by masking the lack of it.

Such debates show that there is no simple opposition between 'rhetoric' and 'reality'. Rhetoric is an aspect of discourse, no less 'real' than other social practices. It evokes the values of the particular discourses with which it is associated. For instance, the metaphors of 'market' rhetoric frame a particular capitalist discourse. I will define 'rhetoric' here as persuasive communication. There is an intrinsic sense of the *strategic* use of communication in this definition, but it does not necessarily imply deliberate insincerity, as is often implied in the common opposition of 'rhetoric' to 'reality'.

The battle over EEO is largely a rhetorical battle, and EEO discourse is an important site of conflict between competing rhetorical claims over equality, gender and ethnic difference, and the values we ascribe to these. As Yeatman points out, 'it is in linguistic practices that certain claims, and not others, are valorised' (1990, p.1).

The rhetoric of EEO can be found not only in the 'official' discourses of government organisations, including policy documents, speeches, and EEO programmes themselves, but in the talk, 'official' and 'unofficial', used by EEO practitioners in the course of their work and in reflecting on their work.

An analysis of the rhetoric of EEO helps us to identify the shifting meanings and power relations within the field of EEO. The rhetoric of equality is effective only where it evokes a discursive context in which appeals to equality are seen as authoritative. In this context it would be effective to appeal to 'fairness', for instance. In a bureaucratic discourse the idea of appointing 'the best person for the job' would be seen as more 'efficient', and could also have the advantage of seeming to sidestep questions of political outcomes. In practice rhetorical strategies often work best when they cover multiple bases: the word 'merit' for instance could evoke 'fairness' as well as 'efficiency'.

EEO practitioners must use effective rhetorical strategies with a wide range of audiences, ranging from grass-roots networks of 'EEO groups' to senior managers. In communicating with these audiences they see themselves as choosing the language – the rhetoric – that will be most effective in persuading a given audience to implement EEO practices. As well as changing their rhetorical strategies from one audience to another, many practitioners see themselves as having changed their communication strategies over recent years as the policy environment has changed. While once the talk was of 'social justice', now it is more likely to be of 'efficient business practices'. As well as reflecting the increasing power of managerial discourse, these rhetorical shifts raise ethical and strategic questions discussed in more detail below.

Current Issues in EEO Discourse

I asked EEO practitioners to reflect on the way they talk of EEO, and the communication strategies they use as EEO advocates. I created a pattern of key issues from their responses. Some of these 'issues' could be seen as points of current debate about the nature and goals of EEO, while others represent differences in strategic approaches – how to reach those goals.

Ethical issues in EEO communication

Many practitioners frame communication strategies in ethical or political terms, or both. In ethical terms, some wonder how they can maintain personal integrity when they are required to put aside their own personal philosophies and use the language of their audiences in order to be effective. This may mean that they have to argue on the basis of values that may be in conflict with their 'own' values. For instance, some believe that the philosophy of 'market forces' can never produce social justice, yet they feel they have to use 'market forces' rhetoric to persuade managers to adopt some EEO practices. Some practitioners resolve this concern by separating strategies from outcomes, ends from means. They do not see themselves as having changed their beliefs, but as adopting necessary strategies to put their beliefs into practice. Alternatively, some refuse to adopt certain strategies, and describe others as having 'sold out' by having abandoned original equality agendas for 'market' values.

The idea of 'integrity' implies a unified 'genuine' self, with an ethical commitment to consistency of values and practices. But if, in contrast to this humanistic view, the self is seen as constituted in discourse – in multiple, often conflicting discourses – the picture is quite different. In this alternative picture the self is seen as moving from one discursive field to another, and each discursive context has its own 'ethics'.

The self is not separate from discourse, so that as I might move, for instance, into the managerial discourse of 'human resource management' (HRM), in 'using' the rhetoric of HRM my subjectivity is in turn being created by the same rhetoric. For example, in using the argument that EEO is a 'better business practice' a practitioner will frequently come to 'really believe' this claim, as some have put it. This reconciliation of two discursive positions, previously perceived as in conflict, is another example of how discursive conflict is reconciled from the perspective of an individual. To an outsider though – perhaps one who retains her or his position in a discourse of social justice – this reconciliation can again be seen as unethical or perhaps as 'selling out'.

A variety of strategies are used by practitioners to resolve these conflicts between discursive positions, ranging from the deliberate maintenance of an 'outsider' status, to various degrees of identification with organisational discourses. Discourse theory has been criticised by feminists because it does not provide a basis on which to make ethical and/or political judgements. Discourse theory does not allow us to evaluate whether a move from the ethics of one discourse into those of another is 'good' or 'bad', because no universal ethical basis is recognised, only the ethics of a particular discursive context.

However, I believe the recognition that the self is always and inevitably situated in multiple and conflicting discourses helps us keep questions of ethical communication open. This recognition is similar to that which allows Pakeha feminists to acknowledge that 'feminism' in our context may not be 'feminism' in a Maori context, and that for each of us our 'feminism' changes as we move from one discursive context to another.

It is this same negotiation between conflicting discourses of the self that allows us to recognise contradictions, that triggers 'consciousness raising', and creates openings in discourse that enable social change.

Strategic Issues in EEO Communication

Some practitioners are concerned with strategic rather than ethical issues, with outcomes rather than processes. They ask whether it matters what we say as long as we get the results we want. If talking about 'managing diversity' will achieve results more effectively than talking about 'eliminating discrimination', why not? The question then is not 'is it ethical?', but 'will it work?'

Some activists argue that the terms in which the debate is framed cannot be separated from the outcomes. They argue that the use of rhetoric that may be effective in convincing politicians or senior managers may also end up changing the whole basis of the political agenda. To talk about 'managing diversity' is to shift the discussion to the managerial perspective, away from the perspectives of the EEO groups who originally defined the EEO issues. What effect might this have on the policies developed, and who drives them? Similarly, the concept of 'diversity' shifts the discussion away from concepts of inequality and discrimination for specific groups towards a more individualised concept of 'difference', floating free of issues of power.

The 'strategic' use of managerialist rhetoric may result in unintended outcomes. One such outcome may be the 'capture' of EEO by senior managers. Some practitioners argue that EEO outcomes will be best achieved or only achieved if EEO is seen as a management function rather than as the 'empowering' of EEO groups. Discourse theory can help us to identify the crucial shifts of meaning that are taking place here, and evaluate them in terms of our own agendas.

I think it is also important to reconsider what we mean by 'strategy'. From an organisational point of view the use of 'strategic planning' is a key rhetorical move to incorporate the subjectivity of all members in the identity of the 'corporation'. Its effect is to erase differences of interests between groups and to subsume them in corporate outcomes, represented as being in the interests of all.

From the point of view of a change agent such as an EEO practitioner, this 'strategic' approach may be resisted, incorporated, or both. Yet even those who resist corporate strategic planning will usually frame their own practices in terms of 'strategy'. For instance, many EEO practitioners see themselves as 'using' the language of human resource management for 'strategic' reasons, to achieve certain goals.

'Strategic' action is differentiated from other kinds of action, and strategy is seen as a kind of functional, rational and outcome-oriented political process that somehow lies outside discursive positions, and from which various rhetorics can be 'used' to achieve political goals. Critical analysis of functionalist approaches which invoke seemingly neutral goals such as 'efficiency' can create convincing arguments that such neutrality always masks political interests. For instance, EEO practitioners have critiqued a concept of 'merit' which acts to perpetuate the exclusion of women and Maori. We cannot use 'strategy', or any other social practice for that matter, as a neutral 'tool' for change. In the name of 'strategy' we are always invoking some discursive context or another, along with the illusion that change can be a simple, rational and functional matter.

The 'Privatisation' of EEO

Until recently, EEO initiatives were largely confined to government organisations, and were a function of government policies. More recently, the National government has resourced private sector EEO programmes through creating the EEO Trust. At the same time, changes in the political climate have meant that government organisations themselves have increasingly used the language of private sector human resource management models. The 'managing diversity' debate is one indicator of the discursive changes that may occur as the model of EEO is 'privatised'.

The concept of 'managing diversity' originated in the United States (US), and is associated with far-reaching demographic changes that are predicted for the US workforce. The workforce will be more culturally diverse and include more women than it has in the past. The 'managing diversity' argument is that managers have no choice but to respond positively to the challenge of effectively managing this new workforce. In New Zealand 'managing diversity' is the theme of the EEO Trust, and has been adopted by some EEO consultants and EEO practitioners.

The people I interviewed raised two main critiques of this concept from an EEO perspective. The first centres on the idea of *managing* diversity, which clearly puts a management perspective at the centre of the discussion. Historically it has been the groups who have defined themselves as 'oppressed' or 'disadvantaged' (depending on their discursive context) who have put EEO on the agenda. Resistance to EEO has primarily, though not solely, come from managers who tend *not* to belong to these groups. The idea of 'managing diversity', however, addresses 'difference' in terms of the needs of managers, not of the groups traditionally marginalised by 'difference'.

The question can be asked: can a perspective in which workers are viewed as 'human resources' be reconciled with one from which marginalised groups seek equal power and participation? In a 'human resources' approach the efficiency of the organisation depends on drawing from the most 'diverse' possible range of skills and viewpoints, and on the ability to, in turn, draw on the most diverse possible market share of clients or customers.

Some practitioners do argue that the use of the term 'managing diversity' can be effective as long as it is used to advance an equality agenda. In other words, the managerial rhetoric in a sense provides an opening for social justice.

The second critique of 'managing diversity' scrutinises the concept of *diversity*. The word 'diversity', and its twin, 'inclusiveness', are increasingly replacing terms such as 'non-sexist' or 'non-racist' or 'non-discriminatory' in EEO discourses. Both concepts separate issues of difference and inclusion from a political agenda, whereas the term EEO was originally introduced into government organisations as part of an agenda of social equality. Cut free of their roots in discourses of feminism and anti-racism, 'diversity' and 'inclusiveness' are terms that can apply to all of us. They can imply that we are all equally entitled to be included and all differences are equivalent. It could be argued that the non-threatening nature of these terms makes them rhetorically more effective. It could also be argued that they avoid fixing rigid identity categories of the 'disadvantaged' into discussions of difference. This argument raises the whole question of identity.

EEO and the Question of Identity

The term 'EEO' encompasses a range of 'EEO groups'. The answers to questions of how these groups are defined, of who defines them, and their order of priority, varies from one organisation to another. Practitioners are in a constant process of negotiating these highly difficult questions, which address not only the identities of the groups but the conflicts of interest between them.

The construction of these categories is backed up by increasingly extensive 'data' which seeks to establish the degree of disadvantage qualifying each group for inclusion. But the identities of these groups are generally taken as 'givens' within which we work to create an equality agenda. However, it is useful to recognise that the discourse of EEO itself is an important field within which the categories of difference – gender, ethnicity and others – are being discursively created and valued. As feminists we might ask when we want to accept this process of categorisation, and when we might prefer to undermine the categories which lock us into 'difference'.

Feminist philosopher Judith Butler's influential book *Gender Trouble* (1990) challenges the categories of difference that many feminists have taken for granted as the basis for political work. She articulates the concerns of a body of feminist post-structuralist theorising in which gender itself is seen as a problem, rather than taken as given, and which concerns itself with creating 'gender trouble', asking which is the 'best way to trouble the gender categories that support gender hierarchy...?' (ibid., p.x). Butler sees gender as a kind of performance, as a series of social practices (ibid., p.33). She stresses that we *create* gender through the way we act and the way we communicate. If we create gender, so we can disrupt it, and she advocates the disruption of gender categories as the most effective feminist strategy.

Butler challenges the 'strategic' need to use the category of 'women' in furthering political agendas, believing instead that as soon as we make a claim on behalf of 'women' we necessarily exclude 'women' who do not associate themselves with our claim. An example would be the decision of many Maori women not to identify themselves as part of EEO target groups. Butler also believes that to perpetuate 'gender categories' is to perpetuate power imbalances.

We can go on to apply a similar approach to other categories of 'difference', asking how they might work to maintain categories that perpetuate power hierarchies. From this point of view it could be argued that recent moves away from the concept of 'EEO groups' in fact 'trouble' the boundaries of the categories quite effectively. The focus is switched to 'EEO issues' and on single issue-based groups such as 'people with family responsibilities' rather than on identity-based groups.

At the same time the range of groups included as 'EEO groups' continues to be contested, as members of those groups see political advantages in such inclusion. For instance, lesbian/gay networks have recently been recognised in some government departments as representing a new 'EEO group', although not one of those which was identified in the State Sector Act 1988. By entering the discourse of EEO, lesbian/gay groups can draw on the rhetoric of equality to counter their marginalisation. At the same time, the validity of their claims is acceptable within EEO discourse only to the extent that they are equivalent to those of legitimised categories. For instance, lesbian/gay relationships might be seen as equivalent to heterosexual marriage for superannuation purposes, while such equivalence might be strongly contested in other contexts.

In defining 'EEO groups', a highly diverse range of social categories is yoked together on the premise that the groups are those to whom 'equal opportunity' has been denied. EEO discourse creates and regulates categories of difference which are reduced to a kind of equivalence. The paradox is that although recognising a type of difference – unequal access to certain 'opportunities' available to dominant social groups – EEO erases others. Each EEO group has its own discourses, which may be more or less compatible with the discourse of EEO as a regulating concept. This is most evident in the case of 'EEO Maori'.

EEO is a discourse that draws on the Western liberal political tradition. Any meaningful recognition of cultural difference puts the universal applicability of this tradition into question. In particular, Maori claims for both participation and autonomy within the framework of the Treaty of Waitangi and of recognition of tangata whenua status draw from a radically different discourse than that of EEO.

Most practitioners I talked with agreed that there needs to be more discussion of the relationship between 'bicultural' or Maori development programmes (as they are variously defined) and EEO. Is 'EEO Maori' a sub category of Treaty of Waitangi Initiatives, for instance? One argument is that EEO Maori relates to Article Three of the Treaty, which confirms the rights of Maori as citizens, but does not address the central issue of te tino rangatiratanga as affirmed in the Treaty. In this argument EEO Maori can provide openings for Maori in Pakeha institutions, but does not give away arguments for partnership or for forms of separate development.

While some practitioners have argued that it is essential to keep arguing for Treaty initiatives in human resource management, focused around concepts such as partnership and biculturalism, others feel that talking of EEO is a more effective strategy for empowering Maori in a climate where 'Treaty discourse' is less likely to be recognised, but the concept of EEO is already to some extent legitimated.

The concept of 'EEO Maori' is used in reference to the 'good employer' provisions of the State Sector Act 1988, which identifies the 'employment requirements of the Maori people', along with the 'employment requirements' of other target groups. While this provision is seen by some EEO practitioners as an opening for Maori in the public service, many Maori reject categorisation as just another target group. An alternative approach to 'EEO Maori' is being considered currently by some Maori EEO practitioners. This approach takes its cue from references in the State Sector Act 1988 to the 'aims and aspirations of the Maori people' (s.56). This provision could provide an opening for iwi-defined agendas that, rather than framing Maori as just another EEO group, refer back to Maori discourses within and beyond the organisations. In particular, it could invoke Maori perspectives on the Treaty of Waitangi.

Concluding Questions

Reflecting on this chapter, I see discourse theory as helping me to question my own assumptions about the way I frame political issues and my own and others' strategic and ethical positions. For me one of the strengths of discourse theory is that it encourages us to rethink our own discursive positions. In the case of EEO, this rethinking reminds me how easily I myself can argue for equality in terms of efficiency, or of market forces, when it seems to me that *really*, like nearly all the EEO practitioners I talked with, my own commitment comes from my desire to advance the interests of my own group and those I care about. What price do I pay when I abandon the rhetoric of radical change for that of a 'rationality geared to efficiency, practicality and control?' (Ball, 1990, p.157). Do I believe that I am being strategically effective, or is the discourse of 'the level playing field' the only show in town?

As well as rethinking our positions from new, critical perspectives, discourse theory must enable us to generate alternative positions and strategies. It releases us from the requirement to work from a set of universally applicable principles, by subverting our belief in the 'one way' approach. We can recognise that 'feminism' or 'EEO' changes as we move from one discursive context to another. The recognition of contradictions within and around us need not lead to despair or a simplistic strategic opportunism, but to the constant revision of our agendas and to an experimental approach which allows us to identify new and shifting openings for changing power relations.

Note

1   What I have characterised as 'discourse theory' here is actually a complex field within which there are many different perspectives and debates. I urge readers to follow up some of the references cited to find a 'way in' to the literature from a feminist perspective. My paper 'A beginner's guide to feminism/postmodernism' (Jones, 1993) is also intended as an introduction to the field.

References

Ball, S. (1990), 'Management as Moral Technology: a Luddite Analysis', in S. Ball (ed.), *Foucault and Education: Disciplines and Knowledge*, London: Routledge.

Butler, J. (1990), *Gender Trouble: Feminism and the Subversion of Identity*, New York: Routledge.

Diamond, I. and Quinby, L. (1988), *Feminism and Foucault: Reflections on Resistance*, Boston: Northeastern University Press.

Eagleton, T. (1983), *Literary Theory: an Introduction*, London: Basil Blackwell.

Foucault, M. (1965), *Madness and Civilisation: A History of Insanity in the Age of Reason,* New York: Pantheon Books.

Foucault, M. (1978), *The History of Sexuality,* New York: Pantheon Books.

Game, A. (1991), *Undoing the Social: Towards a Deconstructive Sociology,* Milton Keynes: Open University Press.

Jones, D. (1993), 'A Beginners' Guide to Feminism/Postmodernism', *New Zealand Women's Studies Association Newsletter,* 14 (1), 22-24.

McNay, L. (1992), *Foucault and Feminism: Power, Gender, and the Self,* Cambridge: Polity Press.

Sawicki, J. (1991), *Disciplining Foucault: Feminism, Power and the Body,* New York: Routledge.

Weedon, C. (1987), *Feminist Practice and Post-structuralist Theory,* London: Basil Blackwell.

Yeatman, A. (1990), *Bureaucrats, Femocrats, Technocrats: Essays on the Contemporary Australian State,* Sydney: Allen and Unwin.

12

Through a Glass Ceiling Darkly: Equality Versus Difference in the EEO Debate

Nicola Armstrong

My first experience of EEO occurred while I was working for a government department in the mid-eighties in Wellington. One of the members of our unit had been reappointed as the EEO Officer and on the first day in her new job had constructed a graph of the occupational location of women and Maori in the organisation. What was sobering about these figures was the way that they starkly revealed the lack of women and Maori in the higher levels of the organisation, despite the organisation's stated policies supporting the movement of such workers into these senior positions. I remember also thinking, as I located myself in the largest group at the bottom of this hierarchy, that such policies had little impact on the bulk of those in EEO 'target' groups, for whom the dizzying heights of the higher grades were but the distant glimmer of a far-off glass ceiling.

Cynthia Cockburn suggests that, if nothing else, equal opportunities says to those at the bottom of hierarchies who have not traditionally been represented in senior positions that 'there is room at the top'. EEO is about breaking down the *vertical segregation* which limits and confines certain groups to low paid, supposedly low-skilled jobs, preventing their progress to higher positions in organisational hierarchies, such as the public service where, in 1988, only 7.6 per cent of all those in the top of the executive clerical grade were women (Ministry of Women's Affairs, 1992, p.38).

EEO is also about edging workers into areas of non-traditional employment where *horizontal segregation* of the labour force has constricted them to a narrow range of occupations. For example, 38 per cent of Maori women and *almost half* of all Pacific Island women in full-time employment are production workers in factories, transport equipment operators or labourers, although only 15 per cent of the total full-time labour force is engaged in these occupations (Novitz, 1987, p.32). Cockburn suggests that opening these opportunities for employment is the 'first item for positive action on any organisation's list' (1991, p.46).

Positive actions would include: fair recruitment practices, supplementary training courses for EEO target groups, reviewing of procedures for appraisal and promotion and ultimately acknowledging the authority and abilities of successful individuals.

And yet here lies the heart of the dilemma that is central to the theoretical development of this debate. There is a disjuncture between the so-called *liberal* emphasis on *individual* achievement and the removal of impediments to the operation of *free and equal* competition and the *radical* emphasis on *positive discrimination* to enable *disadvantaged groups* to be distributed fairly across organisational hierarchies through *varying* entry requirements and creating different criteria for their appraisal and promotion (see Walsh and Dickson chapter).

In this chapter I want to develop in more depth a discussion of the dilemmas this distinction between liberal and radical perspectives raises and particularly the problem of 'equal' versus 'special' treatment. In making this argument I want to suggest that neither position is adequate and that the debate must move beyond this unhelpful straitjacket. This movement, I suggest, could be assisted by contemporary developments in poststructuralist thought which offer insights into the use of language and the formation of identity which go beyond the unhelpful binary opposition of liberal versus radical perspectives.

The Liberal Perspective on EEO

The liberal perspective on EEO is based upon social contract theories of the sixteenth and seventeenth centuries which emphasise the 'fundamental equality of all men (sic) based on men's (sic) alleged equal potential for rationality' (Jaggar and Rothenberg, 1984, p.83). In particular this notion of equality refers to the equal capacity of individuals to compete in the marketplace as economic self-maximisers able to rise in society as far as their talents allow.

Coupled with this notion of equality is the concept of liberty, which is conceptualised as freedom from interference, particularly the interference from illegitimate authority of the state. According to this view the state can legitimately act as arbiter between conflicting interest groups in the public area of the economy and politics, while the private world of home and family are seen as beyond the boundaries of state intervention. The link between these concepts and equal opportunity is that the state is thus seen as responsible for ensuring that individuals are given equal opportunity to enable them to compete in the public arena of the market economy, irrespective of gender, class and ethnicity (ibid.).

The role of equal opportunity programmes is central for two reasons. First liberals, particularly liberal feminists, argue that the state is not neutral and that through equal opportunities the number of women and other marginalised people such as Maori who are in powerful positions, needs to be increased. This increase in numbers, it is argued, will remedy distortions in the operation of decision-making in the economy and in politics caused (in part) by the preponderance of white middle-class men in powerful positions. Second, EEO is central to the pursuit of equal citizenship and fair competition in a civil society based on merit. That is, equal opportunity needs to be guaranteed to allow individuals to exercise their talents freely and to allow society to harness the skills of all its members.

However, as I noted in my opening anecdote, the attention given to the advancement of women, Maori or disabled professionals up the career ladder excludes the bulk of those workers who do not have the qualifications or talents which are deemed necessary for such advancement. Furthermore, it excludes all those whose labour-power is determined to be 'economically interchangeable', in a market where many compete for unskilled or semi-skilled work (Franzway *et al.*, 1989, p.16).

In addition, liberal theory pivots on a notion of self-interested *individuals* competing in the public world. This is important because it runs counter to the identification of EEO *target groups*, focusing instead on outstanding individuals competing in the public arena; individuals who are, ideally, unfettered by responsibilities for the caring work associated with the private sphere. As Middleton's (1990) commentary on Treasury briefing documents indicated, having children is seen by this important policy-making institution as 'irrational desire' because of the costs of the child's dependency on the family. She notes that according to Treasury the 'rational' individual competes in the market place. Having children is an irrational decision because it prevents this.

The liberal model of EEO thus focuses on talented individuals being assisted in their career advancement in the hope that their presence will correct any imbalances in decision-making at the top levels within organisations. However, those able to succeed using this strategy would appear to be those who can best mimic the full-time, continuous service model of employment usually associated with professional men who have the support of a full-time partner at home.

This paradox creates a contradictory outcome for those who achieve within this framework because such achievement may be won at the cost of distancing themselves from aspects of their identities associated with being a woman or being Maori, such as care of children or participation in marae activities. A good example would be the portrayal of senior women in politics as masculine or male in cartoons, underscoring the contradiction between femininity and the supposedly masculine characteristics required for top political office. Achievement in the arena of politics is portrayed as contradictory for women, because the characteristics of a good politician (rationality, unemotionality, freedom from domestic constraints) are seen as contradictory with the characteristics of a 'good woman' (caring for others, being emotional, being dependent, etc.).

Consider for example the cartoon overleaf portraying Jenny Shipley in her capacity as Minister of Social Welfare. It shows her as an aggressive, uncaring person of masculine appearance, holding a 'cocked' gun! Interestingly she is portrayed as much larger than the downtrodden, physically diminished male beneficiary, suggesting a reversal of the conventional gender stereotype of the weak woman and the strong man.

The significance of such portrayals are the ways in which they reflect the no-win dilemma for those who succeed 'in the system', because the organisational context they enter remains the same. To use the example above, if women enter as a minority into 'toxic' environments, where they are encouraged to emulate male career patterns and male styles of operation, little of the world glimpsed beyond the glass ceiling is likely to change. If, on the other hand, they organise around their *difference* as women, does this make them vulnerable politically and subject to additionally heavy workloads as they fight for wider change within the system?

Reprinted with permission of Anthony Ellison

The second horn of the dilemma then, suggests that where women approach their work using the *different* viewpoint gained from being a woman, they are likely to increase their political vulnerability. It is this 'problem of difference' which is emphasised by the second dominant perspective within EEO, the radical approach.

The Radical Perspective on EEO

This radical perspective on EEO emphasises the political nature of difference, particularly *embodied* differences such as gender, ethnicity and disability. In contrast to the argument for equal treatment, the radical perspective *celebrates* and *politicises* the importance of difference as a basis for special treatment. In a context where liberals have argued successfully that gender (or ethnicity or disability) are irrelevant and that individuals should receive equal employment rights and privileges, the radical perspective embraces difference as enriching the social and cultural diversity of the workplace.

At a theoretical level, radicals claim a new political vision where liberalism is rejected as disassociating individuals from the context of their families, ethnic or religious groups and class. In this sense the radical perspective problematises the distinction liberals draw between the public and private sphere and argues instead for the politicisation of the 'personal' and a valuing of it, whether it be women's ability to bear children or the diversity of cultural experience within the workforce.

Theoretically then, the radical perspective opposes the abstract individual who lies at the heart of liberal theory, as a character who is curiously disassociated from the responsibilities of home and health and as a model which implicitly supports white, male, able-bodied workers as the norm.

This analytical divergence between liberal and radical perspectives is sharply drawn in feminist theory. In the 1960s Betty Friedan's pathbreaking book *The Feminine Mystique* (1963) was urging women into the public arena of work, decrying the waste of talent that their confinement to the home represented. A decade later, radical feminists were embracing female psychology and physiology not as an 'oppressive construct' but as an 'oppressed reality' (Bunkle, 1980) offering a superior ethic of caring and co-operation embodied in maternity and motherhood (Baachi, 1990).

Furthermore, the divisions between the two perspectives are 'ideological as well as tactical' (Goodman and Taub, 1986, p.23). The radical rebellion against the 'system' and the values of the marketplace opens up for political inspection the *context of inequality* which stimulates the need for EEO programmes (ibid., p.23). Thus the radical perspective suggests purposeful intervention in the employment process to ensure EEO target groups are fairly distributed across organisational hierarchies.

Furthermore, the radical perspective does not focus on equality of opportunity, but rather on equality of *effects* or *outcomes*, arguing that to fully include the human diversity within the labour force, the object is to remove barriers to the full participation of all groups.

At this point the average liberal becomes very nervous. The cornerstone of the liberal debate for equal rights and freedoms is the notion of equal talent and equal ability to compete. The notion that 'like should be treated alike' (Fiss, 1977) is the fundamental principle in the liberal fight for anti-discrimination before the law. Anything which suggests that those represented within EEO target groups cannot compete *on the same basis* as other workers, is seen as technically dangerous, that is, as one more reason for not hiring women, Maori and the disabled, etc.

The fear is that the radical perspective's endorsement of the recognition of the seemingly 'natural' differences of gender, ethnicity, etc., will return the debate to a conservative dogma where discriminating against EEO target groups is justified as simply a recognition of their 'natural' differences (Scott, 1988). Joan Scott provides the example of this dilemma in her discussion of the famous *Sears, Roebuck and Co versus The Equal Employment Opportunities Commission* (1986). The case concerned women who were excluded from selection for highly-paid commission sales jobs on the basis that due to cultural differences and long-standing patterns of socialisation, women were simply not interested in such jobs.

The case showed that the psychological tests the women were obliged to take to apply for these jobs were clearly discriminatory, including a 'vigour' scale asking such questions as: 'Do you have a low-pitched voice?' 'Have you ever done hunting?' 'Have you participated in wrestling?' 'Have you participated in boxing?' 'Have you played on a football team?' (Milkman, 1986, p.382). Despite this, the court found in favour of the Sears company and judged that they had not intentionally discriminated against women. In her commentary on a case where feminist historians had testified as expert witnesses on *both sides* as to women's 'equal' or 'different' nature, Milkman notes the perils of arguing *for* 'difference' or 'women's culture' within a conservative political climate. In Scott's words the argument for women's *difference* from men in this case, underscored the 'stigma of deviance' (1988, p.39) from the male norm. Alternatively, the argument that women and other EEO target groups are *equally* talented and deserve equal opportunity to pursue any job, leaves in place a 'faulty neutrality', according to Scott where the real differences in the life opportunities of subordinate groups are rendered invisible.

So what is to be done? First it is important to point out that neither of these strategies operate in a pure way and, as Sayers points out, the two are routinely confused with the 'preferred procedures of the liberal approach widely assumed to result in the preferred outcomes of the radical approach' (1994, this volume). Taub and Williams (1985, p.835), go further to ask:

> ... are we doomed forever to oscillate between dualities – group vs. individual equality, assimilation vs. accommodation, 'formal' vs. 'real' equality?

Poststructuralisms and EEO

The problematic nature of this duality between the notion of 'equal' versus 'different' treatment invites a third developing perspective on EEO. Poststructuralist theories have arisen as a response to some of the theoretical shortcomings discussed above and focus on the importance of language, the instability of identities and a conception of knowledge as inherently unstable and entwined with power relations. While this is not the time or place to deal in detail with the complex and diverse corpus of poststructuralist thought, I would note three important contributions poststructuralisms could make to the present debate regarding EEO. These are the dissolving of the binary thinking that exists in distinctions between 'equal' versus 'different' treatment, the reframing of identity politics at the heart of the notion of EEO target groups and a reformulation of the state as a social and political site of contestation.

First then, poststructuralisms offer an insight into the constitution of binary or oppositional constructs such as the 'equality' versus 'difference' debate. Such dualities would be rejected from a poststructuralist position as inherently unhelpful categories which do not acknowledge the *interdependence* of the two positions and which ignore the power invested in each term, where one is usually dominant and one subordinate (i.e. equality = rights or privileges of the male citizen; difference = stigma of deviance from this norm). As Scott (1988, p.48) suggests, there must be a resistance to the 'operation of categorical difference', in this case the seemingly bipolar opposition of liberal and radical approaches to EEO, and the kinds of 'exclusions and inclusions – the hierarchies – it constructs'.

Rather than choose *between* liberal or radical perspectives, Scott (1988, p. 48) suggests a refusal of the power of such oppositional thinking:

> ... not in the name of an equality that implies sameness or identity, but rather ... in the name of an equality that rests on differences – differences that confound, disrupt, and render ambiguous the meaning of any fixed binary opposition. To do anything else is to buy into the political argument that sameness is the requirement for equality... .

As Jones suggests (chapter in this volume) EEO practitioners in practice also move *between* the discourses of equality and fairness and the acknowledgement of difference. Poststructuralisms offer insights into how these discourses are constructed, how they might intersect with other discursive formations and the contradictory and often complex political positions in which this places those who work within organisations promoting EEO.

Second, poststructuralisms offer an alternative to the view of identity at the centre of both liberal and radical perspectives, namely that identities are unified, self-conscious and rational. For poststructuralists, identities are seen as unstable, contradictory and fragmentary. That is, the identities represented in the notion of EEO groups, are not in themselves stable and exclusive; individuals may be members of several groups simultaneously and may coalesce around these identities in different ways. Poststructuralists ask that these identities be interrogated for their investments in power relations. For example, we need to ask the following questions: what is the meaning of these identities? How are they ranked and how does one come to have priority over another (e.g. Maori/woman/lesbian)? How do such identities become fixed and how does this fixing deny their historical, cultural and political construction? (Guy *et al.*, 1990).

Fuss has suggested that the central category of difference under consideration, whether it be gender or ethnicity or disability, 'blinds us to other modes of difference and explicitly deligitimates them' (1989, p.116). That is, the focus on particular EEO target groups may force individuals to make invidious decisions around which identities take priority, usually focusing on only one aspect of their identity, that which is most visible. If EEO is based on identity in this way the dominant question to be asked is 'which identity comes first?', rather than 'how do those competing and sometimes contradictory identities interact in my/our lived experience?'

For example, the bifurcation of ethnic politics into Maori/Pakeha in New Zealand leaves non-Maori people of colour placeless and without a voice, occupying an identity lacking both political analysis and attention. Anne-Marie Jagose (1992, p.54) writes as a non-Maori woman of colour:

> When what is not Maori is Pakeha and what is not Pakeha is Maori, I occupy the gap between the two, that black hole in which nothing can be seen and nothing can be heard.

Furthermore, some important identities such as being a man or being Pakeha remain intact in such an analysis, so that women's continuing association with domestic work and childcare remains unproblematised and Pakeha remain a people without a culture.

Third, and finally, poststructuralisms offer a view of the state as a dynamic process of power alignment and realignment, an analysis which offers possibilities for intervention, such as EEO initiatives. This is not the liberal model of the pluralist state adjudicating between competing interest groups, nor is it the co-opted state of the radical model, furthering the interests of the powerful élite. Rather, poststructuralisms offer a view of the state as the institutionalisation of power relations formed by the practices, processes, relationships and agents which constitute it. From this perspective the form of state power is understood as:

> ... an outcome of particular social struggles. What kind of state we have depends on who was mobilised in social struggle, what strategies were deployed and who won (Franzway *et al.*, 1989, p.35).

So, poststructuralisms offer a view of the state as both a *determinant* of the struggle for EEO (particularly in the legislative framework it creates to facilitate or prohibit these initiatives) and as a *product* of this contestation, for example, in terms of the prevalence of EEO units and practitioners in the executive bodies which constitute the state itself. This vision of the state as both '... *an actor* in social struggle and *at stake* in social struggle' (Franzway, 1989, p.40) provides a dynamic conceptualisation offering opportunities for intervention as well as suggesting the costs of engagement.

Conclusion

For those who work for EEO in this country, as practitioners, students, administrators and business people, a discussion of the theory which underpins the EEO debate may seem like a luxury they can ill afford at a time when EEO is under threat from a more conservative legislative framework. I would argue, however, that at such times it is even more strategically important to clarify the analyses we work with, to avoid *isolation* from other issues (such as the link between managerialism and a much more restricted model of EEO) and to avoid the distorting effects of operating with an *implicit* theoretical perspective on EEO without being aware of its implications.

In this chapter I have reviewed the apparently contradictory positions of 'equal' versus 'different' treatment and have suggested that both positions are highly problematic. As new theoretical positions emerge they may offer alternatives to the restricting bipolar opposition of radical versus liberal perspectives on EEO and we may see through the glass ceiling *less* darkly.

References

Baachi, C.L. (1990), *Same Difference: Feminism and Sexual Difference*, Sydney: Allen and Unwin.

Bunkle, P. (1980) 'A History of the Women's Movement – Part 5', *Broadsheet*, January, 20-22.

Cockburn, C. (1991), *In the Way of Women: Men's Resistance to Sex Equality in Organisations*, Hampshire: Macmillan.

Fuss, O.M. (1977), 'Groups and the Equal Protection Clause', in M. Cohen, T. Nagel and T. Scanlon (eds), *Equality and Preferential Treatment*, Princeton: Princeton University Press, 84-154.

Friedan, B. (1963), *The Feminine Mystique*, Middlesex: Penguin.

Franzway, S., Court, D. and Connell, R.W. (1989), *Staking a Claim: Feminism, Bureaucracy and the State*, Sydney: Allen and Unwin.

Fuss, D. (1989), *Essentially Speaking: Feminism, Nature and Difference*, New York: Routledge.

Goodman, J. and Taub, N. (1986), 'For Women Only? The Recurring Debate Over Sex-Specific Laws', *New Jersey Law Journal*, 117 (25), 22-23.

Guy, C., Jones, A. and Simpson, G. (1990, Autumn), 'From Piha to Post-Feminism: Radical Feminisms in New Zealand', *Sites: A Journal for Radical Perspectives on Culture*, 20, 7-19.

Jaggar, A.M. and Rothenberg, P.S. (1984), *Feminist Frameworks: Alternative Theoretical Accounts of the Relations between Women and Men*, New York: McGraw Hill.

Jagose, A. (1992), 'The (W)hole Story: Lesbians of Colour in Aotearoa', in P. Rosier (ed.), *Broadsheet: Twenty Years of Broadsheet Magazine*, Auckland: New Women's Press.

Middleton, S. (1990), 'Women, Equality and Equity in Liberal Educational Policies 1945-1988', in S. Middleton J. Codd and A. Jones (eds), *New Zealand Education Policy Today: Critical Perspectives*, Wellington: Allen and Unwin.

Milkman, R. (1986), 'Women's History and the Sears Case', *Feminist Studies*, 12 (2), 374-400.

Ministry of Women's Affairs (1992), *Status of New Zealand Women: Second Periodic Report on the Convention on the Elimination of all Forms of Discrimination Against Women*, Wellington: Ministry of Women's Affairs.

Novitz, R. (1987), 'Bridging the Gap: Paid and Unpaid Work', in S. Cox (ed.), *Public and Private Worlds: Women in Contemporary New Zealand*, Wellington: Allen and Unwin/Port Nicholson Press.

Scott, J. (1988), 'Deconstructing Equality – versus – Difference: or the Uses of Post-structuralist Theory for Feminism', *Feminist Studies*, 14 (1), 33-50.

Taub, N. and Williams, W.W. (1985), 'Will Equality Require More than Assimilation, Accommodation or Separation from the Existing Social Structure?' *Rutgers Law Review*, 37 (4/1), 825-844.

13

A Reasonable Request? A Reasonable Response? EEO and Cost-Benefit Analysis

Rae Torrie

Introduction

As we have moved into the era of arguing the business imperative for EEO, practitioners have been confronted by a clamour of calls for a 'cost-benefit' analysis of individual EEO activities or of the entire EEO programme.

This chapter attempts to 'deconstruct' this trend. It begins by backgrounding the EEO environment in the state sector in which the call for cost-benefit analysis has emerged. This chapter aims to clarify what is actually being asked for and to demystify and simplify the whole issue of costs and benefits. Additionally it provides some strategies for dealing with requests for this type of information. For the future I suggest that as organisations begin to understand and practice EEO as an integral part of their business, the discussion of the costs and benefits of EEO will be located in a broader awareness of strategic human resource development.

Background

Since 1984 successive governments have radically reshaped New Zealand's economy. In the state sector, government economic policies have been backed by the legislative imperatives of the State Sector Act 1988 and the Public Finance Act 1989 to create workplaces with a focus on increased efficiency and productivity. Add the rise of managerialism, total quality management (TQM), and workplace reform initiatives and the environment in which EEO is practised has changed markedly in the last decade.

Requests to cost an EEO programme and to measure the benefits of these programmes in monetary terms have arisen, in part, because of this general pressure on all work practices to become more efficient and effective. Another reason however, is the way in which EEO was initially approached by departments, as an 'add-on' rather than part of the business of the organisation. With the passing of the State Sector Act in 1988 each chief executive was required to develop a departmental EEO programme. However, unlike other areas of government activity, EEO was neither taken seriously nor given much priority in many organisations. EEO was seen as peripheral to, and a cost on the 'real' work of the department, rather than a strategy to assist in achieving its business goals. So in the early 1990s EEO became one of a number of 'projects' within departments competing for limited discretionary capital.

My own experience of dealing with EEO cost-benefit requests is useful in illustrating how the nature of requests has changed over time. I worked as the sole EEO practitioner in the Ministry of Commerce in Wellington from August 1989 to September 1992. In my first annual negotiation of the EEO budget, I advised that the EEO programme would likely be a significant up-front cost for the Ministry. However, I also argued that initiatives such as EEO training for all staff needed to be seen as a long-term investment, with savings that would be realised over time in such benefits as reduced absenteeism and a more productive and committed workforce (Torrie, 1991).

At first this argument of short-term costs and long-term gains was sufficient. However, as pressure grew in the state sector for increased and measurable productivity in all aspects of the organisation's business it was no longer sufficient. A microscope was placed on all corporate activities (including EEO) in an attempt to make savings in areas which did not directly or obviously contribute to the Ministry's core outputs. While not specifically required by management to 'prove' the monetary long-term benefits of EEO, justification in monetary terms was sought for particular activities, such as the development of a childcare programme.

Such justification in monetary terms was sought from other EEO practitioners on a range of different aspects of their EEO programmes. For example, cost-benefit analysis was requested on the establishment of procedures for dealing with sexual harassment, and for career development courses for one of the EEO-designated groups.

In other organisations the call for a cost-benefit analysis was of the entire EEO programme. One department which was in the process of restructuring asked the EEO practitioner for an in-depth cost-benefit analysis of EEO over 'x' number of years, apparently for use as the basis for a decision about the level of resources (if any) that would be committed to EEO in future.

This preoccupation with the cost-benefit analysis of EEO has not been limited to New Zealand. As Australian Clare Burton notes:

> The task of implementing Equal Employment Opportunity (EEO) programs at times seems so daunting, and the benefits so intangible, that some have sought justification of EEO programs in the simplest terms available, on financial grounds (1991, p.1).

EEO practitioners in the United Kingdom and the United States have also experienced similar demands.

Several overseas writers have attempted to grapple with this vexed question of EEO cost-benefits. In Australia Burton has argued that 'it may be possible to make some estimates which give an approximate indication of the economic impact of EEO programs' (1991, p.1). However, fellow Australians Poiner and Wills (1991) identify the difficulties of tracing the sources of increase in labour productivity and therefore, of assessing the benefits of EEO. United States commentators have also devoted some attention to understanding the economic impact of EEO programmes and their findings are discussed in more detail below. However, first, we need to look closely at the term 'cost-benefit analysis' and at the general field of human resource accounting as both relate to EEO.

Making Sense of Costs and Benefits

So where does one start when faced with such a request? Is it possible to measure the financial gains or benefits of an EEO activity or programme against the cost: in short, some form of cost-benefit analysis of EEO? The framework or idea of weighing the cost of an EEO activity against its benefits is a useful one, but the reality of attempting to accurately measure the benefits is problematic.

Cost-benefit analysis is an accounting term and refers to a purely technical method of translating particular activities into equivalent monetary values and assessing the costs against the benefits. Measuring the cost side of an EEO programme or a specific EEO activity is relatively simple. Organisational accounting systems for measuring costs are quite sophisticated. There are the direct costs, such as the costs of consultants, materials to be purchased and the salary of the EEO practitioner; and the indirect costs, such as the equivalent salaries of staff who participate in the activity, or the cost of overheads such as the lease of the room or the cost of heat and lighting.

Measuring the benefits of an EEO programme or activity is less simple. In essence there are two possible approaches; measuring the cost of *not* doing EEO and measuring the benefits to the organisation of implementing EEO.

The first way is to measure the cost of not doing EEO. Direct costs will occur to organisations if they are charged under statute about workplace discrimination (Cull, 1991). This can include fines, monetary settlements, legal fees, etc. *The Human Rights Commission vs Air New Zealand* case is one of the clearest examples of this. The award for damages for the seventeen women concerned was referred to the High Court because the amounts involved were in excess of the $12,000 limit of the Equal Opportunities Tribunal (Human Rights Commission, 1990, p.7). Another way of measuring the cost of not doing EEO is to measure the cost of lost opportunities. High turnover of staff in an organisation can be indicative of discrimination in the workplace. In the US the cost of replacing 'a skilled manager can cost an organisation around 93 per cent of an annual salary in recruitment, training, and learning curve costs' (Knight, 1991, p.2). In New Zealand the Treasury and the Inland Revenue Department have calculated that it costs an average of $18,000 to employ a new analyst (Lampe, 1993, p.6).

The second approach to measuring the benefits of EEO is to assess how these will accrue to organisational outcomes such as reduced absenteeism and turnover. Substantial research has been conducted on cost-benefit analysis in some areas of EEO activity, particularly family-friendly programmes, in the United States and the United Kingdom. In a recent visit to New Zealand, Arlene Johnson of the Work and Family Institute in New York advised of two studies that looked at the effects of work/family programmes on non-traditional measures of productivity. These studies proved that such programmes enhanced the employee's ability to be psychologically present at work, to be creative, innovative, to be better able to work in teams and to be comfortable with change. Furthermore, some programmes were simply easier to measure when the costs and benefits were made explicit; with emergency childcare provisions, for example, where it is clear a cost is incurred through parents being unable to attend work (Families and Work Institute, 1993; Lambert, 1993).

Other areas of EEO however, have proved difficult to measure. Accountants argue that it is possible to ascribe some value or dollars to any behaviour or practice, so an exploration of the field of human resource accounting (HRA) is a necessary adjunct to this discussion.

HRA is a particular branch of accounting that has emerged to deal with measuring this type of information. HRA is a collaboration between accounting and behavioural science and has been designed to develop concepts and methods of accounting for people as assets. It is, at least in part, a recognition that the skills, experience, and knowledge that people possess are assets that can be termed human capital. One of the primary purposes of HRA is to help management plan and control the use of human resources effectively and efficiently (Flamholtz, 1985; Pallot, 1990).

So where does one start when faced with a request for a cost-benefit analysis of EEO? Is it possible to measure the financial gains or benefits of an EEO activity or programme against the cost? HRA has been used to attempt cost-benefit analysis of EEO activities. Such an analysis may be useful as it can help justify the implementation of EEO programmes and other human resource initiatives. However, the reality of attempting to accurately measure the benefits of EEO is problematic.

At first glance HRA appears to offer hope for analysing such information and measuring the benefits of EEO. However, there are two major difficulties with HRA when it is applied to EEO. First, it is difficult to isolate the specific reason for improved productivity, and whether this can be tied to an EEO initiative. Poiner and Wills (1991, p. 28) argue that:

> The first difficulty in determining whether EEO/AA [Affirmative Action] programs have achieved anything derives from the impossibility of isolating those programs from other programs and from general movements. If change (using whatever indices we might agree on) has occurred we can never say that it was the result of the AA programs and those programs alone.

The second difficulty relates to problems in ascribing monetary value. Take the issue of reduced turnover for example. It is very difficult to weight and ascribe a monetary value to the different factors which may influence why people choose to stay in the organisation. These reasons may range across a variety of areas; promotion, family-friendly initiatives, personal support, sexual harassment procedures, personal interest, and transparent and rigorous human resource practices. Even where it is possible to be precise, the cost to an organisation of collecting and analysing this information would be prohibitive. Until the accounting systems in departments are developed to address such issues, it will be difficult for EEO practitioners to 'prove' justification for a particular activity using a cost-benefit analysis approach. Currently measures are too crude.

There are a few areas of EEO activity where it is possible to measure or argue effectively in cost-benefit terms. These are where sufficient investment has been made in research or where anti-discrimination legislation makes not addressing the issue a high-risk activity. Two of the most obvious examples of this are family-friendly programmes and programmes to address sexual harassment. Burton, in a preliminary analysis of the economic impact of these two EEO initiatives, reached this conclusion:

> ... a prima facie case can be made that Equal Employment Opportunity programs *of the type and scale described* [in the paper] at least recover their costs, as well, of course, as seeking to meet important equity objectives (1991, p.6). (My emphasis).

However, many areas of EEO activity are not as easy to measure. How does one differentiate between an activity that can be measured and that which cannot? Furthermore, what is the process for dealing with requests for a cost-benefit analysis when the identified EEO activity does not obviously lend itself to such an analysis? The next section provides some guidelines as to how to deal with requests for cost-benefit analyses of EEO activities. These strategies may help to provoke discussion and debate about these issues and about the underlying agendas of those requesting EEO cost-benefit analysis.

Strategy and Questions

So you are confronted with a request to present to management a cost-benefit analysis of your EEO programme or an EEO activity. Where do you start?

The strategy comprises two main parts. The first is to be clear about the request. In my experience a cost-benefit analysis of an EEO programme or activity is often asked for to address a perceived problem that has not been clearly identified. Being clear about the request involves asking a number of critical questions.

• What are they asking *for*?

As I have noted earlier in this chapter, cost-benefit analysis is an accounting term with a technical meaning. Is this what is required, or is a discussion of the likely costs and benefits of the EEO activity in social, organisational, developmental, as well as financial terms, what is intended? Ensure that you get a clear brief and ask for further detail or specificity if necessary.

• *Why* are they seeking this information?

Is this a legitimate query that is being asked of other areas of the organisation or is EEO the one area of government activity being singled out? Is EEO being made the whipping girl for other organisational initiatives which have failed? Check that the call for a cost-benefit analysis is not a strategy for blocking that project. Understanding the reasons the information is being sought can assist in determining how to respond.

Without being paranoid, it is important to consider that one of the reasons might be to limit the role and authority of the EEO practitioner, or to keep her or him busy. Johnson (1993) noted that in the United

States EEO jobs are more clearly defined and bounded by legislation. In New Zealand the jobs are broader, more difficult, less defined, and the EEO practitioner has the opportunity to play many roles – censors for organisations, visionaries, change agents and bridge-builders. These activities do not always meet with favour!

• Is it possible to provide this information about your organisation?

Does your Human Resource Management Information Service collect sufficient information on staff – are the systems in place, are they sufficiently sophisticated to extract the information you require? Is this information regularly monitored and easily accessible?

• Is there research which has been conducted nationally and internationally on this issue?

If not, is it possible to contract or encourage new research which explores the linkage between productivity and human resource policies and practices on this, or any other issue?

• Is it possible to provide the type of analysis being requested?

The second part of the strategy is to locate the request for a cost-benefit analysis of an EEO activity within an organisational and business context and to make explicit the connectedness and interrelationship of EEO with organisational goals. At the bottom line, departments are concerned with achieving their outputs, i.e. with productivity. It is critical that organisations recognise that their biggest asset in the productivity equation is their people. EEO is aimed at redressing discrimination which inhibits performance and at establishing an environment in which people are encouraged and enabled to reach their full potential. It needs to be acknowledged that *not* doing anything or not addressing the issue, is costly. The request for a cost-benefit analysis must be considered in this context.

One of the most important requisite skills for EEO practitioners is the ability to 'see' EEO activities and programmes as tools for achieving organisational objectives by most efficiently and effectively utilising the workforce available. It is vital to remember that this does not mean inducing burn-out in staff. Greater productivity is achieved by people who lead balanced lives, who are not over-stressed, and who are valued and recognised in their workplace. The increased facility which EEO practitioners have had to develop in analysing organisational information makes it possible to use these techniques and skills to pinpoint problem pockets and suggest action that might be taken. For example, if there is a high level of staff turnover in a particular work area, the manager can be given a rough estimate of the cost and encouraged to try some EEO strategies to solve the problem, 'You have nothing to lose – try this!'.

The other key skill for EEO practitioners is the ability to convey and argue this vision. Many strategic planners and managers are able to see organisational goals but often cannot see the relevance of EEO to those goals. Making the links explicit is one of the vital roles of EEO practitioners.

In the past couple of years in the state sector some understanding has developed of the way in which a department's human resource strategy and EEO programme is tied to the business of the organisation. Recent discussions with chief executives about their progress with EEO has emphasised the way that EEO strategies can assist in achieving overall strategic goals. As the level of understanding about strategic human resource development increases, it is my expectation that the attempts to reduce an EEO activity or programme to purely financial terms will decline.

Conclusion

Initial requests in the state sector for cost-benefit analyses of EEO grew out of increasing pressure on departments to become more productive and efficient within current funding, and out of the way EEO developed as an 'add-on' to core organisational activities. Many of these cost-benefit requests were unrealistic, asking for a standard of proof or rigour not required in other parts of the business. In many cases there simply was not sufficient data nor techniques available to fulfil the request, and attempting to collect the required information would have been at an exorbitant cost.

The strategy outlined in the paper for dealing with such cost-benefit challenges is essentially a method for 'seeing' an EEO activity or programme in the context of the organisation's strategic direction and goals. The challenge to make a business case for EEO has put EEO practitioners in the vanguard of thinking about strategic human resource development and achieving a high level of rigour and analysis in planning and monitoring human resource practice (see Burns chapter).

It is my view that as organisations begin to recognise the ways in which their human resource strategy and EEO programmes dovetail with their organisational objectives, there will be less call to seek justification of EEO programmes on purely financial grounds. In the meantime EEO practitioners should be aware of the issues around the requests for cost-benefit analysis and be ready to respond.

Note

The views expressed in this chapter are those of the author and are not necessarily those of the State Services Commission.

References

Burton, C. (October, 1991), 'EEO at the Dingo Fence Maintenance Authority' Unpublished paper, Sydney.

Cull, H. (1991), 'What Penalties and Damages do Employers Face – Recent Rulings from the Equal Opportunities Tribunal and the Labour Court'. Paper presented to the Preventing Discrimination in the Workplace Conference, Wellington, 11 March.

Families and Work Institute (April, 1993), *An Evaluation of Johnson and Johnson's Work-Family Initiative*, New York: Families and Work Institute.

Flamholtz, E. (1985), *Human Resource Accounting*, San-Francisco: Jossey-Bass.

Human Rights Commission (February, 1990), *The Human Rights Commission vs Air New Zealand*, Wellington: Human Rights Commission.

Johnson, A. (1993), Presentation to EEO Practitioners at the State Services Commission, 23 June.

Knight, A. (1991), 'Addressing Employment Equity in the Current Climate'. Paper presented to the Labour Relations Reform Conference, Auckland, 11 April.

Lambert, S.J. (1993), 'Added Benefits in the Link Between Family-Responsive Policies and Work Performance at Fel-Pro Inc.', unpublished report, School of Social Service Administration, University of Chicago.

Lampe, C. (1993), *The Design and Management of Part-time Work Within the Public Service – a Resource for Managers*, Wellington: State Services Commission.

Pallot, J. (1990), 'Pitfalls and Potential: Human Resource Accounting in the Public Sector', *Public Sector*, 13 (2), 10-13.

Poiner, G. and Wills, S. (1991), *The Gifthorse: a Critical Look at EEO in Australia*, Sydney: Allen and Unwin.

Torrie, R. (1991), 'Measuring the Costs and Benefits of EEO', unpublished paper, State Services Commission, Wellington.

14

What Price Educational and Industrial Reform? EEO for Women in Education in the 1990s

Marian Court

The contention is that equal work merits equal pay, therefore our first enquiry must be: what is the comparative value of the work... Men are no more ambitious to teach infants than they are to teach sewing. By one of the stupid conventions governing the world it is assumed that all women can fulfil both these duties, while no man may be supposed capable of either ... (Miss Bain, Southland Educational Institute, August 1893).

Introduction

This chapter examines the issues surrounding EEO and women in the education sector in the 1990s. Inequalities, such as those identified by Miss Bain 100 years ago, between men and women in teaching still exist despite equal pay and equal employment opportunities legislation. Some reasons for the persistence of these problems are identified. Issues such as resource allocation and the perceived status differential between administrative and teaching functions are illustrated in the light of both industrial and educational reform. This chapter argues that EEO has been difficult to advance in an environment which ignores or sidelines equity issues as being tainted with the evils of 'social engineering' and where equity in education is expected to arise out of natural market forces,

Background

During the late 1970s and the 1980s, as part of the second wave of the women's movement and within largely liberal feminist strategies, increased efforts by women to improve their position and working conditions resulted in several gains (Steele, 1981; Watson, 1988; 1989).

However, after a wave of 1988 policy initiatives – the introduction of the State Sector Act and the publication of both the *Picot Report* and *Tomorrow's Schools* – many women expressed fears about the possible negative effects on women teachers of the devolution of educational administration within the context of free-market economic policies and industrial relations. For example, Travers (1989, p.36) argued that under Tomorrow's Schools women would have to:

> ... fight all over again to win rights such as maternity leave provisions, permanent part-time work, domestic leave (for caring for family members), preference to get a job back after childcare leave. Women will be negotiating with predominantly male Boards of Trustees for such rights, and without the right to compulsory arbitration, since the State Sector Act removes this right (s75). History has shown that women have rarely won in negotiating situations with employers under so-called neutral conditions... and some women may not even get to the negotiating stage ... the employing Boards will prefer to employ men for the very reason that they will not press for the same conditions of service which women need.

Some of these fears may have been allayed by the passing of the State Sector Amendment Act 1989. Boards of Trustees were required in this Act to put in place equal employment opportunities policies and programmes, to be 'good employers', and to specifically address 'the employment needs of women' (s77D). Women, along with Maori, people of ethnic and other minorities, and people with disabilities, were to be the beneficiaries of programmes which would aim to remove discrimination in employment policies and practices. School charters would include specific equity goals for both equal educational opportunity and equal employment opportunity.

However, since 1989, contradictions inherent in equal employment opportunities legislation have been identified and political commitment to equity concerns has been superseded by an emphasis on competition. Further, gender gaps in pay and status across the whole of the labour market have not been eliminated. In fact, in February 1993, 'for the first time labour force statistics showed a slight widening of the gender pay gap' (Hill, 1993, p.101).

Although in education equal pay for women and men in the same positions exists in theory, in reality men as a group still earn more than women as a group across all sectors of this workforce. When we consider the present position of women in relation to that of men working in the field of education, it appears that there have been few enduring gains made for women, despite some improvements following EEO legislation and affirmative action programmes in the 1980s.

Where are Women Currently Placed in the Teaching Services?

Surveys across the education sectors show that the gendered nature of a teaching hierarchy, from early childhood to tertiary workforces, is not breaking down. In fact, the differences are becoming increasingly marked.

In the area of early childhood education (including kohanga reo and Pacific Island language nests), the area of least pay and ascribed low status, women still make up the huge majority of workers. For example, women make up 99 per cent of kindergarten teachers. The proportion of women in the primary, secondary and college of education teaching workforces has been steadily *increasing* over the last decade, while in polytechnics and universities the proportion of women has *decreased* during the last two years. In 1992 78 per cent of primary teachers were women (up on 76 per cent in 1990); 51 per cent of secondary (50 per cent in 1990); and 60 per cent in colleges of education (49 per cent in 1990). In polytechnics 40 per cent of teachers were women (down from 41 per cent in 1990) and 24 per cent in universities (down from 28 per cent in 1990) (Slyfield, 1992; 1993).

What factors contribute to this situation? Why have there been so few gains for women? The rest of this chapter discusses issues related to who controls knowledge dissemination and creation, the continued status gap between teaching and administration, equal pay and issues related to Maori and education, particularly in the critical early childhood sector of employment.

Knowledge Dissemination and Creation

There has been an increased feminisation of the teaching workforce in areas where it is commonly perceived that knowledge is *disseminated*, while women are losing ground in the traditional areas of knowledge *creation* (the universities and increasingly polytechnics). History has shown how women's contribution to knowledge has been overlooked and marginalised (Spender, 1982). If attempts to change persisting and destructive gendered inequalities in education (and indeed in society as a whole) are to be successful, women must be fully represented in all areas of knowledge creation, especially in universities – the traditional centres of control over knowledge discourses.

Of particular concern here is the silencing of tangata whenua women. As a consequence of colonising practices in Aotearoa/New Zealand, their voices have been marginalised in dominant knowledge discourses. The distribution of Maori staff in 1990, as shown in the following table, reveals their under-representation, on a population basis, as employees in most branches of education.

Table 14.1:
Distribution of Maori Teaching Staff by Branch
1 March 1992

Branch	Proportion of Staff who are Maori
Kindergarten	4.5%
Primary	7.0%
Area	14.1%
Secondary	5.5%
Polytechnic	7.0%
College of Education	12.5%
TOTAL	6.5%

Source: Dunn *et al.*, 1992, p.23.

In 1987 there were only 48 academic Maori staff in New Zealand universities (Pohatu, 1988). Maori women then held only four senior lecturer positions, eight lecturer positions and two assistant lecturer positions.

Until very recently, little space or resources have been given to Maori to enable them to develop and disseminate their knowledge within state educational institutions. The education developed and practised within Pakeha views of reality, has clearly controlled and limited the participation and achievement of tangata whenua. In 1993 however, there are a growing number of Maori challenging this situation. Maori women in particular are working from 'a diverse range of cultural considerations' to describe and analyse 'differences which count' for them; and are attempting to invert dominant discourses (of both white patriarchies and white feminisms) and assert 'our own definitions as opposed to those constructed outside of us, and re-present our realities through analyses in which we are at the centre' (ibid.). This work has the potential to dramatically alter the monocultural nature of education and the work of teachers in this country (Johnston and Pihama, 1993, p.18).

The experiences of Maori women in education illustrate how there are not only differences between the experiences and status of women and men, but also between different groups of women within education. This needs to be kept in mind as we consider the gendered nature of educational work.

Gendered distinctions exist both *across* the education sectors and *within* each part of the service, operating on both vertical and horizontal planes. In particular, sexual divisions of labour result in women and men often being segregated into different *kinds* of work which are also *valued* differently. The resulting dynamics not only affect the working conditions and career opportunities of many women, but also restrict women's opportunities to bring about change. An example from within universities may elucidate this dynamic. A recent survey of academic staff confirms earlier local and international findings that women in universities are more heavily involved in teaching than in research and publication (Vasil, 1993). Research and publication are significant knowledge creation and legitimation activities, and opportunities for involvement here can be jeopardised when women take on (or are given) heavy commitments in teaching. Research and publication have also been accorded more weight than teaching for academic staff promotion. Despite recent trends to officially value teaching equally, the long-held status of research and publications continues. So, if women are not enabled to undertake more research and writing, not only are women's voices silenced in those areas, but their individual careers suffer. A further consequence is that women are likely to remain heavily underrepresented in the universities' spheres of authority and decision-making and thus marginalised in the processes of policy formation and resource allocation. This, of course, impacts on wider groups of women both within and outside the university.

The Teaching/Administration Divide

Value distinctions between the work of men and that of women in the educational services can be illustrated by looking at their relative placements within career hierarchies. Men still dominate the 'top' leadership positions while more women are placed in the 'lower' levels of teaching/administration hierarchies. The following tables detail the position of women teachers relative to those of men in primary schools, secondary schools and universities.

Table 14.2:
Distribution of Primary School Teaching Staff by Gender,
1 March 1992

	Female	Male	% Female
Designation			
Principal	595	1582	27
Deputy Principal/Assistant Principal, 2nd Deputy Principal	1350	853	61
Senior Teacher	1274	495	72
Teacher	14022	1978	88
Other	123	17	88
Tenure			
Permanent and Provisional	12274	4538	73
Part-time	3767	175	96
Relieving	1323	212	86
Total	17364	4925	78
Mean Age (as at 1 July 1992)	40.7	42.9	
Mean Salary ($ permanent)	32828	39008	

(Slyfield, 1993, p.22)

Table 14.3:
Distribution of Secondary School Teaching Staff by Gender, 1 March 1992

	Female	Male	% Female
Designation			
Principal	59	257	19
Deputy Principal	126	253	33
Assistant Principal, 2nd Principal, Senior Mistress	155	113	58
Position of Responsibility, Head of Department, Senior Teacher	2090	3189	40
Teacher	5888	4213	58
Other	23	4	85
Tenure			
Permanent and Provisional	5579	6912	45
Part-time	2351	907	72
Relieving	411	210	66
Total	8341	8029	51
Mean Age (as at 1 July 1992)	41.5	42.1	
Mean Salary ($ permanent)	41025	43640	

(Slyfield, 1993, p.23)

Table 14.4:
Distribution of University Teaching Staff by Gender, 1 March 1991

	Female	Male	% Female
Designation			
Vice Chancellor/Deputy VC	1	17	6
Professor	16	384	4
Associate Professor/Reader	36	379	9
Senior Lecturer/Senior Tutor	283	1548	15
Lecturer/Tutor	588	755	44
Assistant Lecturer	220	239	48
Other	28	27	51
Employment			
Full-time	857	2664	24
Part-time	315	685	31
Total	1172	3349	26

(Slyfield, 1993, p.24)

Over the last five years, there has been little change in the proportion of women holding principals' positions, in both primary and secondary schools. In 1992 there were still only three per cent of women teachers who were principals in primary schools, while 32 per cent of men in the primary service held principals' positions. Women remain more heavily represented in the smaller school positions, while most of the G4 and G5 large city primary schools have male principals. In 1992 only 15 of the 220 state and integrated co-educational secondary schools (seven per cent) had principals who were women (Slyfield, 1993).

Thus, although there has been a slight improvement in both applications and appointments of women at the lower levels of primary and secondary positions of responsibility, this improvement is not 'trickling up' as many have maintained would happen. Between March 1989 and March 1991 only three women, in comparison with 20 men, were appointed to principals' positions in secondary schools (Slyfield, 1993). Women's applications and appointments to the 'top' principals' positions in the primary service are fewer than men (despite the fact that women make up 76 per cent of the primary service). It is worth noting here that an advertisement for one of these G5 positions, which stated, 'Applicants must demonstrate a commitment to equity in education and equal employment opportunities', had 15 women applicants and nine men, while the median number of applicants for all G5 positions was one for women and 14 for men (Slyfield, 1993, p.15). An influence on women's applications is their own (realistic) appraisal of their chances of positive consideration.

If we examine the secondary service in more detail we can tease out some of the ways gendered dichotomies and value distinctions work against women teachers. In this sector, the distinctions made between the so-called soft areas of the curriculum (e.g. humanities, arts, typing, home economics) where many women teach, and the hard areas (such as maths, physics, chemistry, engineering and technology) which are more often taught by men, are reflected in the different responsibility levels and monetary rewards often allocated to people heading these different department areas (see O'Neill (1992) for an analysis of the historical development of these gendered distinctions). For example, heads of departments in home economics, typing or social studies have been more likely to be awarded a PR1 or PR2 status. PR3 and PR4 status has been more commonly given to heads of maths, science/physics, technical departments, or to those with responsibility in administration. A PR1 position is the first step on the career ladder into senior administration positions.

Another distinction is the lower value given to the work of nurturing, as in pastoral care, (e.g. in dean's work in secondary schools) in comparison to the 'technical' (and until recently male-dominated) work of timetabling or the managing of aspects of the school's finances. Working in pastoral care positions such as guidance and counselling has been considered to be a stuck career route for secondary teachers, from which it has been difficult to gain promotion, while the technical tasks have been considered as administration apprentice experience (Neville, 1988). There are links here between the so-called male areas of work and career advancement in education (Court, 1992).

The Equal Pay Myth

The fact that more men advance up educational career ladders than women results in some marked gender differences in average salaries for men and women. It is somewhat misleading then to assume that equal pay for men and women in education exists. Although within each sector, particular steps on salary scales are paid the same, regardless of whether the teacher is male or female, when the figures for mean and average annual salaries are compared, men, as a group, are paid more than women as a group. This reflects not only their representation in more of the management and senior positions within each sector, but also men's concentration in the higher status areas (working with older learners) in the secondary and tertiary sectors, rather than in the primary and early childhood sectors.

For many women working in the early childhood sector, the issue of women earning less than men is allied to that of the low status of early childhood education in relation to the other education sectors. Dunn *et al.* (1992, p.35) point out that:

> As kindergarten teaching has remained an overwhelmingly female domain, this highlights a serious issue of gender-related income inequity for this branch of the teaching service.

The average salaries for teachers in 1990 were as follows: kindergarten – $28,371; primary – $34,697; secondary – $42,671; $45,138 in polytechnics; and $47,460 in colleges of education. Despite the fact that most university teachers are required to gain graduate qualifications, the difference between the status and incomes of women in the top positions in early childhood education and that of those in university professorships is stark. In 1993 a kindergarten senior teacher (working with Associations and many kindergartens, and carrying responsibilities in policy, staffing decisions, professional development and advice on curriculum development) could earn between $38,668 – $41,858. A university education professor (responsible for a department's policy, staffing decisions and professional development and development of research in education) could earn between $80,000 –$99,000. Miss Bain's question of 100 years ago is worth asking again here: 'What is the comparative value of the work?'.

Within the early childhood sector, there are also differences in the resourcing and remuneration of those working in particular sections (such as those of kindergarten, childcare, playcentre, kohanga reo and Pacific Island language nest centres). The huge amount of voluntary assistance given in these centres is not reflected or taken into consideration in official reports on the labour force in the various centres and it is largely women who work in these ways. Further, differential funding has placed a heavier burden on Maori women (and those of Pacific Island descent).

The ways in which factors of ethnicity and socio-economic status compound gendered factors can be illustrated in the experiences of those involved in the development of kohanga reo. The first kohanga reo opened in 1982. In 1991 there were 630 kohanga reo in operation, with the enrolment of Maori children having more than doubled from 4,132 in 1983 to 10,451 in 1991 (Davies and Nicholl, 1993, p.27). The huge increase in centres, all of which 'are based on the concept of whanau', was made possible by the unpaid work of many Maori women (Ministry of Women's Affairs, 1990, p.20). Irwin states that Maori women were significant in leading the movement from their positions of being 'the people at the cutting edge of social and cultural development' (Irwin, 1992, p.86). For all Maori working in kohanga reo, issues of cultural and language survival and development are inextricably bound up in political struggles (with Pakeha) over who makes the decisions. As Johnson (1993, p.3) argues, 'In order for Te Kohanga Reo to be of any value and worthwhile for Maori interests and aspirations, Kohanga had to be controlled, defined and legitimated by Maori for Maori'.

Johnson argues that within present interpretations of the Treaty of Waitangi as a 'partnership' document, the rights of Maori as tangata whenua have been overshadowed, with the 'partnership between Maori and Pakeha being defined on Pakeha terms and proceeding only as far as Pakeha will allow it to' (ibid., p.5). Struggling under severe financial hardships to support te kohanga reo outside the state system, Maori agreed to the movement's legitimation under the 1990 Education Amendment Act, 'bringing it into line with the various other pre-school facilities' (ibid., p.9). In Johnston's view, this has been at a cost for Maori, with integration into the state system meaning that accountability structures have reversed. Rather than decision-making and policy coming from the 'grass roots' of the parents and whanau of each kohanga, policy is now handed down from the Ministry. Accountability is now also required by Social Welfare through the Income Support Services subsidies that some kohanga reo centres receive for their children. Here, Johnson (ibid., p.12) points out that:

> The criteria for the Income Support Subsidy will exclude many Maori parents from access to the finance which they will need to pay for their children's fees at Kohanga Reo .... The emphasis of the changes is 'retraining' and employment for parents encompassed within the notion that Te Kohanga Reo is a childhood care facility which will look after the children of parents who retrain and are 're-educated' (to enter the workforce).

This example illustrates how the situations and experiences of Maori women working within education cannot be equated with the position and experiences of Pakeha women. The issues of gender are complicated and compounded by those of culture and tino rangitiratanga and struggles for resources. As Johnston and Pihama (1993) point out, within a Pakeha system, those whom the dominant group define as 'different' have to constantly justify their very existence, let alone their claims for equity.

Equity and EEO: Where to in the 1990s?

Under the Employment Equity Act 1990, the female-dominated areas of the education workforce (early childhood and primary) could have sought parity with the secondary and tertiary sectors. However, it is clear that pay equity would have been at a cost to employers, and groups such as the Business Roundtable focused their efforts on defeating this legislation. Hill (1993, pp.100-101) argues that submissions made to the incoming National government in 1990 were:

> ... framed in terms of costs to an economy in recession ... and part of a more general lobby for a deregulated more competitive labour market and enterprise based bargaining. Employers' organisations not only opposed a state-regulated increase in women's wages, but were seeking a shift to wage rates determined by competition, market forces and an employer's ability to pay.

The National government accepted these views and argued that the introduction of pay equity legislation was not a necessary intervention on the part of the state to achieve social justice in labour relations. Rather, it was an unacceptable form of 'social engineering' that would interfere with individual rights and the working of a 'free' market. The Employment Equity Act was repealed within three months of the new government taking office and work began on the introduction of the Employment Contracts Act 1991.

However, the EEO requirements in the State Sector Amendment Act 1989 were retained. Although there was much discussion about this at the time and the Minister of Education suggested making the equity goals of the school charters optional, these moves did not eventuate.

At least part of the reason for the retention of EEO requirements appears to be that EEO was not a threat to the dominant market discourse. That is, EEO strategies could be used to 'enhance the business' and could be accommodated by employers within particular labour market sectors. Unlike pay equity, EEO does not challenge the economic bases and financially discriminatory nature of gender-segregated labour markets (for example, it will not challenge the different pay scales between early childhood and other sectors in education, or the higher rates paid for management positions in relation to those paid to teachers). Pay equity had the potential to alter these long entrenched differentials in salary packages and could, in the short term, have cost employers some considerable amounts of money. It is not surprising then, that the pay equity legislation was quickly repealed under the National government.

Although EEO legislation was not removed, the way the law has been framed has been problematic for women from the start. Embedded in the State Sector Act there is a contradiction that reflects the liberal dualism between 'the public sphere of the market and the private sphere of the household/family' and between 'two different *kinds* of "human nature"' (Else, 1992, pp.240-242), that is, between traditional conceptions of 'market man' and 'family woman'. Within this framework, employers are required to provide for 'the employment needs of women'. Unnamed here is women's delegated primary responsibility for childcare and the persisting assumption that it is women, not men, who 'choose' to be responsible for childcare. Thus equal opportunities for women in educational institutions can be interpreted as meaning only that ways have to be found by employing agencies (boards of trustees) to provide 'flexible' working arrangements so that women can fit the care of their children around their paid employment.

Although equal employment opportunities legislation has remained, it has little visibility in education. There is a requirement for institutions to annually report to the Minister of Education (through the Education Review Office) on their implementation of EEO policies and programmes, but there are no real sanctions against those who do nothing. The history of the EEO personnel in the Education Review Office illustrates a political lack of commitment to EEO. Thirteen EEO Review Officers were appointed when the Review Office was established in late 1989. In 1991 their titles were changed to Personnel Reviewers, signalling a removal of their specialist focus. In 1993 these positions were dis-established. These changes occurred within two staffing cutbacks in the Education Review Office in response to government fiscal requirements. However, the removal of the EEO Reviewers' specialist positions was also related to ideological forces which 'saw EEO as an issue best pursued voluntarily' (Hill, 1993, p.103).

The removal of the EEO Reviewers also needs to be placed in the context of other cutbacks in areas where women had gained some ground for collectively identifying and voicing concerns about learning and work contexts for girls and women in education. In 1991 the Women's Advisory Committee on Women and Girls was disestablished. This was followed by the splitting up of the Girls' and Women's Section of the Ministry of Education which took effect in 1993. In late 1993 the EEO Officer in the Ministry of Education left her job and at the time of writing, this position had not yet been advertised. These changes have occurred relatively quietly, with little public attention being drawn to them.

In the early days of my experience as an EEO Reviewer in the newly established Education Review Office, reviewers were often asked by teachers and board members for advice and assistance in developing their policies and programmes. It seemed then that there were many people interested in developing change in this area. However, after the National government took office, it was not long before a strong statement was issued to us that the Minister of Education was the primary client of the Office. Reviewers were told that school reviews were an output of the Review Office; reviews were being purchased by the state under the terms of the Chief Executive Officer's contract and the Office's Corporate Plan. Thus, reviewers' responsibilities were to serve 'the Crown's interest in education (as investor and purchaser)' (Education Review Office, 1992, p.4). It was expected that reviewers, many of whom were ex-teachers and Department of Education inspectors, would shift their stance from that of working with teachers in a collegial model of co-operative review and assistance, to one of external 'objective' reporters to their primary client, the Minister of Education.

Given the change of emphasis in the Review Office's view of its role, and the Minister of Education's attitude in 1990 that EEO and the equity charter goals could be considered 'not compulsory', it is not surprising to find ambivalence within school boards' implementing of equity requirements in their personnel policies. In the fourth quarter of 1992-3:

> ... 41 per cent of boards of trustees of schools had no policy to address the intent of the Treaty of Waitangi; 43 per cent did not operate a personnel policy that met the principle of being a good employer; 73 per cent had not implemented an equal employment

opportunities programme; 32 per cent had not developed effective procedures to eliminate sexual harassment (Education Review Office, 1993a, p.3).

Furthermore:

[In] free kindergarten associations, 11 of the 14 associations which employ staff in kindergartens, had not complied... with the State Sector Act personnel management provisions. These provide for the fair and proper treatment of employees in all respects of their employment (Education Review Office, 1993b, p.3).

Although in 1992, the Waikato Monitoring Today's Schools Project (Ramsay and Oliver, 1992) found that there seemed to have been a raising of awareness about equity issues (Maori trustees in particular were committed to equity goals and determined to take advantage of the opportunities these afforded for them), few of the equity questions were answered in the Waikato questionnaire survey. From the responses that are discussed in the Equity Report, it is clear that there were both positive and negative opinions about the value of the equity goals. The study found that there had been little evaluation of the implementation of the equity requirements of the school charters. Although the time frame is still perhaps too short to expect that schools will be undertaking self-review of this kind, the ambivalent messages about government's commitment to equity concerns must have influenced boards' prioritising of their efforts within what have been enormous work demands.

The requirements of the Employment Contracts Act have added another confusing dimension to the context of equity issues in education.

The Employment Contracts Act

The various ways the Employment Contracts Act 1991 has accelerated privatisation, contestability, site-based negotiations, competition for 'scarce resources' and a shift of negotiating power towards employers are now becoming clear (Harbridge, 1993). In their analysis of this legislation, Hammond and Harbridge (1993, p.15) point out that one hundred years ago, 'New Zealand was internationally heralded as a "social laboratory" for its determination to achieve equity through a raft of legislation, social and industrial policy developments'. They argue that:

> The introduction of a legal regime based on the principles of collective labour law was an acknowledgement that the earlier regime based upon principles of 'freedom of contract' was an inappropriate mechanism for the governance of the employment relationship. This had been well illustrated in the findings of the 1890 Sweating Commission. 'Freedom of contract', it had found, resulted in the exploitation of many workers, particularly women (p.15).

Hill and Du Plessis (1993) also locate the worsening situation for many women workers in the reviving of contractarian rather than collective labour law. The Employment Contracts Act is grounded in a legal liberalism which assumes that the law provides a neutral mechanism (free from values and particular sets of interests) to support the exercise of individual 'choice' and 'freedom' in market bargaining and negotiation. However, the idea that this kind of free enterprise is the most appropriate for the efficacy of the market and the promoting of a general 'social good', masks the inequalities it both supports and produces –inequalities of gender, ethnicity and class.

In particular, within Western gendered power relations, divisions in the labour market have been constructed in ways that channel many women into 'low-paid, dead-end occupations' (see Hammond and Harbridge, 1993, pp.16-17 for a discussion of these factors). In Aotearoa/ New Zealand, Maori and Pacific Island women are disproportionately located in many of those 'low-paid dead-end occupations' and these are areas where union protection has been largely lost. Hill (1993) has analysed how the introduction of the Employment Contracts Act has impacted on unions' power to negotiate national awards. Many of these awards have been fragmented into enterprise negotiations.

Within the teaching service, the beginning of such fragmenting processes can be detected in the 'picking off' of the kindergartens for the imposing of bulk funding of teachers' salaries. It is not surprising that it is this labour force (made up of 99 per cent women) which has been the first to bear the brunt of bulk funding and attempts to drive down teachers' salaries and working conditions.

This aspect of bulk funding of teachers' salaries is explored in more detail in the next section.

Bulk Funding and Enterprise Bargaining

The 1993-94 Corporate Plan of the Ministry of Education listed the government's fiscal and debt problems and education industrial issues as significant factors that will affect education in the coming year. Equity issues are not mentioned in relation to bulk funding; rather it is stated that in kindergartens and schools, 'a higher degree of enterprise bargaining and greater flexibility in teacher's pay and conditions' is desirable and that 'the devolution of responsibility for industrial matters to school boards in the absence of a grant for teachers' salaries, could have results that are contrary to the government's fiscal objectives' (Ministry of Education, 1993, pp.26-27). The National government's economic and managerialist agendas driving the directions of boards of trustees employer/employee relations are revealed in these statements. The intention is perhaps more clearly expressed in a State Services Commission (1993) document about the bulk-funding of teachers' salaries, which in their view could be a way to:

> ... contain spending in the school sector.... Where teacher salaries are centrally paid for on a 'staffing first' basis, Boards would have few incentives to keep costs down .... The devolution of the Teacher Relief budget to schools at the beginning of 1992 led a number of Boards to re-evaluate their policy in this area. In many cases, this has been successful in keeping costs down (quoted in PPTA, 1993, p.12).

This issue of bulk funding is clearly relevant to EEO issues in the education sector because it has differential effects on groups of disadvantaged workers.

In education we already have a gender-divided service that splits the work of (mainly male) administrators away from that of (mainly female) teachers and support staff. During 1993 the funding and negotiation of contracts for senior management positions (such as principal, deputy principal and assistant principal) was separated from those for other teachers (see NZEI, 1992a; 1992b). This drives a deeper wedge between these two areas of work in schools. Already, many principals (who are mainly men) have won salary increases since 1990. The following maximum increases on a range of rates have been available for boards to give principals (subject to the principal's performance review): 1 July 1990 + 4.04 per cent; June 1991 +0.64 per cent; July 1992 + 6.86 per cent (Middleton, 1993). During these three years however, the salary ranges for teachers (who are mainly women) have stood still. This is a real change in industrial relativities within education, one which reflects the growing emphasis on managerialism as the way to enhance 'the marketplace'.

The introduction of the salaries grant for management and negotiation of a separate collective contract for senior staff in schools has also opened up the way for further attempts to introduce individual contracts for all staff. As yet, the unions of the New Zealand Educational Institute (the primary teachers' union), Post Primary Teachers Association and Association of Staff in Tertiary Education have held off attempts by the State Services Commission to end collective contracts for these groups. These have been hard won victories though, and not without cost to employment conditions of teachers. Some of the changes do not bode well for women in the light of documentation of men's advantages over women in terms of both negotiating power and positions of authority. It is likely that other distinctions between the salaries and conditions of men and women in the education service will occur if site-based bargaining becomes the model for bulk funding of teachers' salaries.

As part of the last round of contract negotiations for primary teachers, annual service increments as of right were lost; these increments are now dependent on yearly appraisals by the principal who is required to attest competent performance. NZEI was required to concede performance appraisal linked to salary increases in the first three years of a principal's appointment (1992a, Section 5.4.2; NZEI 1992b, Section 5.11.1).

Further, within the contract for senior positions, although these staff may have had an excellent appraisal, primary boards are empowered now to grant salary increments for these teachers according to 'whether funding is available for the purpose' (NZEI, 1992b, 5.3.1). That is, boards can now argue that such increments may not be justified within their budget priorities. Thus market factors are now built into recruitment and retention at this level. Boards can determine the initial salary of senior managers on 'the ability of the employer to recruit the specific skill and/or experience required for the job' (Section 5.4.1). They are also able to pay more for some jobs/people according to the board's 'ability to *retain* the specific skills/experience required for the job' (Section 5.5.1). Given the predominance of women in skill and subject areas that are not considered as an appropriate 'training ground' for management, that men are the relatively 'scarce resource' in primary teaching and that there is a prevalent perception that the particular skills required for management are more likely to be held by men than women, it is easy to see how these clauses could work heavily against women in the future.

Most teachers will probably agree that bringing in appraisal requirements may be one way to help identify areas of weakness which need development and also bring pressure to improve on those people who are not providing an adequate teaching service. However, gender issues related to performance appraisal need some more research before we can be sure that these processes will not further disadvantage women teachers. In the past, male perceptions of merit have been shown to be highly problematic for women (Burton, 1988). In the labour market of the 1990s, Hammond and Harbridge (1993, p.28) report that, 'Men are more likely to receive productivity-based payments. This indicates a failure to resolve sexist notions of skill and productivity assessment'. For example, feminist analyses of job evaluation schemes have shown how skills associated with human relationships are valued less highly than those to do with technical areas. How then will pastoral skills used by a woman dean in a secondary school be valued by a principal who perceives the counselling of a distressed pregnant schoolgirl and her parents, not as work requiring skilled and sensitive interactions and judgements, but rather as part of a woman dean's 'natural' sphere of influence, something that she is inherently suited to and good at as a consequence of her femininity? In thinking about who carries out performance appraisals, how these are done and what the results are likely to be, there are many issues which need more research.

Within the tougher negotiating conditions that have emerged under the Employment Contracts Act, some other employment provisions for women working in primary schools have been changed for the worse, for example, with maternity leave. The previous maternity grant was paid to a woman on the birth of her child, but from 1 May 1993, the grant will not be paid until six months after her return to work (NZEI, 1992a, Section 6.3.7). The previous timing of this grant helped many families meet the costs of a new child when the money was needed. There will undoubtedly be savings to the government under the changed scheme if women do not immediately return to work. A related area which is being increasingly contested is the preferential provisions for re-entry after childcare. Under Section 2.3 of the primary teachers' collective contract, a woman can apply for the priority right of getting her job back after childcare leave. However, it is reported by union officers that schools are becoming highly resistant to this, making it difficult for some women to negotiate (Middleton, 1993).

Conclusion

This article has focused on particular areas of concern for women working in education, providing a partial view of some of the structural divisions and inequalities of gender, ethnicity and class that exist in this workforce. It is clear that complex hierarchies of status and reward persist within and across the educational sectors.

The implementation of EEO has been particularly difficult in the education sector because of the scattered nature of work sites and the lack of EEO knowledge amongst Boards of Trustees and those in top management positions. These problems have been exacerbated by massive reform in the education and industrial areas which is impacting on the ways that inequality is created and maintained.

As 1993 drew to a close, many people were expressing concerns about increasing social inequalities, unemployment and impoverishment in this country. The restructuring of the Welfare State has been seen by critics to be motivated as much by central government's wish to absolve itself from fronting up to responsibility for social justice and equity, as by the stated need to cut costs. In education, the bulk funding initiative has been criticised in this way by early childhood workers and Maori in particular, for its 'deceit' (NZEI Rourou, 1992, p.3). In the aftermath of the general election, it remains to be seen how far the 'new' political climate of 'consultation, co-operation and consensus' will develop a commitment to resolving historically entrenched inequalities in women's employment opportunities and conditions in education.

References

Bain, Miss (1893), 'The Remuneration of Teachers', *The New Zealand School Master*, August.

Burton, C. (1988), *Redefining Merit*, Monograph No.2. Canberra: Australian Affirmative Action Agency.

Court, M. (1992), 'Leading from Behind', in S. Middleton and A. Jones (eds), *Women and Education in Aotearoa 2*, Wellington: Bridget Williams Books.

Davies, L. and Nicholl, K. (1993), *Te Maori i Roto i Nga Mahi Whakaakoranga/Maori in Education*, Wellington: Ministry of Education.

Dunn, A., Pole, N. and Rouse, J. (1992), *The Education Sector Workforce*, Wellington: Ministry of Education.

Education Review Office (1992), *Report of the Education Review Office for the Year Ended 30 June 1992*, Wellington: Education Review Office.

Education Review Office (1993a), *Fourth Quarter 1992-93: Overview Analysis Assurance Audits and Effectiveness Reviews of Schools*, Wellington: Education Review Office.

Education Review Office (1993b), *Fourth Quarter 1992-93: Overview Analysis Assurance Audits and Effectiveness Reviews of Early Childhood Centres*, Wellington: Education Review Office.

Else, A. (1992), 'To Market and Home Again: Gender and the New Right', in R. Du Plessis, P. Bunkle, K. Irwin, A. Laurie and S. Middleton (eds), *Feminist Voices: Women's Studies Texts for Aotearoa/New Zealand*, Auckland: Oxford University Press.

Hammond, S. and Harbridge, R. (1993), 'The Impact of the Employment Contracts Act on Women at Work', *New Zealand Journal of Industrial Relations*, 18 (1), 15-30.

Harbridge R. (1993), 'Collective Employment Contracts: a Content Analysis', in R. Harbridge (ed.), *Employment Contracts: New Zealand Experiences*, Wellington: Victoria University Press.

Hill, L. (1993), '100 Years of the Vote: 80 Percent of the Pay: The Politics of Pay Equity', *Women's Studies Journal*, 9 (2), 87-113.

Hill, L. and Du Plessis, R. (1993), 'Tracing the Similarities, Identifying the Differences: Women and the Employment Contracts Act', *New Zealand Journal of Industrial Relations*, 18 (1), 31-43.

Irwin, K. (1992), 'Maori Education in 1992: a Review and Discussion', in H. Manson (ed.), *New Zealand Annual Review of Education 2*, Wellington: Victoria University Press.

Johnston, P. (1993), 'Examining a State Relationship: Legitimation and Te Kohanga Reo – the Return of the Prodigal Child?'. Paper presented at NZARE Conference, Hamilton.

Johnston, P. and Pihama, L. (1993), 'What Counts as Difference and What Differences Count: Gender, Race and the Politics of Difference'. Paper presented at NZARE Conference, Hamilton.

Middleton, L. (1993), 'Personal Communication', *NZEI*, 9 November.

Minister of Education (1988), *Tomorrow's Schools: the Reform of Educational Administration in New Zealand*, Wellington: Government Print.

Ministry of Education (1993), *Corporate Plan, 1993-94*, Wellington: Ministry of Education.

Ministry of Women's Affairs (1990), *Women in New Zealand*, Wellington: Department of Statistics and Ministry of Women's Affairs.

Neville, M. (1988), *Promoting Women: Successful Women in Educational Management*, Auckland: Longman Paul.

New Zealand Educational Institute (NZEI) (1992a), *Primary Teachers Collective Employment Contract 1992/94*, Wellington: NZEI.

NZEI (1992b), *Primary Principals', Deputy and Assistant Principals' Collective Employment Contract 1992/94*, Wellington: NZEI.

NZEI Rourou (1992), 'Maori Voice Concerns about Bulk Funding', 3 (12) p.3.

O'Neill, A.M. (1992), 'The Gendered Curriculum: Homemakers and Breadwinners', in G. McCulloch (ed.), *The School Curriculum in New Zealand*, Palmerston North: Dunmore Press.

Picot, B. (1988), *Taskforce to Review Educational Administration: Administering for Excellence*, (Picot Report), Wellington: Government Print.

Pohatu, G. (1988), 'The Watts' Report: Implications for Maori in Southern Universities: an Opinion', *New Zealand Journal of Educational Studies*, 23 (1), 75-85.

'Preschool quality threat', *The Dominion*, 28 August, 1993, p.8.

Ramsay, P. and Oliver, D. (1992), *Monitoring Today's Schools: Report No.10, Equity*, Hamilton: University of Waikato.

Slyfield, H. (1992), *An Overview of Equal Employment Opportunities in the Teaching Services*, Wellington: Ministry of Education.

Slyfield, H. (1993), *The Position of Women in the Education Services*, Wellington: Ministry of Education.

Spender, D. (1982), *Women of Ideas – and What Men Have Done to Them*, London: Routledge and Kegan Paul.

State Services Commission (1993), Internal document, July 1993, in *Post Primary Teachers Association (PPTA), Branch Election Kit: 1993*, Wellington: PPTA.

Steele, J. (1981), 'An Evaluation of In-Service Training: Women in Management 1978-1980', unpublished MEd thesis, Education Department, Massey University.

Travers, A. (1989), 'The State Sector Act and Tomorrow's Schools: Implications for Women', *Delta 41*, 33-39.

Vasil, L. (1993), 'Gender Differences in the Academic Career in New Zealand Universities', *New Zealand Journal of Educational Studies*, 28 (2), 143-153.

Watson, H. (1988), 'The Impact of the Second Wave of the Women's Movement on Policies and Practices in Schools', in S. Middleton (ed.), *Women and Education in Aotearoa*, Wellington: Allen and Unwin/Port Nicholson Press.

Watson, H. (1989), 'Getting Women to the Top: the Promotion of Women Review', *PPTA Journal*, Term 2, 1989.

15

Dangerous Opportunities? Women and the Process of Workplace Reform

Rose Ryan

> *The Chinese character for 'crisis' means dangerous opportunity*
> *– a neat way of expressing the prospect of both gain and disaster.*
> *I think ... restructuring is, in that sense, a crisis for equal*
> *employment opportunities, a dangerous opportunity to break*
> *down barriers, and open up careers – or to see the blinds fall on*
> *the missed window of opportunity for a long time (Hall, 1989,*
> *p.3).*

Introduction

In 1991 a high-level group of experts on the role of women in shaping structural change reported to the Secretary-General of the Organisation for Economic Co-operation and Development (OECD) that:

> ... the smooth functioning of OECD societies and their supporting economies in the 1990s and beyond depends on recognising women as principal economic actors and enabling them to realise their untapped potential. It challenges the traditional assumption that equity and efficiency are mutually exclusive outcomes that have to be traded off against each other. Women are not a problem

for the economy. On the contrary, the solution to economic problems depends on enhancing women's economic role. Women are a key resource that is currently under-utilised, both quantitatively and qualitatively.... Meeting the twin goals of equity and efficiency [however] requires significant changes to the 'system'. Those changes represent a major structural adjustment (Blanchard, 1991, p.7).

Since the late 1960s the New Zealand economy, like the economies of all other developed nations, has been changing. These changes have resulted from a number of interrelated factors such as: the influence of new technology, increased competition in product markets, globalisation of trade, the continued shift in employment away from the manufacturing sector of the economy towards the service sector, and the impact of deregulation as neo-classical approaches to economic management have been adopted. The consequences of these influences have been so many and varied that it is often difficult to tell cause from effect. However, one of the more significant influences has been diversification in both consumer demand and production processes, which has put pressure on business organisations and the way they produce goods and services. New ways of working have been needed, and the demand for 'greater labour market flexibility' has become a catch-cry of the 1980s and '90s.

The impact of structural change has, in many respects, been to the disadvantage of women. These negative impacts have been well covered by other writers (Armstrong, 1992; Else, 1992; Sayers, 1993). Hammond and Harbridge (1993) have shown that the Employment Contracts Act 1991 has allowed employers to adopt a short-term cost-cutting approach which has disadvantaged many women. However, other employers have developed quite different strategies for adapting to change, based on what has become known in New Zealand as *workplace reform.*

The analysis of workplace reform in New Zealand is a relatively new field of academic study and the study of the impact of the process on women is even newer. This chapter aims to introduce the reader to the basic concepts regarding traditional work organisation and the debates concerning women's participation in the process of workplace reform. It argues that workplace reform offers an important opportunity for the improvement of equity in employment in New Zealand. This improvement can be achieved in two ways: first through the development of ways of working based on values that are more inclusive than the traditional values of organisations and second, by providing more advancement opportunities to members of disadvantaged groups, such as women and Maori.

The Taylorist Past

Employment in the twentieth century has been heavily influenced by Taylorism. In essence Taylor argued in his landmark work *The Principles of Scientific Management* (1947) that work needed to be made more efficient and this could be done if jobs were designed according to scientific principles. This philosophy led to the very influential notion of scientific management which has dominated management processes to this day.

The application of scientific management to the design of jobs resulted in two distinct trends in the nature of work organisation. The first of these was a fragmentation of jobs into small components requiring very specialised skills. Employees could easily be trained for such jobs, and the continued repetition of one task ensured maximum efficiency in performance. The second trend was a growing gap between the position of management and workers. Under Taylorism the planning and control of the job was a managerial task. However, its performance was the role of workers. Under traditional systems of work organisation, control of the workplace was left in the hands of management, while workers performed jobs which necessitated leaving their hearts and brains behind upon entering the workplace. In other words, workers should work and managers should manage.

Taylorist work organisation has been criticised from a number of perspectives. The most common criticism arises out of the human relations approach to organisation theory. This view sees fragmented jobs as resulting in bored, apathetic employees with little interest in the jobs they perform and little commitment to the organisations in which they work.[1] From a feminist perspective, however, traditional forms of work organisation have contributed to continued inequality in the labour market. In particular, jobs and business organisations are built upon capitalist and patriarchal notions of value, the result of which is gender-based segmentation in the labour market.

Specifically, gender-based segmentation in the labour market has had three consequences for women's employment. First, conceptions of the managerial role and function and ideas about what makes a 'good' manager are based on 'masculine' notions of hierarchy and control. To illustrate this point, research has shown approximately two-thirds of both women and men describe a good manager in primarily masculine terms (Powell, 1988). Second, the fragmentation of jobs has resulted in occupational hierarchies in which women are found mainly at the bottom. As a result women are more often than men found in jobs which are repetitive and boring, with little skill attached to them and with poor wages and conditions. Finally, work which reproduces women's domestic work as part of the production of goods and supply of services (e.g. cooking, cleaning, clothing manufacture) is given little value, is commonly seen as unskilled, and consequently attracts poor wages and conditions.

There is a strong relationship between hierarchical work structures and traditional attitudes towards women. Discriminatory behaviour at work often results from traditional attitudes towards women as secondary earners with less attachment to work and less interest in advancement. These stereotypes are related to women's labour market position rather than gender *per se*. However, they are commonly used to justify the continuance of work patterns in which women are more likely than men to occupy positions in the peripheral labour force. Agassi argues that what is needed in order to break this pattern is:

> ... no less than a break with the traditional work patterns which have developed for boys, men and fathers, who have had the benefits of the (unpaid) domestic services of mothers, wives and daughters and could be exempted thereby from all domestic and childcare obligations.... . To improve the quality of working life... it is necessary to break with many of the outdated rigid categories of the division of labour such as semiskilled and skilled work, machine operative and technician, blue-collar and white-collar workers, rank-and-file worker and supervisor, and clerical and professional employees (1982, p.253).

If, as Agassi argues, a break with the past is needed, what are the features of changes that are occurring at the present time? And how can women use them to ensure greater equity in the world of work? These questions are addressed next.

Workplace Reform in New Zealand

In the New Zealand context workplace reform has been taken to refer to an integrated package of changes involving a number of processes. These may include; the introduction or improved use of new technology, improved training opportunities for workers, new approaches to industrial relations with greater involvement in decision-making from workers and their representatives, and new forms of work organisation (Workplace New Zealand, 1992). Enderwick (1992) describes the process as follows:

> The focus is on reorganising the flow of work, the organisation of tasks, work responsibilities and job content. It generally involves a move towards team rather than individual work organisation, increased employee responsibility for quality and perhaps productivity, broader skill definitions, a closer integration of work goals, appraisal and payment systems and new approaches to employee relations (p. 192).

Many companies and unions in New Zealand have supported the implementation of workplace reform. Companies generally support workplace reform in order to achieve the traditional managerial goals of improved competitiveness, higher levels of productivity, and increased profits (Workplace New Zealand, 1992; Enderwick, 1992). Many workers and unions support workplace reform because it also appears to have many positive spin-offs for workers (New Zealand Council of Trade Unions, 1992).

Whatever the reasons, there is a strong interest in workplace reform in New Zealand. The movement is growing in popularity amongst employers, employees and unions. Taylorist forms of work organisation are being reconsidered and often reversed in the two critical areas of job redesign and workplace structure. First, jobs are being designed so they incorporate a variety of tasks rather than segmented single tasks. This has implications for company training programmes, as these must be designed to broaden the skills and abilities of workers to meet the demands of more complex work. Second, devolution of power and responsibility to individuals and work teams is replacing rigid forms of hierarchical managerial control. This process has commonly involved the establishment of consultative committees or other bodies so that unions and employees have a say in decisions affecting the production process.

Issues for Women

Are the changes involved in workplace reform capable of improving equity in employment? The remainder of this chapter examines two central issues. First, the extent to which equity concerns are currently being integrated into workplace reform programmes. In particular, do companies see improved equity as being a fundamental goal of change and are those groups which have traditionally been disadvantaged in the labour market involved in planning for change?

The second issue involves the extent to which workplace reform promotes more equitable labour market outcomes for women and whether all groups share equally in the benefits of change or some groups receive disproportionate shares.

Integrating EEO with workplace reform

Participants in the New Zealand Workplace Reform Conference noted that:

> It is important that workplace reform link into wider issues of equal employment opportunity. The workplace cannot be separate from employees' personal lives. The workplace should come to value diversity (race, gender, culture, family circumstance) as a source of advantage (Workplace New Zealand, 1992, p.27).

However, the incorporation of EEO programmes as part of the goals of workplace reform is not common. Twenty-one organisations (private and public sector) and two industries provided a summary of their workplace reform goals and achievements at the Workplace New Zealand Conference. Of these, one industry mentioned the percentage of women in the labour force and one organisation (Bluebird Foods) addresses EEO issues. This may suggest that EEO is seen as separate from other changes occurring within the organisation. However, another interpretation is possible. Many organisations emphasise the need to recognise *all* employees in their workplace reform goals. Goals which recognise employees' needs include such objectives as; improved training, increased participation of employees in management decision-making and creating team-based management. By definition, therefore, such outcomes should equally benefit groups which have traditionally been disadvantaged. To find out whether *all* employees benefit in practice would require further detailed investigation within the workplace.

The successful integration of EEO and workplace reform is dependent on the underlying reasons for implementing the process. The critical issue is whether the organisations perceive workplace reform as a programme or as involving a cultural change to their method of operation.[2] Where workplace reform is seen as a management technique, or a fashion to be followed, then the process of EEO and reform integration is hindered. However, if workplace reform is seen to be about changing the culture of the organisation and involving all employees in the process then the integration of EEO into the programme is more likely to be successful. The idea is consistent with Cockburn's (1989) notion of a transformational model of EEO. This idea is discussed in more detail by Walsh and Dickson (in this volume). A transformational model of EEO emphasises the need to critique the 'nature and purpose of institutions and the processes by which the power of some groups over others in institutions is built and renewed' (Cockburn, 1989, p.218).

The transformational model of EEO suggests that EEO should be integrated with workplace reform objectives. Organisational culture is directly influenced by notions of gender transmitted from wider society. As Mills (1988, p.352) argues, 'organisations are ubiquitous, confronting us as "cultural forms", not only as manifestations of social values... but also as transformers of cultural phenomena'. Organisational culture reproduces the values of society. Workplace reform opens up the values of the organisation for scrutiny and seeks to be more inclusive. In doing so it exposes organisational culture to influences from a greater diversity of individuals and groups. In this way, workplace reform offers the potential for achieving Cockburn's 'long' agenda – the creation of organisations that are more tolerant of a range of values and opinions.

Who Benefits from Workplace Reform?

Are the benefits of workplace reform distributed equally across all groups within the workplace? In particular, does reform solve the problems associated with Taylorism such as the fragmentation of skill and the separation between the management and performance of tasks? The following section argues that women may benefit from workplace reform in several critical areas. But we need to continue to monitor the impact of reform on gender relations in the workplace before reaching any hasty conclusions.

A common feature of workplace reform initiatives is that management hierarchies are flattened and team-based forms of management are instituted. Opinions vary as to how beneficial working in teams is for workers. On the one hand it has been argued that teamwork fosters a 'family' atmosphere where people are more likely to be co-operative and supportive of each other. Allocation of work by the team can take account of the strengths and weaknesses of individual members, and supervision of individuals is more personal than managerial or bureaucratic. Others argue that teams encourage conformity and act as an agent of social control for the employer – workers will work harder so as not to let down other members of the team and to 'fit in', and teams will compete against other teams thereby increasing productivity (Garrahan and Stewart, 1992).

A recent report of trade union experts from OECD countries commented that women do much better when teamwork is introduced (OECD, 1993). Evidence from the same report suggests progression at work led to enhanced self-esteem and personal development for women. Research carried out at Nissan New Zealand suggests that both men and women prefer teamworking to other methods of working. In general teamworking was felt to encourage much better relationships amongst employees, who were more inclined to help each other out. While teamworking is not without problems, (for instance, the possibility of resentment towards team members who were slower than others or who had a high level of absenteeism) it is more likely to result in a greater sense of participation in the workplace (Ryan, 1993).

Of particular interest was the number of Maori and Pacific Island employees who suggested in interviews at the plant that teamworking was a more culturally appropriate way of working for them. This was because in their cultures family orientation was central, and other workers argued that the benefits of teamworking had international application. These findings raise interesting questions about the extent to which a strategy such as workplace reform, which was implemented by management for one set of purposes, may be co-opted by groups of employees to meet their own interests.

There are two further means by which workplace reform could improve women's position in internal labour markets. The first of these is through the process of job enlargement. Job enlargement involves the reintegration of jobs which previously had demarcations between them. Workers are then encouraged to be flexible across a range of jobs. This flexibility allows women to perform a wider variety of tasks, including jobs previously considered 'men's jobs'. Second, the increased emphasis on training may benefit women by helping to improve their self-confidence and by providing them with the skills to be able to seek promotion or progression.

The evidence on both these points is, again, that women have benefited from changes where they have occurred. Restructuring of work organisation in the clothing industry in Australia has given women the opportunity to work on a different range of machines (e.g. straight-stitch machines, overlockers) and to perform jobs at different skill levels on the same machine (e.g. sewing side-seams, sewing collars). They also have had the opportunity to learn skills related to the maintenance and operation of their machines. Similarly at Nissan, emphasis on versatility of skills has allowed women to move away from the one area of the plant where most had been employed in the past and provided them with the training that has allowed them to access other traditionally male-dominated jobs in the plant.

Training may also provide beneficial effects for women. In Australia training is provided on an industry basis within an industry-based career path. This includes the identification of skills common across employers and payment systems, based on the skills obtained by employees. This system has provided women with the opportunity both for improved earnings and to move jobs within the industry. In New Zealand the development of industry training arrangements, while similar to that operating in Australia, has not been as comprehensive. Within individual companies skills learned are a mix of those which are company-specific and those which are portable. At Nissan, for example, many workers commented that working on the company's information system allowed them to learn general computer skills.

Improved access to a range of jobs across the plant has also improved access by women to positions as team leaders and forepersons. While in the past, few women were employed in supervisory positions, in February 1993 women held 42 per cent of team-leader, foreperson and supervisory positions, even though they made up only 28 per cent of the total number of employees (Ryan, 1993). This is in contrast to the usual pattern of horizontal segregation where women are more likely to be found at the bottom of organisational hierarchies.

Another issue is the question of re-evaluating 'women's work' in the light of workplace reform. To what extent does reform have the potential to help improve the value placed on women's paid labour? The answer to this question hinges on the extent to which workplace reform is able to be applied to those jobs which have traditionally been performed by women, in female-intensive occupations such as cleaning and clerical work.

The workplace reform model has been applied more commonly to the male-dominated manufacturing sector of the economy. Women in female-intensive manufacturing industries may benefit from changes that accompany the reform process. For example, the restructuring of the textiles, clothing and footwear industry in Australia has led to increased recognition of the skills required in such jobs and a subsequent increase in pay for those workers employed in that industry. However, it is in the service sector where the majority of women work and where, although there are several important examples of workplace reform such as the Christchurch Park Royal, Manukau City Council and the New Zealand Qualifications Authority, reform programmes are considerably less common. The reasons why this is the case are complex and relate to such differences as: greater success of alternative employment relations strategies, different competitive and economic environments, less interest from unions, the nature of the industry and the workforce employed in it. In particular, the problems which workplace reform are designed to solve (particularly strict demarcations and tight managerial control) may not be significant issues in the service sector where arguably, jobs have been less subject to managerial scrutiny, and where flexibility in the performance of tasks has been more common.

Consequently it is difficult to make any firm predictions as to the impact of workplace reform on the value placed on women's work in female-intensive industries.

Conclusion

This chapter has considered some of the main issues of concern to women in relation to the process of workplace reform. It has argued that workplace reform offers women and other disadvantaged groups a 'dangerous' opportunity to redress some of the inequities that have resulted from systems of work organisation based on Taylorist principles. Whether such opportunities result in positive outcomes for women will depend largely on two conditions. First, the extent to which the workplace reform model is adopted throughout a range of different types of organisations; and second, the extent to which traditionally disadvantaged groups are involved in structuring the agenda for change.

Notes

1   For a general discussion of critiques of Taylorism, see Grint, K. (1991).
2   I am grateful to Judy Nicholl, from Air New Zealand, for this insight.

References

Agassi, J. (1982), *Comparing the Work Attitudes of Women and Men,* Massachusetts: D.C. Heath and Company.

Armstrong, N. (1992), 'Homeworking and Gender Relations: a Return to the Sweatshop or the Workplace of the Future?', in S. Olsson (ed.), *The Gender Factor : Women in New Zealand Organisations,* Palmerston North: Dunmore Press.

Blanchard, F. (1991), 'Shaping Structural Change: the Role of Women'. Report by a high-level group of experts to the Secretary-General, Organisation for Economic Cooperation and Development, Paris.

Cockburn, C. (1989), 'Equal Opportunities: the Long and Short Agenda', *Industrial Relations Journal,* 20 (3), 213-225.

Else, A. (1992), 'To Market and Home Again: Gender and the New Right', in R. Du Plessis, P. Bunkle, K. Irwin, A. Laurie, S. Middleton (eds),

Feminist Voices: Women's Studies Texts for Aotearoa-New Zealand, Auckland: Oxford University Press.

Enderwick, P. (1992), 'Workplace Reform and International Competitiveness: the Case of New Zealand', *New Zealand Journal of Industrial Relations*, 17 (2), 185-206.

Garrahan, P. and Stewart, P. (1992), *The Nissan Enigma*, London: Marsell.

Grint, K. (1991), *The Sociology of Work,* Cambridge: Polity Press.

Hall, P. (1989), 'Award Restructuring and Equal Employment Opportunities', 'Dangerous Opportunity: Industry Restructuring and Equal Employment Opportunities'. Papers presented to a seminar held by the Women's Directorate, New South Wales Department of Industrial Relations and Employment, April 21, Sydney.

Hammond, S. and Harbridge, R. (1993), 'The Impact of the Employment Contracts Act on Women at Work', *New Zealand Journal of Industrial Relations*, 18 (1), 15-30.

Mills, A. (1988), 'Organisation, Gender and Culture', *Organisation Studies*, 9 (3), 351-369.

New Zealand Council of Trade Unions (1992), *Building a Better Workplace,* Wellington: New Zealand Council of Trade Unions.

OECD (1993), 'Women and Structural Change in the '90s'. Report on a meeting of trade union experts held under the Labour/Management Programme, 25-26 June 1992, Paris.

Powell, G. N. (1988), *Women and Men in Management,* California: Sage Publications.

Ryan, R. (1993), *Japanisation or a New Zealand Way?: Five Years on at Nissan New Zealand,* Working Paper 5/93, Wellington: Industrial Relations Centre, Victoria University.

Sayers, J. (1993), 'Women, the Employment Contracts Act and Labour Flexibility', in R. Harbridge (ed.), *Employment Contracts: New Zealand Experiences,* Wellington: Victoria University Press.

Taylor, F.W. (1947), *The Principles of Scientific Management* (Revised Edition), New York: Harper.

Workplace New Zealand (1992), *Quality Through Partnership: Successful Workplaces of the Future.* Report of the Workplace New Zealand International Conference on Workplace Reform, 27-30 September 1992, Rotorua.

Part Three

Viewpoints

Equal Employment Opportunity in the Public Sector

'The most amazing thing [that has happened] is that people now know what the words mean. They don't know the details and they get hung up on things. But, I hear all over the country people saying, 'we believe in EEO'. They didn't even use the words in 1986, they didn't know what EEO meant.'

Diana Crossan
Group Manager, Human Resources, Justice Department

Interviewed by Janet Sayers

Diana started her working life as a probation officer in the early 1970s. There were very few women probation officers then and the job was as 'Probation Officer for Women'.

Diana pinpoints her decision in 1974 to go to Britain and do a social work qualification as critical in her own working life as it gave her a qualification. While she was overseas she met and married an engineer and when they came back to New Zealand they lived in a variety of places, including Tokoroa, and Diana continued her probation work.

In 1980 Diana moved to Wellington and became a senior probation officer. This was her first experience as a manager. Two years later she became a Student Unit Supervisor. Two to three years after that she applied for further promotion, several times, but it was made clear to her that the Probation Service was not interested in promoting women.

She moved to the Labour Department as the manager of Group Employment Liaison Service – a national organisation of community workers working with gangs, street-kids and groups of unemployed workers.

249

In 1986 Diana was approached by Diane Candy who, in 1984, had been appointed at a clerical grade to bring about EEO in the public service! Diana was approached because someone was needed at management level to set up an EEO Unit at the State Services Commission (SSC). Diane had realised shortly before applications for the position closed that if they did not encourage women to apply they would be getting a male section head. So Diana, along with several other people, quickly applied.

Diana was manager of the EEO Unit from 1986 to 1990. These were critical years for EEO in New Zealand. Some of Diana's experiences there are explored in more depth below.

Diana was appointed Director of Policy at the Ministry of Education in 1990. In February 1993 she began work as Group Manager of Human Resources with the Justice Department.

You were involved with EEO in New Zealand right from the start. Can you elaborate on your first involvement with EEO? How did you first come to understand the term?

My first EEO job was to set up the EEO Unit. The people who interviewed me for that position had little understanding of EEO. My understanding was formed from being in the workforce and watching some of the things that went on.

One of the most important things that happened in terms of how I came to understand EEO, and the decisions that were made about how the Unit was run, was that shortly before I began at the Unit I went to Adelaide to represent New Zealand at a conference on EEO. I went there without any knowledge of what structures were needed for the introduction of EEO. So, I decided to talk in the breaks to each of the Australian States' representatives to find out their structures for EEO and why they had done what they did.

I can pinpoint two critical ways this conference influenced my thinking about EEO. First, I got the message at this conference that EEO in Australia was about women only. It was important that it be different in New Zealand.

Maori public servants were sending out some strong messages. There had been several hui of Maori public servants and they had sent a delegation to the Commission and said, 'you need a separate unit for Maori'. Kim Workman, at the SSC, had drafted a design of a Maori Unit and a separate EEO Unit. The Commission turned that down and said they could have a senior Maori person in the EEO Unit.

The other important influence of the Conference was on the structure of the Unit. In Australia they had a director, senior analysts and junior specialists – the generalists were more senior. One of the selling points of EEO, I believed, was having EEO encompassing several groups, not just women. So we went the other way and had a director, four senior specialists and a couple of generalist advisory staff underneath. This fitted with the EEO Maori senior position.

I went back to the Commission and said, 'We can't have a senior Maori without a senior woman'. They agreed to that. The disability and ethnic minority positions were created one grade below the others, but still far above anything there had been before.

Diane Candy left the SSC soon after my appointment. So, the original staff of the EEO Unit were myself, Shayne Mathieson (she was already in Auckland and a skilled generalist), Moana Herewini got the Maori position, Joan Stone was appointed to work in the disability area, Danna Glendining for women, and Marilyn Kohlhase for ethnic groups. Robyn Hunt joined us later, as did Janice Burns, Jody Tapiki and Stella Thorpe.

This culture for EEO – including other groups as well as women – has been very influential on the development of EEO in New Zealand. It set the parameters in many ways didn't it?

I think it made a big difference.

Our first ever meeting was at Pirinoa, at Joan Stone's place, as a type of retreat. This was the first time we all met. Two important things came out of this meeting. First, we decided to pick several words that were central to our understanding of EEO. We asked ourselves, 'What is feminism? What is biculturalism? What do we mean when we talk about an ethnic group? What is working class? What do we mean by religious identity?'. And we had a long session on these things. So when we came back to work we had an understanding of these important concepts. We also discussed each other's role and how we could help each other. The other important thing that happened was that it helped break down barriers between the groups and gave us some legitimacy with each other.

So, what happened from there in setting up the EEO Unit at the SSC? What were some of the critical incidents that occurred during your time at the Unit?

I do think that one of the reasons we started getting EEO in New Zealand was because other commonwealth countries were ahead of us. Our representatives at the commonwealth public servants' meetings had to admit, each time it was on the agenda, that New Zealand hadn't done much. Margaret Bazeley and the Commissioner of the Canadian Public Service Commission were also important in influencing action.

My first job at the Unit was to set up systems. The first document was put out in 1984 – the Government Statement on EEO – which was done under National, in Muldoon's time. This was a signed agreement amongst state employers to do something about EEO, and was the base document that we used to help set up the EEO processes.

We also realised we needed a communication strategy. There were big gaps in people's understanding of EEO. People had no real understanding of how structural inequality stops people from participation.

From about 1987 we started to realise that changes in the state sector legislation were likely. We talked long and hard about whether we wanted to get EEO into this legislation. We decided that the most powerful thing we could do was that – it almost didn't matter if we didn't do anything else.

We looked at every bit of Australian legislation we could. We asked, 'Did it make a difference?' We got a lot of help from the Australians on the wording. They kept saying, 'Get the target groups named. If you get them named other people can pick up the issues'. And this is what has happened.

Is there any particular achievement in terms of EEO that you can look back on, and take strength from?

The two clearest for me are the legislation and the words. The legislation is self-explanatory.

But the most amazing thing is that people now know what the words mean. They don't know the details and they get hung up on things. But, I hear all over the country people saying, 'we believe in EEO'. They didn't even use the words in 1986, they didn't know what EEO meant.

I have watched people gain strength from it. It allows people to say, 'I am going to do that because I'm allowed to do it, because there's meant to be EEO and I am going to have that'.

I am also proud of a lot of the process and structural stuff; putting EEO into CEO's contracts, progress reports, statistics, getting political support through fair means and foul ...

What do you see as the main advantages of EEO and disadvantages. Or, in other words, its limitations as well as its ability to create positive change?

The limitations have got nothing to do with EEO itself. EEO is only a concept. It is taken on as if it is more than a concept – as a structure. But it isn't a structure.

I have asked other people what they think it means and they often say it is a planned, systematic programme of structural change ...

The limitations have come from what people have put on it rather than EEO itself. Some people say that EEO Maori doesn't work –well that's a load of rubbish. EEO is just about equal employment opportunities, and if there are different ways of doing that, let's look at them. The words themselves don't have any constraints – its the constraints that other people put around them.

The advantages are that I think there is a concept we can talk about. I mean, no one now is going to say, 'we don't believe in EEO'. They might want you barefoot and pregnant in the kitchen, but they're not going to say that anymore.

I can sit in a senior management meeting and say, 'we don't have EEO because of this'. Now managers will look at the problem, and act on it. Not because of legislation, but because they can accept it will disadvantage staff and EEO (getting the best person for the job) is good business.

Do you see any techniques that work particularly well in EEO?

The top level support is important, as is experience and understanding the issues. From this seat as Human Resource Manager, the fact that I have all this experience in EEO and 15 years in Justice before, is very important. And so, that combination means they can't negate that experience. As well, the Chief Executive was very supportive.

Do you see any difference between the private and the public sector models? If so, in what way are they different?

Two things – legislation and the culture of the public service. Legislation leads to far stronger incentives and people all through the organisation feel they can push the issue.

Also, most of the public service has a social service bent, so people who work there have a natural affinity for the issues for target groups. I mean people don't go into social work, probation and health to make money. (Well, some of them might.) Basically EEO fits the culture a whole lot better.

As the public sector disintegrates you see that culture having more to do with the Chief Executive. In the private sector it is the same – if the boss opens the doors then it is a lot easier. The acceptance of EEO has a lot to do with the person heading the organisation.

So, as the public sector is being driven towards more private sector models, what do you see happening to EEO? Has it lost impetus, do you think?

It lost a bit for a while, during restructuring and redundancies. Lots of the target group people were fired. Part of it was that people seemed to think, if you are lean and efficient, then you treat your staff badly. There was a lot of that going on. Not in this Department, but I saw that in other places. I think it was also the opportunity for some quite clear discrimination to happen in the guise of down-sizing – that was across the board, not just target group discrimination.

Do you see conflict between the private and public sector models? Between the business drive for EEO and the legislative, justice and equity drives for EEO?

I don't see a problem. In fact I think it is an insult to think there might be a problem as it suggests women, Maori and other groups, aren't up to it. The suggestion that the structure and the way that things are being done currently is best, is arrogant. There are many ways to get from A to B. Things that were out are now in. The ways there are contestable.

What I think happened for a while was there was perceived to be only one way to set up the new public service. That you had to be lean, mean and market-driven. There was no room in that for diversity. You had to do it this way and that is the only way. That approach is not compatible with EEO. In the pure deregulated market there is no room for EEO at all. This is because women have to become like men, to give up their families and so on.

I don't think the country can last like that. There are other aspects to life. Where people are saying, 'life is more rounded than that'; that is where EEO can come in.

One of the central tenets of EEO in New Zealand has been the focus on 'merit' and a move away from quotas and firmer forms of affirmative action as there are overseas. But, if you look, say, at the number of women in management in Australia, America and New Zealand, you find that New Zealand is dragging the chain quite badly.

Yes, quotas and so on have been more effective. But EEO was introduced into those countries in a different era. I do think quotas work and they are the only way to go. But, the timing was bad here politically and I don't think EEO would have taken off if we had taken the same approach.

What do you see as the future of EEO in New Zealand?

I think it depends on the energy of the people. Some people say, 'EEO is hopeless in our Department'. What they mean is that there is no support from the managers, that the co-ordinator is unskilled, that there are no resources or that it is not supported by the chief executive.

I think that we have made a lot of progress in some ways, as I have outlined. But then we haven't in others. I just think that we need to keep at it. We get better and better at understanding EEO.

People get upset that EEO hasn't delivered this, and EEO hasn't delivered that. But, it's the people that haven't delivered. EEO is only equal employment opportunities. That's what it means. EEO itself is only a concept – it can't do anything on its own.

Equal Employment Opportunity – The Maori Perspective

'Sometimes results come in unexpected forms or unexpected ways. You can't assume that someone who responds in a redneck way is not able to grow beyond that – I've seen enormous shifts.... If you raise issues people go away and gnaw at them and come back for more'.

'What I'd like to see is a higher level and a better spread of Maori in the public service. At the moment Maori staff are clustered in Justice, Health and Education. We need the influence of that Maori perspective everywhere that policy is being developed.'

Joe Doherty
Senior Advisor, Strategic Human Resource Development Branch, State Services Commission

Interviewed by Marianne Tremaine

Joe Doherty's tribal affiliations are with Tuhoe. He comes originally from the Ngaputahi community on State Highway 38 in the middle of the Ureweras. The little community numbered only 20, so Joe went to school in neighbouring timber milling communities; primary schooling at Te Whaiti Native School and secondary schooling at Rangitahi College, Urupara.

Afterwards he went on to study at the University of Waikato and Auckland University towards a Bachelor of Arts in Geography. He is two papers away from completing a degree and has been studying extramurally at Massey University.

Tell me about your work background?

My working life began, from a career perspective, when I joined the Department of Labour as a factory inspector. I got to know the heavy industrial areas of Penrose and had a lot of contact with the Southdown Freezing Works. The powerful union at Southdown would call me in for support on safety matters and would be irritated if my measuring instruments did not back up the case they wanted to make. After six years in Auckland I was a factory inspector in Rotorua for two and a half years, then transferred across to the Employment Service, still in Rotorua. I was part of the first moves to encourage community involvement in creating employment. During that time I became concerned about the policy development process in Wellington which seemed to have a very centralist bias and took very little account of our input from the regions about local needs.

So in my naïvety I thought I should get closer to the bureaucracy and influence policy-making. I applied for a job in Wellington helping to manage the field-workers of the Group Employment Liaison Service. This service helped those who were so severely disadvantaged in terms of seeking employment that they couldn't access the services available to them. From working with the employment problems of gang members and street kids, I moved to a position as a Senior Management Advisor in the State Services Commission.

The job involved looking at the social impact that restructuring was having on the wider community and my particular brief was to focus on the Maori. We would make recommendations to government. The organisations affected by the first round of restructuring were the Forest Service, Energy, Lands and Survey and the Ministry of Works, all employers of significant numbers of Maori people. In some cases, I had to advise government on what to do with whole communities such as Kaingaroa and Minginui villages. I was concerned that the communities themselves should have a chance to decide their own fate and in most cases this is what happened.

When the Social Impact Unit was disbanded I applied for another job in the Commission looking at structures and systems and advising the government on how it could carry out its business more effectively and efficiently. Then I took time out from the Commission and went to the

Ministry of Maori Affairs to work for about 14 months. I went there specifically to set up the monitoring of the Treaty responsiveness of state sector agencies. Monitoring was shared jointly by the Ministry of Maori Affairs and the Commission; work which I had started before I left the Commission then carried on at the Ministry.

After going back to the Commission to the same section I'd left, I found that I soon had to make choices when our structure changed with reorganisation. Two of the newly-formed branches interested me. Both areas were important in terms of the Treaty. One was the state sector development branch and of course the strategic human resource development branch where I am now.

In broad terms what I do can be called policy analysis (with a human resources slant) that takes account of the Treaty of Waitangi. But on a more specific level, my job is to design a management development programme that will equip Maori managers with skills to make them more competitive in the job market and enable them to achieve a higher level of participation in decision-making processes.

Do you think there is any answer, as a Maori, to the problem of how to keep in touch with who you are and where you're from?

Yes, there is – I really believe there is. Every two or three months I go home to Te Urewera for short breaks. The reality for the people there is totally different from the reality I experience in Wellington. You need to be able to keep in touch with your own people and you need to be able to keep faith with your background in the way you approach your work.

For instance, this organisation is finally doing something about both recruitment of Maori and making the Treaty a focus of our work. There's a deliberate attempt to get more Maori staff into the organisation and some of the things I've been on about for the last several years are finally beginning to happen. For instance, one of the projects I'll be leading off next year is to do an audit to see just how responsive public sector organisations are, principally to Maori as employees but also how responsive they are to Maori as clients. From that survey the Commission will then do some strategic thinking and provide some guidelines that public sector agencies can work with.

So senior management is taking its statutory responsibilities for this whole Treaty area into account and finally we'll be doing something. I'm hoping that we'll be picking up more on the monitoring of responsiveness. It's even more important that the Commission gets involved now that the Ministry of Maori Affairs and the Iwi Transition Agency has been disbanded and the new Ministry of Maori Development (Te Puni Kokiri) has embarked on a programme of mainstreaming. Programmes for Maori in fields such as social welfare, housing and education funding, which were part of the Ministry's workload, are now being mainstreamed back into the departments.

As part of mainstreaming there's a transition arrangement where Te Puni Kokiri keeps a watching brief and monitors programmes which have been transferred across to departments. But those contractual arrangements with the Ministry of Maori Development are for a finite period – three to five years – so in anticipation of the contractual period coming to an end, someone, perhaps the Commission, needs to take account of how well this whole process is working. Is it effective? Is it more efficient for Maori?

What do you see as the links between the Treaty and EEO?

Well, I do think that the government has fallen down on its statutory responsibilities in this area. The state needed to take account of the Treaty much earlier, long before EEO became an issue. It was exciting for me when the Labour government introduced their Maori policy Te Urupare Rangapu. The government's objectives were spelt out. Public servants had a written statement on what the state sector should work towards achieving in terms of the Treaty.

Basically that was honouring the principles of the Treaty and setting out the state's responsibility to assist Maori development in terms of education funding and social welfare programmes. At last there was the feeling of a way forward. After my experience with the Department of Labour in the early to mid-80s when I felt very dependent on the Department's employment programmes for things like marae development programmes and employment creation for Maori, this was a significant turning point. With Treaty responsibilities there were huge gaps that needed to be plugged through state agencies.

In terms of EEO I was aware of the statutory regulations when the State Sector Act came into being and knew about some of the initiatives of departments. My current personal view is that EEO for Maori is quite a useful mechanism for achieving change, but it doesn't provide a complete solution to the tensions that exist at a practical level. There is some resentment about being identified as an EEO group. It is felt that this denigrates the position of Maori as tangata whenua and Treaty signatory. But EEO is reasonably well understood in the public sector and senior managers have a clearer understanding of equity issues that confront Maori as an EEO target group, but very little understanding of the same issue in its broader context under the Treaty. There is no monitoring process for picking up on what is happening with the Treaty, whereas for EEO the systems and processes are in place with the EEO Unit in the Commission and there is a statutory requirement for managers to present EEO plans and have them monitored by the Unit.

Among some managers there is a realisation that in the wider context of our New Zealand society, they could exercise control and work towards developing Maori autonomy and that the government is serious about assisting this process with its focus on Maori development. The EEO community is prepared to acknowledge that there is a tension there between Treaty responsiveness and EEO Maori and that there's a need to do something about it.

At a recent EEO conference Maori practitioners caucused to talk about EEO and the Treaty. They were concerned too about creating an appropriate body for Maori EEO practitioners. Some alternative structure such as a Maori EEO practitioners' association was discussed but the decision of the group shifted in favour of looking at the key issues rather than being separatist. There is currently a group comprising equal numbers of Maori and non-Maori planning the next national EEO practitioners' conference.

With day-to-day issues relating to EEO and the Treaty, there is a common perspective that can be applied which looks at comfort zones which in large part are defined by managers, in the work environment. They need to extend their own comfort zones by coming out of them. In thinking about this I'm influenced by the story of a young Maori woman who came to talk to me. Through sheer frustration, she was going to leave the public service. She had set up a conference for Maori women in her department at her manager's request. But when she went ahead and began organising the hui she was told that since it was to be part of suffrage year, and to be a high-profile meeting, it wouldn't be appropriate to meet on a marae. The marae wouldn't be sufficiently prestigious. The criterion for selecting the venue seemed to have nothing to do with the fact that the people attending were Maori women. She was disillusioned and felt her only alternative was to leave or be seen as having 'sold out'.

There is an expectation that people will conform to the culture of a public sector organisation. But as far as Maori are concerned there's a lot that can be done to accommodate a Maori perspective. The bottom line is accepting that you do have a diverse public sector and that to get the best value for the taxpayer's dollar you need to get the best out of all your people. For Maori you also have to take account of the Treaty.

You need to look at the articles of the Treaty as far as government departments are concerned. They (departments) are the main representatives of the Crown, therefore they have to meet Treaty obligations. Maori are the other signatory to the Treaty and taking into account Article Two and the obligation to protect tino rangatiratanga means that the way in which public sector organisations operate in terms of service delivery and development of policy has to take the Maori view into account. The way of doing that is to encourage greater participation of Maori in the public service so that Maori are involved in the development of policy and delivery of service. There is a dual accountability for Maori in the public service to their iwi and the Maori community as well as to their managers and the state. Trying to satisfy both can lead to serious dilemmas.

One of the solutions has been the setting up of separate Maori units in some departments of the public service as a kind of transitional arrangement until a bicultural workplace is achieved. Maori units function well when they can be a source of expertise. There is a problem about sharing the more esoteric Maori knowledge too widely, however. Taha Maori, or knowledge at the level of general awareness, should be freely available to Pakeha and others, but tikanga Maori belongs to Maori and cannot be shared. I can see that in the cases of some departments, such as the Department of Conservation and the Ministry for the Environment, tikanga has to form an aspect of their work. The very nature of this work demands a level of understanding of the world as Maori see it, for the environment and conservation are key concepts. So if tikanga is not to be shared then perhaps not all cultural units should be transitional. In areas such as conservation, Maori need to be involved because of the particular work of the department and its closeness to Maori concerns.

But there are strains for Maori and others who work to make the public service more bicultural. It can be depersonalising to work as a change agent within the public service because you are dealing with areas that affect your own values deeply and yet you have to work in terms of a rationalistic process. This problem won't ever be entirely overcome. My own way of measuring how bicultural an organisation is, is to feel comfortable within it. But true biculturalism is probably not achievable. It is always an ideal. The closest for me would have been the time I spent in Manatu Maori, though such an environment is quite taxing in its own way. The successes in this organisation are that the Treaty is being taken into account in all descriptions of branches that have been established. There is an acceptance that we need to have more Maori working here and there is a proactive recruitment drive to increase our numbers of Maori staff. We know that Maori have skills that the organisation needs. There is a generic set of competencies that advisors need and then there are specialist skills such as an understanding of Maori culture and values and the Treaty of Waitangi.

How do you see the future for EEO Maori? What would you like to see happen?

For EEO Maori a tribal approach is needed. That would be the ideal. Pacific Island people are working in groups according to their countries of origin. We need to work in a tribal way. But there aren't really enough of us to achieve that. Realistically we need to concentrate on a Maori perspective and look for the opportunities that pop up under EEO.

But we must be mindful of political implications all the time. We need to think about the Treaty and plan the future beyond the three-year term of any government. We need to think longer-term about what sort of society we need or want. We need to think about the position of Maori relative to the rest of society. There's a huge gap there. How's it going to be plugged?

How do you cope with ignorance and racism and redneck attitudes?

Sometimes it makes me angry but anger uses up the energy you need to do other things. You have to accept that change is painful for people, that they resist change. You need to try to determine the nature of resistance and the level of resistance and plan to achieve change by countering their resistance. You need to know the people in your organisation. Part of the change strategy is to identify influential people who can effect the change and work on them to get them to be sponsors and support the whole change process. It takes time just chipping away at the areas of resistance until you shape the organisation into something closer to your ideal. Sometimes results come in unexpected forms or unexpected ways. You can't assume that someone who responds in a redneck way is not able to grow beyond that. I've seen enormous shifts. In the Commission there's a high level of intellect among the staff. If you raise issues people go away and gnaw at them and come back for more.

It even works with people in Treasury. I single them out because they too are a control agency like the Commission who are often seen to be divorced and different from mainstream public sector activity. If you make suggestions about things that might happen, often the brief time it takes people to shift is quite amazing. Considering how emotive some of the issues are you would expect it to take ages before anyone could process the information and make an attitudinal shift. People who are able to make this kind of shift are good people to nurture and sometimes they can become change agents too. Part of the shift comes from their level of trust in you.

When I get discouraged I look back on an older Maori guy who, with just a few words, took me to a new level of understanding. He took me aside and said that he used to think about giving up when he couldn't achieve a particular goal. He'd get angry and strung out and feel responsible for failure and get into the self-blame trip. But he learned to think of it as a strategic withdrawal. 'When you think about it mate, the future really looks after itself. It's a cycle – all you need to do is wait for the cycle to come back around again. There's no need to give up. The one thing you can count on is that you'll get another chance'.

The Pacific Island Voice in EEO

'My background has given me a strong commitment to social justice, a desire to make a difference.'

'The key factor these days in the success of business is how people are used and valued and how their potential is recognised.'

Marilyn Kohlhase
Employee Development Manager, Auckland City Council

Interviewed by Marianne Tremaine

Marilyn Kohlhase grew up in Auckland in a large working-class suburb. Her ethnic background is German/Samoan and she was born in New Zealand to migrant parents who were ambitious for her future. She walked to church every Sunday along a street divided into state houses on one side of the ridge and private houses on the other, so she has always had an awareness of class and known that there are haves and have-nots in society.

Tell me about your work background?

At university I'd been on a studentship, so when I finished my degree I should have gone to teachers' training college but my parents paid off my bond and I went fishing. I saw the effect of multinationals at work in the fishing industry and I became interested in the impact of overseas capital on New Zealand's economy. So it was probably not surprising that my next move was to CORSO as a youth education officer. I worked in schools around New Zealand talking about the causes of poverty. My background has given me a strong commitment to social justice, a desire to make a difference.

After CORSO I was fairly burnt-out, so I worked on a short-term research project on fishing in the Pacific. Then I went as an administrator to Continuing Education at Auckland University. Then I was in the Clerical Union for a short while. From the Engineers' Union I was tapped on the shoulder to apply for a job at the State Services Commission as Ethnic Minorities Co-ordinator.

The position was surrounded by controversy. Some in the Pacific Island public service community felt that a particular Samoan man should have got the position. I felt very vulnerable in the middle of this debate. But some of the opposition died away when the mother of a women who had been to school in Samoa recognised me as 'Lizzy's daughter'. So I have my mother to thank for gaining a degree of acceptance from the community in that job.

What was your first involvement with EEO? How did you first come to understand the term?

My first involvement with EEO was when I was working for the Clerical Workers' Union in 1983. We promoted the Working Women's Charter in the late seventies and set up the Working Women's Resource Centre in 1983. In the mid-1970s I was also involved in the first black women's group in Auckland along with Ripeka Evans. However, it didn't last long in that form. There was a parting of the ways between Pacific Island and Maori women and Ripeka went on with others to form a black unity group. Then I was part of the FOL [Federation of Labour] Maori and Pacific Island Committee which was set up in 1980. So with one thing and another you could say that I've been involved in equity issues since the late seventies.

As for defining EEO, the first time I thought about a formal definition was when I was with the unions and I read the blue glossy publication on EEO put out by the Employers' Federation. From that publication I took EEO to mean positive action to get more women, Maori and Pacific Island people into the workforce. Of course in those days I was sceptical about a publication on EEO put out by the Employers' Federation, just as I was sceptical about the EEO job in the Commission.

I felt nervous about the EEO job both from the point-of-view of whether it would be possible to achieve change within the bureaucracy, and also because of the attitude towards me by some of the people in the Pacific Island Community. As an Aucklander I had few supporters in Wellington at first, because people didn't know me and I wasn't culturally strong, so there was always a question even within myself about whether I was the appropriate choice.

Throughout my first year I felt very unsure, but the thing I could do, that Diana (Crossan) had seen as my great strength, was to get things to happen in a bureaucracy. Increasingly I did find support from others working in the field, especially when I was working on the Pacific Island Senior Management Programme and setting up Pacific Island networks for public servants.

Because I was sufficiently articulate and confident, I would stand up in front of people and say, EEO has provided us with an opportunity to get in touch with our roots again. This type of public relations exercise is the 'soft' side of EEO and depends a great deal on personalities. All the time, in the background, there were certain traditionalist Samoan elders who disapproved of having someone like me in the position. It was stressful, but I survived. My support came mainly from friends, family and the then Pacific Island Affairs Unit.

Is there any particular achievement in terms of EEO that you can look back on?

The career development programmes I ran throughout the country for Pacific Island people in the public service. The courses identified those people with leadership potential and helped them to recognise that they could make the move to become managers. We tried to show them that they didn't need to operate in the traditional humble Pacific Island way within the public service. Some of these people went on to apply for the Senior Management course and ended up with promotions. Seeing that happen was the most wonderful thing for me.

There were three of us involved in running the Career Development courses. I was born here and the other two were born in the Islands but all of us were university educated. We were role models and could say things based on our own experiences. It was exciting, powerful stuff but an administrative nightmare. We didn't want to turn anyone away and 30 people would come on the courses planned for 15 and we would cram them in. We didn't have the resources we needed to be running courses on this scale. State Services Commission support staff were pushed to the limit. It was a real strain. But in EEO you're always trying to do more and you do put pressure on others – it cuts across our being nice people. If you're committed to change, change comes first.

The other achievement was building the networks of Pacific Island women. They were very successful because of the people-orientation of the Pacific way. That support and sharing was very important and it was one of the most significant things from that time of intense activity.

Having worked in social change in CORSO and the unions and Continuing Education, I was used to working against time. In the EEO Unit we always had the knowledge that 'our cause would be watered down' and that we had to achieve as much as we could before that happened.

What do you see as the main advantages and disadvantages of EEO – or perhaps rather its limitations as well as its ability to create positive change?

Well, I could be cynical and say that it's created an industry. We've created employment for ourselves, it's something of a bureaucracy. However, more seriously, the main advantage has come from the introduction of the State Sector Act which has helped the groups named in the legislation to come together and promote their visibility, difference and worth. Now, you can hear the voices for change. Now people are able to say, 'we are here, we will stay here, demographics show we will grow in number'. Because the legislation identifies the haves and the have-nots, the employers have to make some provision for these people who have been ignored and used and often abused in the workplace.

For people from the Pacific Islands imbued with the feeling of gratitude to the colonial government of New Zealand for bringing them 'civilisation', the colonised mindset carries over to work. Pacific Island people are grateful to get basic jobs in the public service. It's difficult to bite the hand that feeds you, especially for those with a traditional conservative upbringing. The colonised mindset can lead to conflict when there is resistance to new ideas. For me it was hard to build adequate alliances or to teach people to strategise to help them move up the career ladder. But the legislation has helped to bring people together to network and talk through new directions.

As far as the negative aspects are concerned, there can be a difficulty in working with other groups for EEO. At one stage I wanted to work more closely with the PSA (Public Service Association). The PSA had set up national working parties for EEO groups: Pacific Island people, Maori, women and people with disabilities. I felt that we could have worked together on things like recognition for cultural skills, proper payment for language interpretation for Pacific Island staff in the public service. I wanted to do this through the Human Resource Division at the State Services Commission but it wasn't so easy with some of the personalities involved. They couldn't see that we could work together to achieve the same ends. It was utterly frustrating.

Perhaps another limitation was the obsession with EEO plans. They were a useful tool to draw attention to the need for specific goals and objectives, but the EEO Unit within the State Services Commission came to be seen as police checking up on whether or not plans had been implemented. Sometimes too we became rather precious if the plan didn't conform, if people didn't say things in the right way. But if good things were happening in terms of EEO, did we have any business to complain about minor details in plans? Looking back I think more flexibility was needed, the recognition that EEO was being done differently according to the different cultures of different organisations.

Where do you think EEO is at present? At the moment do you see any particular trend emerging in terms of EEO?

Human resource management styles in New Zealand are being examined in the context of looking at teamwork and coaching and delegation and leadership and visioning and strategic planning. All of us EEO gals have been doing that stuff for a long time. We were doing it out on a limb, but we were making a contribution to human resource practices in Aoteoroa. Our EEO philosophy, both theory and practice, needs to influence human resource management if human resource management is to be really successful for organisations. EEO is the 'magic ingredient' that will help the cake rise to perfection

The trouble with us [the EEO co-ordinators in the EEO Unit of the Commission] was that we were like princesses on stallions charging through the public service with that 'holier than thou' attitude that tends to get up people's noses. We knew that our cause was pure. There's a particular style that goes with being a social change agent which can be confrontational. You show people what is wrong with their way of doing things and you know all the answers. It makes it hard for people to like you.

So where EEO is now is different for different sectors. For example, local government is doing very little for EEO. But local government organisations aren't the only ones that are dragging their heels. At a seminar on the amendment to the Human Rights legislation which was attended by 400 people, the audience was asked how many of them belonged to organisations which had EEO plans and only ten hands went up. Mind you some of them may have been doing EEO stuff without calling it EEO. For example, Dominion Breweries' career management programme benefits the whole of the organisation and I would call that EEO. EEO is done under different names in different organisations.

I think too that the issue of where women are in the hierarchy of organisations is of concern to management. But when you begin to talk about sexism, people go a bit funny and feel very uncomfortable. Yet until you can address the issue of sexism in some way, you are stuck and you get the feeling that it's going to exist for a long time. There are challenges there for EEO. We need to find ways of talking to the people in power about how to make changes that will help bring people from disadvantaged groups into the organisation and have them survive without being marginalised or being merely token.

How do you feel about the relationship between EEO and the Treaty?

I feel that EEO and the Treaty were lumped together in the early days in the public service. I think EEO is about equity and access in the workplace and the Treaty of Waitangi is about power in this country and should influence how we work together, but I think that EEO for Maori people is a different issue and not understood by Pakeha. Being prescriptive won't work. We need to be able to approach things differently with different people and with different organisations.

For Pacific Island people it can be difficult, because sometimes the Maori approach to EEO may seem not to be understood. And so when it comes to looking at the Treaty I think we all need a good understanding of what it means in terms of the history of this country and our historical relationships. There are going to be some significant changes in the economic balance of power, with greater Maori prominence in the ownership of fisheries, for example. But also with New Zealand developing an identity appropriate to the next century, the outcome should mean that we are seen as a bicultural/multicultural nation where Maori have high visibility and influence.

In terms of EEO and the Treaty new models have to be found. EEO has been dominated by Pakeha women and now there is a real need for Maori people to develop their own approach. I think there is a maturity of analysis coming from some Maori EEO practitioners and a diversity of models to accommodate different perspectives is emerging.

What sort of models and techniques do you see developing?

I haven't thought much about a model as such but I see a strong link with the idea of TQM (total quality management). If we think of the designated EEO groups as separate entities on one side and the organisation on the other side, it's difficult for communication to get under way between them, sometimes simply because of problems in the organisation. If the organisation is struggling with bad management, a lack of communication, no career paths and lack of trust, then it's not possible to begin talking about what's wrong for designated groups.

But back to TQM. Often it fails because people don't become empowered to make changes – EEO processes could make that change, but their role is misunderstood or ignored. Changes can be made by looking at particular issues that are global issues for the organisation, career management for example. But you need people with equity concerns too for there to be a change in the power dynamic as a result of this kind of global strategy.

Sometimes you feel that so many groups are discriminated against in organisations that it's hard to restrict your work to the groups which are designated in the legislation, but often something which is introduced to help a designated group can help others. For example, we have introduced a literacy programme here at Auckland City Council primarily for

Maori and Pacific Island staff and it's been extended to Pakeha people too. And there are some changes in personnel policy that are beneficial for everyone, improved recruitment and promotion procedures, for example. So you may focus on designated groups but the disempowered in the whole workforce benefit.

By and large EEO in wider terms is élitist. The people who benefit from it tend to be the few who are already advantaged within their EEO group. I always felt that the people in the public service were very lucky, comparatively speaking. They had good jobs, working for an organisation which had a concern for employee rights. When I was in the Clerical Workers' Union, I'd go to places where the employer was so hostile to the union we had to meet in the toilet.

There seems to be a type of hierarchy in EEO. People with disabilities often feel that they are given much less attention than women and Maori. Do people from the Pacific Islands feel a similar sense of frustration?

Yes, I sensed it while I was at the Commission even though we used to say, and I agree, that a victory for one group is a victory for all, because it moves our cause forward. But what else can you expect when EEO is dominated by Pakeha women – naturally they see and act from their own viewpoint. That puts an extra burden on someone like me to try to redress the balance and get the message across about the Pacific Island community. However, there are a group of Pacific Island women at the State Services Commission who have kept an eye on me although they are all younger than me and they keep reminding me of what reality is like for them. They say, 'Marilyn, we are the poor relation'.

But we know we have to support Maori staff, our understanding of their struggle means that we have to hold back sometimes when we're ready to go ahead, because we want them to develop an initiative first. Sometimes you are walking a tightrope because you want to develop programmes for Pacific Island people, but there is a need to recognise the special position of Maori in the public service and other sectors first.

As for people with disabilities, they seldom feature in organisational planning. It's accepted to talk about women and Maori, but for other groups, management acceptance is slower. You can of course use whatever available tools there are to push your message home. For example, I talked about Suffrage Year so much in 1993 that in some quarters it became known as 'Suffer Marilyn Year'. You can use fashionable, trendy ideas which are just commonsense EEO, such as family-friendly workplaces.

What have you gained from working in EEO?

Working in EEO has been great for me because I've enjoyed being with people who are passionate about what they are doing. There's an excitement about being involved in change even though it's burn-out territory. Being part of collectives (often voluntary) which have set up new ventures and made a difference – that's been important for me.

I've gained a lot in terms of personal growth from working in EEO with committed people.

What do you see as the future for EEO?

EEO in its pure form is going out of existence. There's a need for human resource practitioners to promote the issues of family-friendly workplaces, of networking, of career management, of sexual harassment under the 'good employer' banner. There will need to be a considerable equity component to human resource management in the future – but by the same token there's got to be an equity component to being a chief executive and manager in the future because of the customer orientation of the new world of business today. You need people with an appreciation of equity issues, otherwise they are going to abuse the market that they arc trying to appeal to.

Even the fact that McDonalds has a Pacific Island burger and Pacific Island employment policies, those are some of the signs that demographics are going to force people to change. So the message of the EEO Trust that diversity is good for business is an important one. Human resource practices need to change the values of the whole workplace.

It seems to me that the philosophy and beliefs and practices of EEO are integral to good human resource policy in both the public and private sector. The key factor these days in the success of business is how people are used and valued and how their potential is recognised.

EEO and People with Disabilities

'For the majority of people with disabilities there are two main survival strategies, denial or allowing your mind to be colonised..'

'Often you can ignore your disability until after your teenage years. With work or attempts to get work, the reality of life hits you. You may have been floating along thinking you were much like everyone else, but this is the time when you come face-to-face with your identity crisis and suddenly, out of nowhere, you are confronted with heaps of issues that can't be ignored.'

Robyn Hunt
Manager, Review and Development, Workbridge

Interviewed by Marianne Tremaine

Tell me about your early life. Where are you from?

I was born in Christchurch but grew up in Hororata, 'a little village of about 500 people halfway between Christchurch and the mountains'. My family are still there farming crops and sheep in Hororata. I went to the same primary school that my parents had gone to as children. Because my parents were known and respected, I had a place in the scheme of things. My first shock was going away to a Presbyterian Girls' Boarding School. I detested being a boarder. It was hard being different in that middle-class conservative establishment, but I loved the academic part of school.

In those days it was hard to demand your right to do something unusual which didn't fit into the prevailing mindset. People's minds were colonised by experts such as doctors and teachers who told them what to think. I wanted to sit School Certificate in three years rather than four and had to fight school policy and the Headmistress. It was a tough battle that I won mostly through passive resistance. But I passed School Certificate and was accredited University Entrance the following year. Thinking back, I can see that I started becoming politicised about disability rights in my UE year when Jim Flynn, an American political scientist from Otago University, came to speak at a seminar about the civil rights movement in America. I recognised the links between people discriminated against because of race and those discriminated against because of disability. Both race and disability were social constructions. That was the dawning of a new understanding for me.

When it came to my last year of school, I said I would go back as a day girl or not at all. Being a daygirl was a good transition from school to life in a university hostel. It took me four years to complete my BA, a double major in English and Political Science. I loved the fun side of university as well as the learning. I went to every party and got into all the hippy stuff of the sixties.

How was it making the transition from university to work?

In retrospect I can see that I was a little naïve to think that with a degree I would be able to get any job my heart desired. When I started to apply for jobs, reality hit me with a smack about the ears. I wanted to be a radio journalist. That dream soon faded. Although there was full employment, I applied for 40 jobs and got nothing. Finally, in spite of being non-numerate, I went to Wellington to work in the Department of Statistics, an awful experience that has left scars. The job was hopeless, the human resource management skills in the department were non-existent. I was very unhappy there. I got sick and lost weight and left after five months.

My father had warned me not to go there. He knew I wasn't the public servant type. But after leaving I had to endure nine months of unemployment and lost a lot of self-esteem. Finally I got a job on a newspaper through a family friend who was related to the editor. Although it was a blow to my pride to have to use a family connection to get a job, I still dreamed of being a journalist. On the newspaper, I began as a clerical assistant in illustrations writing captions for photographs. Later I became a journalist, employed on an under-rate worker's pay because my employer considered my level of production would not justify full pay. But I enjoyed the job and when I was given the chance to write stories, I had good support from two men with disabilities who worked there and the editor of the Women's Page. Nevertheless, the paper wouldn't send me on a journalism course and there seemed no hope of promotion. So I left and went overseas for three years.

In that three years I worked at a variety of different jobs, fought with unenlightened employers, read *Spare Rib*, felt intimidated by the amazing strength of feminists, travelled in Europe, became involved in a left-wing political media group, met my husband and ran away from the English winter with him when he got a job in Wellington. Back in New Zealand, I was offered a job in Broadcasting as assistant to the Public Affairs Manager. At work I met Helen McConnochie and began to write free-lance for *Future Indicative* (a radio news magazine for and about people with disabilities) as well as writing articles for my husband's publication on the ways technology could help people with disabilities.

The International Year for Disabled People in 1980 was a landmark year. The IYDP telethon was a very politicising event which took me forward with my personal analysis of disability issues. I saw it as charity and entirely distasteful. The attitudes were patronising. We were pitied, but not acknowledged as people. Telethon helped me see that disability is not the major problem, but rather the environment. You often have it in your power to find ways around your disability, but you are still handicapped by social attitudes.

How did you come to know about EEO?

Basically I knew what EEO was long before I knew the term and now I can't even remember when I first heard it. I think that's because during the eighties I was involved with so many issues relevant to EEO. I was in women's groups. I was taking time out to have children and go back to university to do English honours and Women's Studies. I was involved in disability issues with the EEO Unit of the State Services Commission even before I went there to work. Having experienced blatant discrimination at first-hand, when a theory like EEO came along it was tailor-made for me.

What is the main message you would like to get across about EEO and disability?

My main message would be that the issues for people with disabilities are similar but different. For us it's much more urgent than for other groups because over such a long time there's been no action. We're so far behind even in the public sector where there has been substantial progress on EEO. But nothing has been done at all in the private sector.

The reason why nothing is happening is partly historical. Between the late 1800s and the 1950s, people with disabilities were shut away in institutions so they were 'out-of-sight and out-of-mind'. So disability issues don't figure in the New Zealand psyche because they haven't been talked about. That's one thing that has changed. People with disabilities have become more visible and currently there is at least a concept of disability that wasn't there in the past.

There are deep problems in attitudes towards people with disabilities. Our issues are trivialised. We are not seen as having ordinary, natural, human aspirations to achieve and meet our personal goals. Until EEO addresses this issue of failing to take people with disabilities seriously, none of the real problems will be solved. An example of this is a newspaper story I read recently, about a woman with cerebral palsy setting up a computer business. When I started reading, I thought it was just another version of the 'super-crip' story. You know, person with huge disadvantages overcomes all, achieves enormous success, clears buildings in one bound, that kind of thing. Now those stories worry me because I'm sure people read them and think, 'If she can do all that, what's wrong with me?' In fact people with disabilities do well managing to live perfectly ordinary lives. Media stories can give people with disabilities the idea that unless you over-achieve, you don't count.

But this particular interview was different. The journalist went through the facts of the woman's entrepreneurship and detailed her struggles and successes, then at the end asked her if, given all that hard work, it wouldn't have been easier just to stay on the benefit and keep her computing as a hobby. I was outraged. Her creative efforts were trivialised because she was disabled. Yet we all know that to an extent your self-esteem and the way you are valued by others is affected by the job you do. We accept that not having work harms the unemployed and can make them feel worthless. Why isn't it obvious that people with disabilities have similar feelings?

No other group is up against that kind of rubbish, although they all have their own rubbish. But disability is more complex because it interlinks with all the other EEO areas, with gender, ethnic minorities and Maori. Yet even if you look at just the area of gender, I don't believe the women's movement in New Zealand has done anything to encompass the interests of women with disabilities in a structured way. Suffrage year is a case in point. Women with disabilities were practically ignored.

By the same token EEO has done very little for the average person with a disability. Part of the reason is that EEO has come at a time when trying to do anything that's not essential is going against the stream. Disability is no longer a cost that organisations feel they can afford. With restructuring, many of the people with disabilities in the public sector who were at the bottom of the heap have lost their jobs. The private sector is irrelevant because many employers are too small for EEO as it's practised at the moment to be of much use and for big employers, EEO is totally alien to the culture.

The private sector may well be starting to look at some groups for good self-interested reasons, but I don't believe that they've begun to look at people with disabilities even as a market. Yet we know that the proportion of people with disabilities in the community is *at least* ten per cent and because of the stigma involved with disability, survey figures are probably very conservative and a more realistic estimate could be as high as 28 per cent.

Are there any particular EEO achievements that you feel have made a difference?

Having a scholarship for people with disabilities in the public service makes a difference. A scholarship gives important messages to people. We need role-models. The award system to recognise the achievements of employers is another milestone and gives valuable examples to organisations who haven't come as far. I'm proud of the work done by people with disabilities themselves, in setting up networks and in organising the first-ever conference of public servants with disabilities in 1993 and in the celebrations of disability pride. Then there are the achievements of people who have worked with us as allies, for example the work of Diane Candy, Diana Crossan and Janice Burns.

But there are disappointments in the wider world. For example, people with disabilities have no voice in the EEO Trust. That's the fault of the way it's been set up. I doubt that many Maori organisations are members of the EEO Trust either.

What do you see as the main advantages of EEO and the disadvantages?

In terms of the advantages I think that EEO has provided the first neutral place for people with disabilities to meet. The disability networks have enabled people to meet in the workplace. Women and Maori have had their own meeting places but we haven't. Interacting with each other is important in the long-term development of a community. People with disabilities are so diverse as a group. We are really a whole lot of smaller groups.

The profoundly deaf can often be quite separatist. They don't necessarily see themselves as disabled. They see themselves as a cultural and linguistic minority. There is rivalry and sniping in the wider disability community. There is the attitude of 'You get more than we do and it's not fair'. But that's historical too, in that we're reaping the fallout from the attitudes of the people who were in control in the past. EEO has taught us to work together, it's shown us ways of meeting and talking around the issues. We don't face only external barriers, there are lots of barriers operating between us.

Many people prefer to keep their disability hidden, which can lead to a lot of pressure, because to deny your disability you may have had to be better and make more effort than everyone else to get and keep your job. Then there's the gulf between employed people with disabilities and unemployed people with disabilities. That gulf is hard to cross except in a service delivery kind of way.

There are so many differences between us: class and cultural differences, educational qualifications, skill levels. EEO tends to help those who are already advantaged, those who have jobs, skills and education. If you are disabled and have no skills then it is difficult to get started in the workforce, especially these days. When I was first applying for jobs it was hard. These days it must be even more difficult and demoralising. Ideally, you hope for a job that is going to enable you to achieve at your highest level rather than a dreary, unsatisfying job that you do purely for the money. But that desire is hard to achieve for anyone and more so for people with disabilities who have to battle with discrimination.

So in terms of your experience and what you've used EEO to achieve, what would you try to enthuse others about using to make progress?

One of the things that I've found most empowering in my own working life is managers who recognise my disability as a positive part of me. Working with managers who see my disability as a strength allows me to give much more energy to my work. I feel passionately about what I do and it's wonderful to work with a boss who sees my emotional involvement as a positive asset to be encouraged, rather than a hindrance limiting my objectivity. Some of the people I've worked with have given me the freedom to take risks and be creative. Few people get that chance, let alone people with disabilities.

My career took off when I finally got myself together about disability and decided that I could be up-front and have a take-it-or-leave-it attitude. But by that stage I also had some skills and experience and qualifications to offer. People might say, 'Well, you could afford to do that'.

But that attitude change is really significant, isn't it?

Yes, it is significant. And so many young people that I've come across are really confused. I believe it holds them back. And it's a result of society's values that they're confused, because they've been given so many mixed messages as they've grown up. They're still getting them. Growing up in the fifties I got heaps of mixed messages and it wasn't until the eighties that I really felt comfortable with myself and who I was.

I think there are a lot of people round who still haven't got that all sussed. But the people who have, seem to me to be really successful.

They are the people who are up-front and feel OK about who they are. They don't make a big thing about their disability, but it's there and it's part of them. For me it's an advantage because I've chosen to work in the disability area, though I have worked in other jobs. The places where I experienced the most discrimination were those other jobs, but I know that people working in the disability area have experienced discrimination too.

But you see, not everyone has the choice of where they work and that's what EEO is all about, in essence, that people need more choices. The whole issue of cost is just a lot of garbage and often the issue of productivity is too. Not always, because there are some people who do have lower productivity. But there are ways of maximising productivity which don't have to cost a fortune; it just needs some creative thinking.

I suppose the thing that worries me most about EEO is that in the area of disabilities, it hasn't been very systematic. It's been very ad hoc, often just a one-off effort with no follow-up. And the ad hoc approach is probably even more prevalent in the private sector, because there's so little knowledge. In some ways, disability organisations are themselves amongst the worst offenders. I don't believe they're necessarily good allies in EEO. You'll always find some individuals within the organisations, but as a group I don't believe they've taken the lead. They have not been the ones who've pushed for EEO. It's been individuals with disabilities. The APD (Assembly of People with Disabilities) is keen on EEO, but even within the APD there's quite a lot of cynicism about it – its efficacy, who it's for, what it really means.

EEO doesn't sell itself well. An advertising agency would say that it has an image problem. Even people in my own organisation don't think much of EEO. How are we ever going to achieve EEO, if people at Workbridge doing their best to place people with disabilities, see EEO as some irrelevant pie-in-the-sky theory? There's also the big debate between EEO and managing diversity. I have a problem with managing diversity because with the downturn in the economy there hasn't been much recruitment. And yet if you're only looking at the way you manage the people already within your organisation, you're not going to make a difference, because EEO is also about who's not there?

It would be nice to be able to say that most of the problem is lack of exposure to people with disabilities, but that's too simplistic. It would be the same thing as taking people onto a marae for a day. People might enjoy the experience but it wouldn't necessarily change their attitudes. There's a lot of tokenism in EEO and issues which need attention. There are issues surrounding access and information. But basically there's the issue in people's minds and that's the hardest issue of all. For example, last year I did an interview with the Evening Post for Braille Week. The journalist who rang me up kept talking about blindness until I said, 'Excuse me, but I'm not blind, I'm partially sighted', and then she went into a complete tizz and wasn't sure whether she should be interviewing me at all.

The problem is that people can only see things in black and white terms. They don't see shades of grey. You're either alive or you're dead, you can see or you can't see, you can hear or you can't hear, there are no in-betweens. We need to get through to people that the differences are more subtle and complex than that. I've even heard of people in wheelchairs parking in disability carparks and being abused when they put their chair in the car and walk round to the driver's seat.

People attack them saying 'You're not disabled, you can walk'. They don't understand that walking round your car after you've put your wheelchair in the back is one thing, but walking for any distance unsupported might be quite another. If you want to know where the bottom-line is on people's attitudes to disability, you only need to look at disability carparks and the way the general populace treats them with contempt.

Do you see any trend emerging in terms of EEO? For example, some people feel that EEO is going out of business and being absorbed into human resource management practice. Would you agree?

The very idea worries me. Allowing human resources to absorb EEO will not be a solution. The problems may be less obvious but they will be exacerbated. If EEO is absorbed within human resources, it will get stuck there and lose its impact to change the whole organisation. EEO needs to be managed as a massive change process extending to all parts of an organisation and changing its culture and values.

What about models – do you see any particular models emerging or any particular techniques that work?

No. I don't. There are examples. The way the Ministry of Commerce has worked has been a good example of what can be achieved, but the trouble is that so many of these things are linked to specific people. Good examples tend to be the product of good management. Good management is a prerequisite for EEO. In the Ministry of Commerce they seemed to be able to make things happen because they had people with vision who were determined to carry things through from idea to implementation. When these people move on, sometimes their ideas are embedded in the structure of the organisation, sometimes a new broom takes over and all the gains are lost.

The problems are often in middle management. What you find with EEO is that often the people at the top say, 'yes' and are very enthusiastic, the people at the bottom say, 'yes, we need EEO desperately', but somewhere in the middle is the great sludge of what I call 'corporate concrete' which doesn't want EEO and doesn't want change. Accountability needs to be pushed down right through the organisation.

In terms of the reality of your job, what approach to EEO works best?

I like to take a very direct approach. I believe that anything is possible and that you've got to take risks in EEO. Some of the people in EEO are not risktakers and I wonder why they're there. Wanting to do nice things for people in a woolly kind of way is not a good reason for being in EEO.

You've got to be there because you have a vision, because you want to carry it through and because you can see the long-term goals and that's the whole business about advantaging people – sometimes you may have to advantage people who already have advantages so you can filter it down – but the important thing is to take that next step.

I don't have problems with rewarding achievers necessarily. Workbridge has a Women's Study Award and we made four awards again this year. I said to the people who got the awards, we don't want your gratitude, we want you to put something back into the disability community. There is no point in advantaging people just to have them become the disability equivalent of the Queen Bee.

Why do you think that Workbridge has been so successful?

Because we're a business organisation and we're very clearly focused. Because we're a service organisation which serves its customers. There are a lot of service organisations out there in the disability sector who don't know what service means. We relate directly to our two major customers; people with disabilities and employers. They are our prime markets.

Our success is partly to do with the people employed here. One of the reasons I love working here is that people with disabilities are seen by the organisation as customers and treated with respect. All our material is good quality. Admittedly we don't have the bottom-line of fund-raising like most of the other disability organisations. But we work on a lesser budget than our predecessor organisation, so we are cost-effective as well.

The service mentality is something really useful that we've taken from the private sector. EEO could gain a huge advantage from adopting a service approach. The people in our management team who came from the private sector don't have any of the baggage surrounding disability and have just seen it as a service issue. To them people with disabilities are no different from anyone else and that has been refreshing and exciting and doesn't conflict with any of my views or values.

At some point EEO will have to come to terms with the service approach and the need to market itself. I think that we tried quite hard to market EEO at the beginning but the emphasis in the public sector has changed. The role of EEO has become more of a monitoring exercise so that marketing has faded away a bit, but there's still a need. The EEO Trust does its best but, given its resources and the amount of work to be done, it's an impossible task to be all things to all people.

What about training? What do you think works best in training sessions?

The problem is that people come with different expectations and they don't always want to hear you. There are specific issues about training in the disability area. We don't have enough quality training available. But I think what works best for me is to keep it light, practical and make sure it doesn't sound frightening or too hard. That's why I use humour a lot, to help people relax and see that there is nothing complicated about what I'm telling them.

Another reason I use humour is to know whether the audience is still alive and alert, because it's not easy for me to read body language if I'm addressing a group. If they laugh I know they're still with me. If they don't laugh I know I'm in big trouble. People with disabilities have little strategies like this that they use. Sometimes we're so unconscious of them, that we're not even aware of using them ourselves. We have to be creative and good at organising other people to give us what we need.

You don't tend to experience much resistance in training sessions because it's one thing to be mean to people with disabilities out in the real world, but no one wants to be seen as 'anti' in a training session with their peers. So people are very seldom up-front about their negative feelings, which of course makes it hard for you to deal with things that are sitting unspoken in their minds.

Looking back over your experience of the last ten years and changes and shifts in Disability-EEO, how do you feel about it now from this distance?

I feel very angry that when the repeal of the employment equity legislation is discussed, it is already being seen as limited to pay equity when its scope was so much wider and I feel very angry about Suffrage Year too. Both of them were lost opportunities for disability. Over this time though, there has been a change. People with disabilities will no longer accept being at the bottom of the heap. Overall we have made some amazing changes in the last ten years, but I question how deep and lasting those changes have been and how we can build on them. One of my big fears, and it's an issue for women as well, is that we will slip backwards. It's so easy to lose ground. People forget. History gets lost.

That's another thing, people with disabilities have no history. We have no past to draw on. Women are discovering their past, but there are no women with disabilities in that past. And I find that harder and harder as I get older and search for my own past. In all the words that have been written about welfare in New Zealand, there's no mention of people with disabilities. We have no role to play. It's as if we weren't even there, except that I know we were. For example, the first blind woman to gain a university degree graduated in the 1920s with a Masters in Latin, but we don't know that. You're not likely to read that anywhere. Yet that was at a time when it was quite exceptional for a woman to get a degree, let alone a blind woman. There is still the view that people with disabilities can't do anything.

More research on our history would help to explain why things are the way they are. I think that the lack of a past is one of the reasons why people are confused. If you don't know what happened in the past, you don't know why things are the way they are and it's hard to know how to make things happen differently in the future. We need the understanding and the lessons to be learned from the past.

Are there any last points you'd like to make?

The new Human Rights legislation offers the opportunity for real education and learning about workplace issues for people with disabilities. It should be seen as a mandate for action, not some kind of legislative clobbering-machine. I would like to challenge everyone who reads this book to commit themselves to make change happen, so that when we look back after the next ten years, we can see real change. If you are committed to EEO, ask yourself what you are going to do about it and what you're going to do in the disability area? Don't leave it all to people with disabilities. We need allies who will listen to us without taking over or giving us tokenism. We want real change. We would have preferred it yesterday, but we'll work for it today or tomorrow. Make yourself part of that change. If you're not part of the change, you're part of the problem.

Towards a More Equitable Society

'Organisations that improve their human resource procedures usually become more equitable.'

'... we cannot expect business to solve all our social and environmental problems. Everyone has to take individual responsibility and the government must help facilitate that.'

Gill Ellis
Consultant, Ellis Walker and Associates, Auckland

Interviewed by Janet Sayers

Gill works as an organisational consultant in equal employment opportunity, management and team development and career management. She is also a part-time lecturer in Management Studies at the University of Auckland. Gill previously had a successful international career in marketing, advertising and management, in 1977 becoming the first Australasian woman director of the international company in which she worked.

Gill became known in New Zealand, in 1986, as a co-author of *Theory K: The Key to Excellence in New Zealand Management* and in 1991 for *Women Managers: Success on our Own Terms.* Gill is active as a public speaker, seminar leader and promoter of women's development in the workforce. She is involved with women's networking groups and enterprise development initiatives for women.

In our initial discussions about this interview we decided to follow a past, present, future format. You mentioned that you were disappointed with the movement that EEO has made in the last six years. As a beginning to discussing the past of EEO could you reflect on why you are disappointed with EEO's progress?

Six years ago I had a sense of excitement at the possibilities of EEO. I really had great expectations. So, when I look back I ask myself, 'how can I justify to myself EEO's failure to achieve what was hoped for it?'

I see two main reasons for this failure. They are, in short, that the priority for private sector companies was economic survival during that period of time, and that the timing of the introduction of EEO was awful.

EEO couldn't have come at a worse time in New Zealand's history for being dropped on infertile ground. There was massive structural adjustment to the economy and the EEO movement has to be seen in the context of that, and the prevailing New Right ideological agenda.

I imagine a concept of 'brain time' for executives, which is how many new ideas they can grasp at any one time. During this time we had deregulation, restructuring, changes in tax policy, and major political changes. This change was coming at people from all fronts and their ability to cope was strained. Personal stress levels have been high. This is not just for executives, but everybody.

Another related issue was that companies became very lean and mean at this time. There were very few resources for *anything,* let alone the introduction of EEO. Companies were trying to do it all on the smell of an oily rag.

So I think the resource constraint was very real. Had things been a little 'fatter', then EEO may have got a few more people and more resources.

Business people were focused on three main strategies – changing work practices, building customer service, and product/service innovation. What wasn't happening was any type of human resource development.

You or I might argue that if human resource development had been the focus, then companies might have been able to do these three things more effectively. But the skills and knowledge weren't available then in

New Zealand. The level of understanding of human potential issues was quite basic.

So you see the problems as much broader than a 'failure' of EEO, and that the human resource issues are critical?

Yes. If, for instance, you want to upgrade your performance management and appraisal systems, and you want the kind of systems that truly measure performance, then you have to overcome bias. If you want really effective recruitment systems then you know that leaving it to untrained individuals to interview someone and make a subjective judgement is not the best way of doing it. And so, EEO is often initially a procedural 'clean-up act'. Organisations that improve their human resource procedures usually become more equitable.

You mentioned that the triumvirate of workplace practice, service and product innovation was 'happening', but that human resource development wasn't...

People didn't acknowledge at the time that the 'people thing' was an important component of those three strategies, except in customer service. Look at what happened – we had 'Kiwi host' programmes and lots of training in customer service. More recently we have seen a focus on TQM or quality programmes, performance management and team-building. It is only now we are hearing people say that quality, teams and performance are about people. Only now are executives saying, 'we need to know more about the people dynamics in organisations'.

In that kind of environment, attempting to introduce EEO for reasons of social justice, equity and discrimination was almost impossible. I mean, the contexts tell you that your chances of success are going to be really slim.

I think this is the reason, or the explanation, for what you call the 'managerial imperative' – the philosophy that EEO was 'sold' as being an effective business strategy. Given these contexts I think selling EEO in this way was a *natural* outcome. In such an environment the only way to get anyone to listen to the message of EEO was to put it in managerial language – that is all that they were able to hear then.

Most importantly, we had a 'New Right' ideology pervading government. We had from Treasury, from the Business Roundtable and other opinion leaders, a very strong message that the only answer to New Zealand's problems was revitalised economic growth through market-led economics. So I think that EEO people tactically allied themselves with that message.

What were the differences in the public sector?

EEO in the public sector was promoted more from the human rights, equity perspective to start with. But, the problem was the ideological contexts were just the same as I described for the private sector. Again, the contexts were Treasury led, aiming for minimising the role of the state, cutting staff numbers for efficiency, cutting national debt, and introducing user-pays charges. So the same philosophy of promoting EEO needed to be done in the public sector, for it to be acceptable to managers who wanted to keep their jobs.

We were unrealistic, I believe, in what we could achieve against that background. We really should pat ourselves on the shoulder for what we have done given the tremendous opposition.

The background you have given helps to lift some of the responsibility for the 'lack' of progress from EEO's shoulders. We tend to look at ourselves and say – we haven't achieved this, and we haven't achieved that ...

Yes, although I feel somewhat cynical about the current state of EEO.

Why is that? Could you comment on the current state of EEO, particularly in the private sector?

I think of the private sector world of EEO and equitable human resource management practice in three groups. First, there is a group of companies who are placing a very low priority on HRM in any way, let alone EEO. They still do not have an awareness of the importance of people. My belief is, they will not survive. The only reason that they are surviving at the moment is because of high unemployment. People are hanging onto their jobs despite the rather toxic work environment. These companies are lost causes because you are not going to convince them about EEO when they don't even believe the fundamental basic of treating their staff as assets.

The second group of companies is numerically fairly big. They are placing a much higher priority on equitable HRM practice. What I see there is growing interest in training and development, participative management styles creeping in as a response to quality programmes, and better systems for recruitment and selection. Companies can see the payback. Also the Employment Contracts Act has had quite a dramatic effect on practices codifying job descriptions, terms and conditions. The Act made people think in more detail about recruitment and has forced a general upgrading of those human resource practices.

Are you seeing this in small businesses as well as large businesses?

No, not nearly as much. But, nevertheless, even small businesses are having to negotiate employment contracts and so they have to be better prepared when recruiting, even if it is fairly minimal.

So this second group of companies has given some attention to human resource practices. What about EEO?

In these organisations there has been some improvement against the worst excesses of subjectivity and personal bias. This is a result of improvement in the human resource systems. But improvements have been very minor.

Why is that?

Part of the reason for the lack of progress with EEO is that it has been problem-based. In explanation: a company may have a sexual harassment programme or a workplace literacy scheme. They haven't introduced these schemes out of the kindness of their hearts. The workplace literacy initiative came from wanting to increase the productivity of non-English speaking workers. Or they have introduced EEO initiatives to appease a women's or union lobby. I can think of three organisations I know where feisty women have moved into senior management roles and have said 'things have got to change around here'. So EEO initiatives have often been reactive; that is, reacting to problems rather than following an agenda to meet certain objectives organisation-wide.

My third group of private sector companies is a very small one. It is primarily made up of individuals in companies who have understood the basic principles of EEO and what it is trying to do. These individuals don't have a problem linking human rights issues with the managerial imperative. They argue, 'human rights might be the reason for doing it, but there are benefits to the organisation as well'. So, it makes sense to do it. They are linking EEO to the organisation's overall competitive advantage.

However, these individuals haven't been able to capture the majority of their colleagues into accepting that you need organisation-wide change.

So, what we have got currently is some very good examples of EEO initiatives, such as those in the EEO Trust 'success stories' booklet. But I don't think most of those companies [illustrated in the project book] are really doing EEO. In the long-term they will find they have had minor change only. This is because the overall premise of an EEO programme, to counter the discriminatory barriers, is not being carried out systematically. The initiatives are ad hoc.

I find it extremely hard to name one company that is a role model of doing EEO well, given the circumstances I have outlined, even though I applaud many excellent individual initiatives.

One of the problems, of course, is the lack of resources in the private sector, and the fact that the Trust doesn't have a monitoring and evaluating function. So that work is not being done.

Yes, but I just want more people to acknowledge these ad hoc initiatives are unlikely to achieve EEO in the long-term. I can't see how it possibly can. All the evidence from overseas and our own evidence – Judy McGregor's work on women in management, the SSC's review of several years of EEO in the state sector – they all suggest very little progress has been made.

We won't go forward unless we are honest about our objectives and failures.

If we could back-track for a moment and clarify how you define EEO. My experience is that people have different ideas about what EEO is.

My definition is a planned, systematic programme of change for the whole organisation with some specific results intended.

How do you see 'managing diversity' programmes – do you equate 'managing diversity' with EEO?

Absolutely not. At least not on its own, because it doesn't effect change. The purpose of EEO is to effect change. So, although 'managing diversity' programmes are useful, they don't fundamentally affect the structural problems in organisations.

I think that managing diversity has one particular strength that EEO does not have. It allows white men to feel included. Many men are also parents, and so it is possible to get them on-side with the objectives of the programme. I am a great fan of 'allies' for change and 'managing diversity' allows us to bring in allies from the dominant, majority groups who are sympathetic.

Could you see EEO linked to a TQM programme or a workplace reform programme?

Yes, but again, there has to be the planning at a systems level.

So you are saying EEO has to be integrated into the whole process ..

In isolation TQM or workplace reform will not solve inequity problems.

What do you think are effective strategies in EEO work?

There are several strategies that I use that I think are very helpful in EEO work.

I have been influenced by Fran Peavey, a social change activist who works internationally. I take from her work the idea of 'multiple strategies'. There are many strategies that can be used in the struggle for equality, not only one. Their validity depends on the contexts. Strategies could be: legislative; change; information; research; education and training; individual change such as consciousness and values work (for instance, school curriculum covering basic issues such as uncovering prejudices and stereotyping); structural change; political activism, and so on.

The second strategy is 'incrementalism' which was recently supported by Angeles Arrien. She argued that successful societies go for step-by-step change. Part of the problem with our modern society is that we want to get results so quickly. But, we need to go through all the important stages. I don't think it works to whip organisations into change too quickly, before they are ready.

A third strategy is 'Walking Our Talk', which is being consistent with our own philosophies. If we want to change the ways that businesses and influential groups are run, then we need to influence them to shift their thinking. The way to do that is to respect them as individuals in the same way that we would like to be respected.

There is a fundamental belief that I have about respect for human beings whoever they are. I understand the role that activists have in change, and the role that anger has in that, but I think that we need a more co-operative approach when we are working within businesses to facilitate change. We must build bridges.

I think it is this approach that works best in EEO training. Don't confront – minimise resistance by trying to find where people are at and work with their frameworks. Where I set the limits of what is acceptable is with their behaviour, not on them as people.

One of the objectives of the book was to ask, 'What is happening? Where to from here?', because, people really are struggling to find answers.

Answering the question 'What is happening?' involves also asking the question 'What measures of success can we give to EEO in the private sector?' The first measure might be to look at how many companies have a full-time dedicated person allocated to EEO. We find very few in the private sector. Telecom has, which you would expect because it's a huge company.

The second measure might be to look at how minority group members are faring and see the failure of EEO having repercussions for companies.

Enterprising individuals find other avenues for their skills. For women it has been self-employment. For Maori it's been gathering their own resources and seeking parallel development using the Treaty as the means of gaining economic independence. The failure of the business world to accommodate Maori aspirations means that they are increasingly doing their own thing about economic development and jobs.

Another example would be people with disabilities. Particularly Workbridge, because they have been very successful. This is principally because they have marketed their people according to business philosophy. They have said – 'OK, this is a market-led, free-enterprise environment. People with disabilities can meet company needs for people with skills'. So they have promoted people with disabilities to business as 'value for money' and 'very committed' (because they are so pleased to have a job).

Self-development is a strong theme for people with disabilities, as well as women and Maori, as traditional corporate structures fail to accommodate their needs.

What about the future of EEO? How do you feel about the future of EEO?

The future I divide into short-term, medium-term and long-term scenarios. In the short-term I will continue promoting 'managing diversity' concepts as I don't think that anything else is going to work. In the medium term I am hanging out for MMP (mixed member proportional representation), a changed political and economic environment, and legislation for EEO. In the long-term I think that a focus on environmental issues and sustainable economics will be more important than EEO in delivering equity. There is a bigger context about what needs to change – not in organisations so much as society.

In the short term we will still have a New Right ideology and its view that a market economy is going to provide the answer to New Zealand's problems. OK, so it has been slightly dented by MMP. But there is not yet a philosophic change in New Zealand. It's a slight accommodation. So, my view of working with equity issues in the next three years, if that's how long we have, is very tactical. I think what will work best is the 'managing diversity' philosophy. The three focuses I mentioned before – improved productivity, customer focus and quality, innovation – will be the themes of the business world in the next three years. And so I will sell improved HRM and 'managing diversity'. The message is: 'People are different. You have to value that difference if you want people to deliver high levels of productivity and gain the competitive advantage.'

These are EEO principles under another name. I still want organisations to adopt the systematic approach, the research, the profiling and discovering what the barriers to individuals and target groups are. I will still promote positive action programmes where they are appropriate. I will still recommend companies review individual policies and practices, assess programmes and so on. So, there is very little difference except EEO is labelled and marketed so that companies can grasp a reason for doing it that they believe in.

Business people are picking up 'managing diversity' from overseas literature and management magazines. They are more open to it. As well, the ethnic diversity in Auckland is increasingly apparent. Now significant proportions of a company's customer base are Asian and Pacific Island people and this has been a catalyst for greater awareness.

Given your comments in your review of the past, it doesn't appear that this approach will work though. Would this be correct?

Yes, there is no way this is actually going to work in delivering equity. So some other response is needed in the longer term.

In the medium term I see three factors as critical: MMP, the likelihood of EEO and pay equity legislation, and demographic changes. First, MMP. Political and economic philosophies will start shifting under MMP. I think they will have to as a result of stronger representation from a range of political parties. I see that there will be a much stronger input from left-centre and green parties. So, I am more optimistic about the possibility of some kind of EEO legislation. That range of parties support EEO, so you have to believe there is a good chance of legislation.

The most likely EEO legislation would mandate certain basic provisions for auditing and reporting and there would be certain incentives for organisations to do it. For example, using publicity and positive role models, rather than the current legislation which penalises those that discriminate. We will always have basic human rights laws and hopefully more of the education work the EEO Trust is currently doing. But this is not nearly enough. The monitoring and auditing work needs to be done.

In the medium term the demographic imperative will also be here. The ageing workforce, multi-cultural diversity and radically changed social and family structures will all require an appropriate work place response.

What about the longer-term issues?

In the longer term I see issues of economic sustainability as critical. Planetary demands rule, OK? Environmental issues are part of this 'big picture'. I feel very passionate about this.

The world scientific community, most of the Nobel-laureates, not just a few eco-freaks, have warned that we are in an environmental crisis. This crisis is world-wide: unemployment due to technology, abuse of human rights, growing millions of refugees, drugs, lack of political accountability, the rich-poor gap, growing numbers of homeless, environmental degradation and so on. This has to be related to employment. We cannot continue to think of EEO in companies without looking at the context that is creating the inequity in the first place.

The problem is world physical throughput. Too much growth – unchecked production and consumption. We could imagine the world as divided into three types of people: a billion over-consumers (like us in New Zealand), a billion marginals living in deprivation like Somalia, and in the middle three billion people who are actually living in a sustainable way. I believe we need to rethink our priorities about the way that we live – I don't see an alternative.

These are very big problems. Almost overwhelming I am sure for most people...

Not so big if you start to consider all the solutions. Part of it lies in re-evaluating how we measure national prosperity; for instance, Marilyn Waring's work on measuring Gross Domestic Product.

Also we cannot expect business to solve all our social and environmental problems. Everyone has to take individual responsibility and the government must help facilitate that.

If we accept environmental issues as paramount then we don't need the managerial imperative for EEO – we don't need the 'it's good for business' argument. Then we are left with the human rights argument. But, that isn't going to be enough. So the environmental imperative, that we are all going to be dead if we don't, there will be no world unless we change, is a pretty powerful argument.

In the long-term you obviously see EEO globally, environmentally and outside the contexts of the organisation. What are the implications of this for EEO in New Zealand more specifically?

I have to ask myself, 'what is the key target group that is suffering inequity in employment in our society at the moment'. And the answer that I keep coming to is, 'the unemployed'. The other large disadvantaged group in the community are caregivers – of the aged, disabled and so on. You could probably add the employed poor to this short list – those below the poverty line on low wages. And so I ask myself, 'if I work in the equity field on issues of employment, what is it that I do to help those groups, and the answer is – not much!'.

Because EEO as we have currently constructed it, only operates within organisations, it doesn't encompass those groups. And so I have trouble sleeping at night thinking, 'what is EEO for?' If it is designed to deal with inequity then we are failing; the work that we are doing in organisations is actually for the privileged few who have got jobs. That is not to say we should stop doing what we are doing. But, in the long term, if it is equity issues we are concerned about, we should be addressing employment per se. I know that some of our push for flexible work, and the sharing of jobs is helping that. But, underlying all the problems is our own desire for material wealth, consumer goods and a salary that gives us a lifestyle we want. In other words, we are not prepared to give up what we need to for there to be enough jobs to go around.

Now, compare this argument with what we accuse the white male power-élite of in organisations. We say that these men aren't prepared to give up what they have got – they aren't prepared to give up power to share it around. How about we apply that same argument to ourselves, in respect to the have-nots. It might be an uncomfortable thing to think about. But it is the truth of it. We are not prepared to give up our standards of living to solve the problem of unemployment in our society. EEO has failed to address this issue.

I think that is also a problem of HRM more generally. There is a psychological emphasis in the theory and practice which tends to focus HRM, and EEO as well, on individual performance, motivation and so on – scientific management. The sociological analysis is important, and you are right, I think, that EEO should be looking at these wider contexts. But, again, these are large problems. What do you see as the solutions?

First, government has a central role in taking on guardianship or stewardship for the whole community and legislate sets of standards that would value human beings more.

Profit-making business that measures the true costs and effects of what it does has an important role in the community. This is what green economics promotes. There is not a problem with making profit per se. But, at the moment the costs of treating people badly, polluting the environment, producing goods and services that very few want and creating waste are problems. There is an inadequate feedback system. Businesses get away with it.

Another solution is what I call 'new paradigm' education. New right ideology has captured the language so that words such as freedom, justice, fairness and individual responsibility, have been distorted or given new meaning. Economics is so full of jargon, and has been captured by experts so most of us feel we cannot participate in debates about our wealth and how it can be equitably shared. So we need education to create awareness around our community's loss of democratic institutions and to inform people about economics so that they can participate in decisions. This informed participation will lead to a more equitable society.

EEO in the Private Sector

'It is very important that employers see EEO as a solution, not a problem. What EEO does is identify the barriers. It is a means of identifying the problems that are already festering'.

'I don't see EEO as a dogmatic, rigid recipe ... EEO is applying some core principles and allowing the organisation to put those principles into practice in a way which is meaningful and relevant to its own employees and to their needs and to their environment'.

Trudie McNaughton
Executive Director, EEO Trust

Interviewed by Janet Sayers

Trudie McNaughton is the Executive Director of the EEO (Equal Employment Opportunities) Trust which is based in Auckland. The Trust promotes the benefits of EEO to employers as a means of improving their effectiveness, efficiency and competitiveness through the successful management of diversity.

Trudie was the inaugural EEO Officer at the University of Auckland for three years. She worked for a number of years with the group of women who developed the first Neighbourhood Support Groups in Auckland and which became models for others throughout New Zealand.

Trudie has previously worked as a researcher, freelance writer and editor. She compiled *Countless Signs, The New Zealand Landscape in Literature* and *In Deadly Earnest, A Collection of Fiction by New Zealand Women, 1870s – 1980s* (1989).

How did you first come to understand the term EEO?

My first involvement in EEO was when I was appointed EEO Officer at the University of Auckland in 1989. The job was set up to look at a range of designated groups but the assumptions of some of the key players who were central in the creation of the EEO position were narrower. Some of them were unsure about the scope of EEO at the beginning. My sense of their intentions was – let's deal with women (academic women) now, this is the burning issue, and we'll deal with the others later.

So you see EEO as relating to a range of groups, not only women. What are the other key features of EEO as you see it?

There are a number of key features. EEO is not about a finite list of designated groups. You should always be able to add other groups that may be disadvantaged, e.g. outdoor workers as opposed to indoor workers, general staff as opposed to academic staff, or whatever. So I think that the definition has to be broad enough to look at any person, or group of persons, who may experience discrimination.

It is also vital that EEO is not only about representation. That is, not just about recruiting and selecting a more diverse range of employees. It means equal opportunities for employees to achieve their potential in the workplace.

So it is about actively recruiting from a diverse workforce and then valuing and nurturing that diversity so that people can retain their distinctiveness rather than feel that they have to assimilate into the dominant group.

What about the classical EEO definition of EEO being about a planned, systematic, results-oriented set of activities?

I take all that for granted. The mechanics of EEO include a planned, systematic, results-oriented set of actions and so on. Those actions are the tools. I do think that it is very important that EEO policies and planning are integrated with organisational policy and planning. I think you need to identify EEO as a means of achieving the organisation's goals, not as an optional, marginal 'clip-on'. I think EEO has to be seen as a business imperative to deliver its potential benefits.

It is, of course, terribly important to acknowledge the human rights arguments for EEO. However, I don't believe that these are enough on their own to change organisations. EEO has to be seen as an integral part of an organisation's way of operating.

Is there any particular achievement that you can look back on and draw strength from?

One of the trends that is very heartening is the increased awareness of the work that has to be done in defining the relationship between EEO and Maori. Not just the recognition that this is an issue, but how the organisation is going to implement that responsibility and carry that through into practice.

The increasing profile for other designated groups such as people with disabilities and lesbians and gay men is also heartening.

Can you be more specific about the relationship between EEO and Maori in the private sector?

Organisations that want to be at the cutting edge have to have an understanding of what the implications of the Treaty are, what the implications of legislation such as the Resource Management Act are, what iwi consultation might mean in practice, what Maori development initiatives and Maori business strengths might mean for the organisation, what Maori as a market means for the organisation, what Maori as a potential labour force means for the organisation. I think that these are all issues that people have to come to terms with. Unfortunately, too many organisations are reactive – they are waiting for a crisis, for a breakdown in communication, for a highly public case of discrimination, before they look at how dialogue and partnership can occur.

A number of private sector organisations have seen the bicultural moves in the state sector organisations as something which they don't need to emulate. There are another group of organisations who are honest in their confusion as to where they should begin. However, generally I do think there is increasing awareness that EEO Maori is a pending issue. There is not a lot of activity, but there is an awareness that they will need to take it on board.

Some of the smarter human resource managers are recognising that responding to the needs of Maori in the workplace not only benefits Maori but also enables the workplace to be more responsive and flexible to other employees in a range of ways in terms of legal provisions, ways of working, team-building, management styles and so on.

What do you see as the main advantages of EEO and the main disadvantages of EEO? Or, in other words, EEO's limitations and its ability to create positive change?

I do not see any limitations or disadvantages to organisations that use EEO creatively. I see EEO as an imperative for organisations that want to attract and retain the best quality, the most productive, the most loyal, the most innovative, creative and flexible employees. I don't see how organisations think they can do that without having EEO. I don't see a downside to that. The commitment in terms of time, information-gathering, development of policies and plans is an investment. Frequently what happens when organisations do data-gathering on EEO is that they find, not only what they are doing well, but where they could improve right across the organisation.

It is not EEO that is the problem. It is very important that employers see EEO as a solution, not a problem. What EEO does is identify the barriers. It is a means of identifying the problems that are already festering.

I don't see EEO as a dogmatic, rigid recipe which organisations have to follow with the same set of ingredients, in the same quantities, in the same order. Therefore I think EEO is applying some core principles and allowing the organisation to put those principles into practice in a way which is meaningful and relevant to its own employees and to their needs and to their environment.

If you had to identify those core principles what would they be?

I think they go back to some basic ideas. Most workplaces are designed consciously or unconsciously for a so-called 'typical worker', who is no longer the norm. Policies and practices in these workplaces reflect the needs of that 'typical worker'. So there are barriers to entry, full participation and the development of workers who are not part of that so-called 'traditional', 'typical', dominant group. In other words, barriers to designated groups.

An organisation that aims to be an EEO employer will seek actively, both through commitment at all levels (particularly senior levels) and through active consultation with all employees, a means of identifying those barriers. It will then work co-operatively to remove those barriers.

Another core principle of EEO in action is recognition of relevant merit as the basis for quality employment decisions. With such quality policies and practices and with unfair discrimination removed, or at least minimised, an EEO employer will have a diverse workforce and a workplace which fosters that diversity.

What is your experience of resistance to EEO?

I think there is a great deal of misinformation about what EEO is, and a lot of the resistance comes from that. Resistance also comes from people not understanding that merit is still relevant. People often think EEO is 'jobs for the girls' and so it is seen as replacing one set of injustices with another. Also, people tend to think that EEO is only about interviews, and not about the whole range of employment policies, decisions and practices.

I think too that resistance occurs because you are talking about fundamental cultural change. You are talking about change in the way that you deal with people. Not change in technology, change with people. And that always leads to resistance. So I think that some resistance is therefore inevitable and people who try to move on EEO and intend to wait until there is no resistance, are naïve, and they will wait forever.

Equally, you have to minimise the resistance. And you do that by clear commitment, good consultation and very effective education and training within the workplace as to the benefits of EEO and the reasons why the organisation needs to move on it.

Another point about resistance is that at the moment many people feel very vulnerable about their own employment prospects. Even if they are in employment, people are very nervous about job security.

There has been an enormous amount of change and so, with an imperfect understanding of what EEO means, a lot of people feel personally quite threatened by it.

People feel under seige at the moment. They feel there is too much change, they feel they cannot cope, and many report feeling unwilling or unable to learn about 'new' things. So the challenge is for people to understand that if they are moving on quality initiatives, if they are moving on workplace reform, if they are moving on restructuring of any kind, then, if they want that to be really effective, they have to build EEO in as part of that change process or it simply won't work. They need to recognise that in many instances EEO is only a more effective way of doing some of the good things already happening in their organisations.

Gill Ellis [see interview in this book] made a similar point about the incredible economic and social change that has occurred since 1984, when EEO first became an issue in New Zealand. People can only cope with so much change at one time.

Yes, a number of people have said, 'we don't have to do it. There are a number of other things we have to do. We are moving on things like occupational safety and health and yes, we might think that EEO is a good idea, but we simply can't look at it at the moment'.

And that's part of the symptom of having EEO as a clip-on or add-on as you termed it earlier.

Yes, but even when people see it as an integral part of the way the organisation works, it is still very difficult for them to move to implementation.

Why is that?

They don't see EEO as a business imperative and they feel there is an option. Employers often tell me that they think EEO is a good idea, but they don't have to do it. They feel that they need to move on things they have to do. So if EEO is not already part of their accountability, or if the organisation doesn't have a statutory requirement to perform, or if EEO is not part of their appraisal systems, or if there is limited senior support and no resourcing, then EEO falls off the end of the list of good intentions.

Presumably legislation would help EEO become a priority on this list?

The new Human Rights legislation is an important catalyst for change because it has forced a re-evaluation of current employment practices. It has highlighted the fact that too many employers have used irrelevant factors like age, gender, disability, but particularly age, in making employment decisions. Now that they are unable to use those factors as shortcuts, they are being challenged to examine their practices and their policies. This has led to an increased interest in EEO. It is still too early to see if it will lead to increased action.

It is quite interesting the way that EEO has acted as a spearhead for good human resource management practices. Janice Burns makes this point in her paper too [see Burns chapter]. It appears that one of the reasons EEO gets a lot of flak is because it pioneers a planned, systematic approach to human resource management.

I think that EEO is sometimes the tail wagging the dog. You come in and say, 'What are the barriers to, for example, women in the organisation?'. You find out what the barriers are, but in the process it throws up all the other imperfections in the system. That's what I meant earlier when I said EEO should be seen as a solution, not a problem. The trouble is that EEO often gets blamed for 'dredging up' the problems in the organisation. But, in fact, it is actually very useful that the information has been gathered up. This is because the problems were there anyway just waiting for a formal or informal complaint, or increased absenteeism, or just for more staff to leave. I agree with Janice – that is what happens.

Where do you think EEO is at present in New Zealand?

Clearly there is a major difference between EEO in the private sector and EEO in the state sector. I think there is a change in the state sector in the way that EEO is seen. There is now a more conscious promotion of the benefits to the organisation as well as the benefits for the designated groups. State sector EEO work is much more advanced than private sector activity.

In the private sector the situation can best be illustrated by an EEO Trust project. The EEO Trust researched and published a 'success story' project in 1993 (funded by the government's EEO Contestable Fund) in which we surveyed all the members of the EEO Trust to elicit successful EEO initiatives. The project showed that private sector EEO activity is almost exclusively ad hoc initiatives. These initiatives are fine: perhaps a literacy programme, or an harassment prevention programme, or some mentoring schemes, or developing support for designated group networks. But there are very few organisations which have EEO integrated into the way that the organisation works.

Very few private sector organisations have effective EEO programmes. Some have EEO policies, but they have not been translated, for most organisations, into action.

The Human Rights Act is creating a lot more interest at the moment. Certainly the demand for information and resources from the Trust continues to grow very dramatically. There is interest particularly in the sexual harassment area.

What about people with disabilities? Are there many positive things happening in that area do you think?

I think there are some. The Human Rights Act has helped. I also think that the Disability Pride Awards have raised the profile of disability issues with employers.

'Managing diversity' techniques appear to be currying more favour in the private sector especially. Do you see this type of approach as being 'at odds' with the traditional EEO focus on designated groups?

I don't think of EEO as 'managing diversity' because that implies a top-down imposition which I think is inappropriate. I tend to think of it as making the most of diversity because that implies reciprocity between management and employees. That is a much more responsive and participative model.

I do see valuing diversity as part of EEO. I believe some early interpretations of EEO were limited. They were just about getting more of particular groups into jobs. I don't believe that gives people more opportunity because if people are recruited into a toxic workplace that has no interest in identifying the barriers to their participation and development then you don't have equal opportunity. So it seems to me that separating out issues of valuing diversity from EEO is a naïve separation. I can't see how you can have equal opportunity – if you look at a specific group such as women – if all you do is identify the barriers to recruitment and selection of women and then assume that women will have equal opportunity once they are in the workplace. That's a false assumption.

One of the reasons people interpreted EEO in the narrower sense is that they were worried about resistance to some of the other components. I don't think that limiting the definition of EEO reduces resistance – I believe that there will be confusion and a loss of credibility later on.

At the moment do you see any particular trend emerging in the private sector.

There is increasing awareness of EEO as an issue in the private sector. There is also an increased understanding of the need to link EEO to strategic human resource management work. But as yet there is not a lot of that happening. I think that private sector organisations are responsive to particular sets of identified barriers such as sexual harassment, or customer complaints, or barriers to effective team-work, or literacy needs, rather than having a strategic overview of the role that EEO could have in the organisation.

Do you think that part of the reason that EEO might not be there is that strategic human resource development issues are so young in New Zealand?

I think what you said earlier is true – I think that EEO is often the catalyst for strategic human resource development work. I think that many employers still do not realise the value of the people in their organisation. Many who say they do, don't actually have quality policies and practices to translate their rhetoric into action.

EEO in the public sector has emerged from a bureaucratic model which is hierarchical, planned, systematic and so on. Presuming that EEO in the private sector is not making such good headway as the public sector, what models might work better? Have you noticed any particular trend towards integrating EEO into initiatives such as workplace reform?

The increased emphasis on quality is important. If an organisation is interested in quality then they must also have quality employment practices and they need to take EEO seriously.

Also workplace reform is obviously a major issue. If you are seriously interested in workplace reform then clearly you need a workplace that is responsive, which is participative and so on and EEO is an important part of that.

Do you think that this is happening?

No, I don't think that many organisations are implementing EEO, and I think that organisations would say that themselves. But that is the challenge. If you want teams to work then you can't have barriers to certain people within those teams.

I think that to achieve workplace reform, EEO is an essential part of the process. Workplace New Zealand is working hard to ensure increased understanding of the need to implement EEO as part of workplace reform.

What about the future of EEO? How do you feel about the future?

I think private sector organisations who are 'leading edge' organisations will take EEO seriously. I think that for the majority of small to medium employers, who employ the majority of New Zealanders, EEO is not an issue currently. The challenge is to tap into that employer community. That will require the provision of resources to enable those employers to assess their EEO performance.

For small employers the fact that there are resources such as this book, or the information on our database, is irrelevant, because they don't see the need and they don't have the time and they don't have the specialist personnel in the organisations to focus on EEO issues. They are too small. And yet, if we are really talking about having an impact in the New Zealand workplace we need to be looking at those organisations, as well as the large organisations.

And so in terms of the future of EEO I would see that as being the greatest challenge – tapping into small and medium workplaces as well as the corporates.

List of Figures and Tables

About the Authors

Nicola Armstrong

Nicola Armstrong is a lecturer in Sociology and Acting Director of Women's Studies at Massey University. She is currently researching home-based work and has recently co-edited the book *Women and Work: Directions and Strategies for the 1990s* (1992), and published a chapter on home work in Su Olsson's (ed.), *The Gender Factor* (1992).

Celia Briar

Celia Briar is employed as a senior lecturer in Social Policy at Massey University, where she has worked since 1988. She completed her PhD on women and employment policy in the UK in 1986 and has since written extensively on employment and unemployment issues, particularly those affecting women. In her spare time Celia enjoys being a mother, a Morris Dancer and exponent of the celtic harp.

Janice Burns

Janice Burns is a senior advisor with the EEO team of the Strategic Human Resources Development Branch of the State Services Commission. She has been involved in EEO research and development work for the past nine years and is co-author of *Equity at Work – an Approach to Gender-Neutral Job Evaluation.*

Marian Court

Marian Court is a lecturer in the Department of Policy Studies in Education at Massey University. She has taught in primary and secondary schools. She is primarily interested in studying gendered discourses in relation to teaching and management. Her recent publications include an article in the new journal *Gender, Work and Organisation* entitled 'Removing macho management: lessons from the field of education', and a study of job-sharing and team leadership *Women Transforming Leadership*, (ERDC, Massey University, forthcoming).

John Dickson

John Dickson is the Research Officer for the New Zealand Nurses' Organisation. He is an Honours and Masters Graduate of the University of Otago. He is a former Research Assistant at the Industrial Relations Centre, Victoria University of Wellington. John's recent publications include work on functional flexibility within nursing, nurses' attitudes towards the health reforms, and occupational regulation governing the practice of second-level nurses.

Deborah Jones

Deborah Jones is a lecturer in the Department of Management Communication at the University of Waikato. She previously worked as a public servant and as a self-employed consultant in various aspects of organisational communication. Her current research is on EEO and biculturalism in the public sector, and involves developing theories of discourse and rhetoric, as well as the connections between gender and ethnic differences. Deborah has been involved in feminist theory and practice for over 20 years.

Bev Marshall

Bev Marshall is a lecturer in the Department of Human Resource Management at Massey University. She teaches mainly in the area of Organisational Behaviour, and serves on the Business Studies Faculty EO Committee. She holds a Bachelor of Business Studies in Human Resource Management and Psychology, and an MA endorsed in Occupational Psychology. Her current PhD research is on the processes individuals go through in ethical decision-making.

Heather McDonald

Heather McDonald is a senior policy analyst for the Ministry of Women's Affairs. Her main areas of interest are early childhood care and education and work-family issues. In 1992 she spent three months working at the New York-based Families and Work Institute, a non-profit organisation that undertakes research on work-family issues. She has been actively involved in rape and sexual abuse services for many years and worked as the first National Co-ordinator for Rape Crisis for a year and a half.

Judy McGregor

Judy McGregor is a senior lecturer in communications in the Business Studies Faculty at Massey University. She holds a BA from Waikato University, an LLB from Victoria University and a post-graduate diploma of legal studies from Auckland University. She is a former newspaper editor and spent 20 years as a journalist. She is doing her doctorate on the making of news during the 1993 election campaign. She chairs Massey's harassment advisory committee and is a member of the university's EEO committee.

Rose Ryan

Rose Ryan is a lecturer at the Industrial Relations Centre at Victoria University of Wellington. She has worked in the industrial relations field since the early 1980s as a union official, public policy advisor and researcher. She has undertaken research in the area of workplace reform and was a facilitator at the Workplace NZ conference in Rotorua in 1992. Rose is currently working on a PhD on the dynamics of change in New Zealand workplaces.

Janet Sayers

Janet is currently a lecturer in the Department of Human Resource Management at Massey University. She teaches courses in equal employment opportunities and industrial relations. She has published several articles concerning the implications of industrial reform for disadvantaged groups in the labour market, labour force demographics, and equal employment opportunities.

Paul Spoonley

Paul Spoonley is an Associate Professor (Sociology) and the Associate Dean at Massey University's Albany campus. He is a series editor for Oxford University Press, an editor of *New Zealand Sociology* and the author or editor of some fourteen books. His current research is focused on changes to employment, labour market deregulation and segmentation and the implications for iwi development.

Rae Torrie

Rae Torrie works as a senior advisor in the Strategic Human Resource Development Branch of the State Services Commission. She has worked as a practitioner in EEO for the past six years. In her spare time Rae likes a spot of golf, tennis, and gardening, and has been known to bootskoot and tap dance.

Marianne Tremaine

Marianne Tremaine is a senior lecturer in the Department of Human Resource Management at Massey University. She was born in Invercargill and her tribal affiliations are with Kai Tahu. Marianne has masters degrees in Philosophy and English from Otago University and a Diploma in Local Government Administration from Auckland University. She teaches cross-cultural communication and is working on a doctoral thesis on justice and the Treaty of Waitangi.

Pat Walsh

Pat Walsh is a Reader in Industrial Relations and Public Policy at Victoria University of Wellington. His principal research interests in recent years have focused on the human resource management implications of public sector restructuring and on issues of labour market flexibility.

Wendy Wicks

Wendy Wicks is employed as a disability policy analyst for the Central Regional Health Authority. Her involvement with equal employment opportunities has been through working as an EEO co-ordinator, and her active participation in and commitment to EEO-disability networks and to disability issues. She has written and trained on disability issues, particularly on employment issues for women with disabilities. Wendy is allergic to any form of photographic reproduction.

Index